SALT MARSH & MUD

A YEAR'S SAILING *on the* THAMES ESTUARY

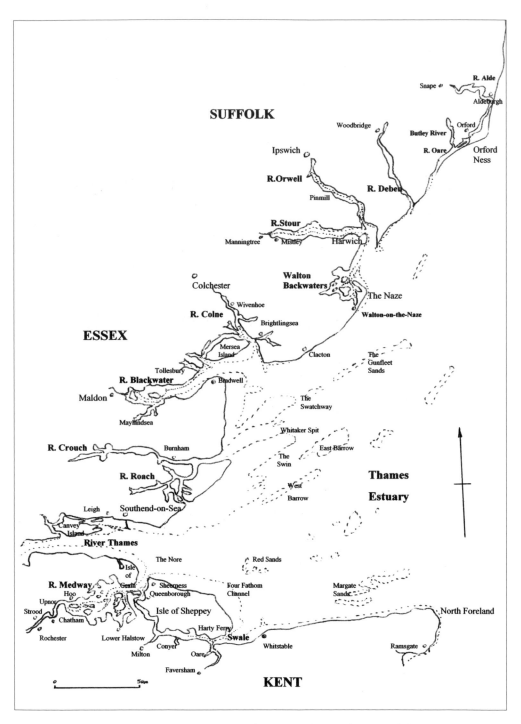

The east coast rivers area of Kent, Essex and Suffolk sailed by the skipper and the mate.

SALT MARSH & MUD

A YEAR'S SAILING *on the* THAMES ESTUARY

NICK ARDLEY

AMBERLEY

To my wife Christobel, the mate, for her belief and the inspiration she has given at all times

First published 2009

Amberley Publishing
The Hill, Stroud
Gloucestershire, GL5 4ER

www.amberley-books.com

Copyright © Nick Ardley, 2009

The right of Nick Ardley to be identified as the Author
of this work has been asserted in accordance with the
Copyrights, Designs and Patents Act 1988.

British Library Cataloguing in Publication Data.
A catalogue record for this book is available from the British Library.

isbn 978-1-84868-491-1

Typesetting and Origination by Amberley Publishing.
Printed in Great Britain.

Contents

Preface
Author's Notes

These tales are set around the low marshland environment that bounds the lower Thames and Medway rivers, which spill out into the greater estuary of the Thames. The stories, based on personal experiences, observations and historical events – with maybe some fiction woven in too – cover the lower coastal reaches of the Thames estuary: the southern coast of Essex, the Medway and the Swale (a body of tidal water that separates the Isle of Sheppey from mainland Kent, along the north Kent coast).

The landscape, in this part of southern East Anglia and north Kent, is indented by numerous creeks, which once hummed with the vitality of water-borne traffic and creek-side industry. Now these arteries are silted and slower running, but the tide still comes and goes; wandering, darting, tentacles appear here and there, on the flood, as it creeps imperceptibly up the rills, through low banks of ooze, mud and clay. Water, just enough, soon allows the passage of pleasure craft, which nose their way up to berths once occupied by their larger sea-going cargo sisters in years of yore: humble spritsail barges, coastal ketches and, in some ports, larger deep-sea traders.

Once within the creeks and gutways, creeping up on the tide, mounds of cord grass and glasswort, the lower growing marsh plants, are met; then too, is the firmer marsh, with its heady flowering plants which fringe the shore, before solid land itself is reached. The land, being solid only by the grace of a man-made sea wall, is itself often of a watery nature. It is this terrain, in many respects a wilderness which lies betwixt land and sea, that the author and his wife have grown to love, for all its ever-changing variety throughout the four seasons of a year.

It is hoped that the reader, too, may come to relish the flavours, scents and scenes that are met in the stories; to tingle at the feel of sailing through channels, at times, barely a metre deep; to witness within, some events, historical or otherwise, both great and small, that have occurred in this little corner of maritime England.

Acknowledgements

To my Mother, Gwendoline D. Ardley, my heartfelt thanks for the companion sketches that echo the stories. My gratitude, too, must go to all those who have been part of my life afloat and have, perhaps, found themselves characterised wittingly or unwittingly.

Photographs and illustrations are from the author's own collection, unless otherwise credited.

Artwork by Gwendoline D. Ardley

I

A Winter's Tale

For a number of years now the skipper and his mate had maintained their little clinker yacht in commission throughout the year, using her on the numerous gorgeous days which nature provides during those shorter hours of daylight, from late autumn through to early spring. Their moorings lay up a little creek within the estuary of the London River, somewhere near its mouth, from which they, or the skipper alone, could often be seen brightening up the water, the yacht's tan sails contrasting with her cream hull, blue boot top and red undersides.

Coupled with their out-of-season jaunts on the tide, they had long desired to sail away, for a quiet night or two, and drop anchor up some little lonely creek over the Christmas period. They hadn't achieved this yet, but one year the mate assured the skipper, 'It will happen!'

Some years back, as an interlude from ditch crawling, the skipper had become involved with club cruiser racing. He raced with the family as crew and mainly, as it developed, his son. The races were largely quite short legs, held locally, round the buoys, achievable in three hours around high water, with some longer day passages.

Although they did quite well with this lark, the skipper found it did not compare to the enjoyment of a few hours' sailing on the tide, often close to the marsh edge, creeping up on the tide with a fickle breeze. It was on one of those excursions, some years back, that a little egret was spotted, long before it was acclaimed as being resident in those parts. The wonderful sight of avocet feeding along the tide edge, their heads dipped, swivelling back and forth as they ran their long curved bills along the tide line, was always a delight.

However, while racing and collecting quite an array of trophies for their efforts, they had become aware of a quaint club trophy which was awarded to the first vessel that visited a particular yacht club in the New Year. This other club was located some miles up the smaller river Medway, a tributary joining the London River at Sheerness.

The skipper, during the autumn of a year or so previously, after returning from a delightful late afternoon sail enjoying the abundant wildlife, was passing the time of day with another club member, who extolled the brave deeds of the Gentleman's Cruise participants during the late spring of that year. Several crews, all made up of men, had made the trip, enjoying a couple of days of male bonhomie.

The other chap went on to say, 'We do our Blue Nose Trophy on our trip and it was so-and-so's turn this time ...'

When the skipper challenged this, it transpired that the little group were keeping the trophy to themselves – generally on a rotational basis! This probably rings a bell with other sailing readers too ...

It was well known that when these robust salty sailors completed their daring deed, they hadn't been out since the last days of the previous fine autumn. The skipper had thought 'Ha!' but had not actually spoken aloud; he responded with, 'I'm glad that you all had a good weekend.'

The skipper's wife, the boat's excellent mate, when this was related to her, snorted and retorted, 'We've got to do it, come on – after all, we sail all year round!'

A year went by but the challenge, silently made, was firmly embedded.

As all sailors would agree, a winter sail, wherever you are, is very much dependent on tidal and weather conditions being suitable. This is especially so if an overnight sail is planned. Sailing, after all, is supposed to be a pleasurable past time. Wind and rain are tolerated, if one is caught out when out on the water, but one does not as a rule purposely go out for a day or night sail in these conditions.

It had been particularly cold on the run up to Christmas, with a deep hard frost. A few days before, a covering of snow gave the hills a playground for children to enjoy a toboggan ride on. A sail had been enjoyed, too, after the decks were swept clear of frozen snow, but the skipper knew two hours out on the tide was a little different from one day through to the next. 'Would it be a white Christmas in southern England?' was the question on the lips of most people. This was a rarity and forecasters were reluctant to commit themselves in this respect. However, the snow cleared away, leaving a warmer, damper period over Christmas. This moved away leaving it cold and settled on the run up to the New Year. They were beginning to feel quietly confident.

During the days after Christmas, the skipper suffered various nags and questions, 'Do you think the weather would hold?' or, 'You could get the gear down to air' and, 'Do we have all we need on the boat?'

The day before New Year's Eve dawned bright with a light breeze. The decision was made by both the crew to load the boat up with the stores that didn't need to go down on the day, leaving the sleeping gear until the final decision was made, to keep the damp at bay.

Were they going to be able to sail out of the creek one year, and come back in the next? With this question sitting silently on their lips, both listened intently to the

... the final decision was made ...

forecast on the following morning. It was as predicted: a moderate south-westerly, becoming a light north north-westerly overnight, then south-westerly again. This was ideal. The sun was forecast to be clear of cloud cover and the night's cold, but just above freezing.

The plan was to reach across the London River, cut over the flats running out from the land between the two rivers and get as far into the smaller river under sail, and then use the iron topsail to run up over the tide to their destination. The return, if the forecast held, would be comfortable and probably enjoyable too.

Arrival in daylight was of the essence – so the skipper coldly planned to use some diesel, something that he was always reluctant to do, unless it was unavoidable. This would surprise the old sages down at the club, thought the skipper. One of those sages, an elderly wise old man, usually commented on the skipper's reluctance to use fuel. The skipper generally retorted, 'Why pollute the environment when a breeze costs nothing?'

The daylight tide for the last day of the year was timed for some thirty minutes past noon. After loading up the boat with the remaining supplies and sleeping tackle, the skipper prepared the mains'l with the first reef tucked in, while the mate prepared other essentials. The wind was a little heavier than expected but the sun was shining. Both looked awkwardly at each other, as if to say, 'Are we mad? Are we doing the right thing?'

The skipper said with much reassurance, 'It'll be lovely out there, look at the wind direction, it'll be a beam reach all the way over to the River Medway.'

The mate replied, 'Let's do it then', her voice somewhat hesitant, but with a little twinkle in her eye.

They departed from the mooring as soon as their little boat was afloat. The mate took the helm. While still in the creek she powered the boat round through the wind; the skipper hoisted the mains'l and then the jib, the mate then shutting down the engine. Feeling that it could be a fast and possibly furious passage, the skipper quietly

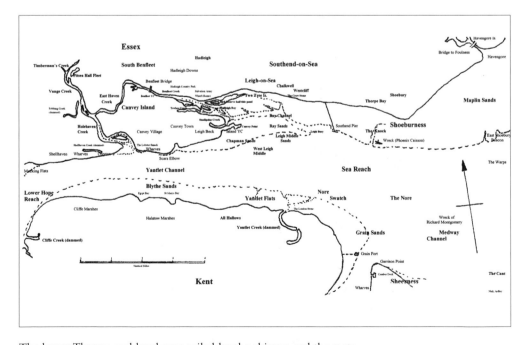

The lower Thames and local area sailed by the skipper and the mate.

dealt with a myriad of other things that when on his own got done later when time permitted, leaving the competent mate to get on with the helming. Keeping her busy was of the essence at this point!

Later, when telling a friend about the passage, the skipper said, 'I didn't relieve the mate until the passage across the Grain Sand was being made –!'

As they ran out, numerous brent geese were seen feeding in the shallows under the marshes; the skipper noticed them bobbing about a bit and looked out over the London River with a little apprehension. There was just a small sign of some white caps; it would be a little choppy along the deep-water channel edge. A flock of wintering knot rose up as if to salute the lonely yacht. They swirled up and around, then settled back on a patch of shingle to while away the time until the tide ebbed to reveal their treasured feeding grounds.

Clearing the marshes and rounding a point outside their creek, with the sails sheeted in, both the crew had felt the boat lean to the breeze as she picked herself up and begin to fly. The crew and boat settled onto a comfortable beam reach, the tiller at times tugging at the helm, calling for attention to the main sheet from time to time. Later their satellite navigation instrument showed them doing a steady six knots over the ground, passing a mid-channel buoy at what seemed a ferocious pace, crashing into the odd roller. It was out here that one of the rollers slapped under the starboard quarter, sending up a cloud of spray and the airborne droplets dashed down onto the mate. The skipper was below making coffee, so missed the excitement!

Once in the shallower water, sailing fast along the southern shore of the London River, almost running, they skirted a ring of buoys marking a firing range. After looking at some shore marks then glancing at his mate, the skipper had said, 'We're fairly "motoring" across here', for the land had passed by at a seemingly impossible rate.

It was not long before they were approaching the old fort that sits at the entrance to the smaller river. It squatted darkly in shadow, a sentinel, a silent dark tribute to countless defences of this land of ours. The skipper noticed the force of the flood tide running past the fort's side; this was now helping them, rather than being on the bow, giving them an extra knot.

The sometimes sinister-looking fort that squats on the edge of the spit that runs out from the Isle of Grain. (Pencil sketch by the author)

The water was a little troubled just inside the entrance. The skipper, noticing a couple of deep rollers approach fine on the starboard bow, watched as the little yacht rose up, then dropped, with that classic clinker scrunch, onto the second crest, sending up a sheet of spray, the droplets twinkling against the wintry sun as they passed over the boat. The mate had her second dousing. The skipper – well he had ducked quickly behind her!

They continued across to the marshes along an island that fringed the river at this point. The island, so legend has it, was the resting place for hundreds of French prisoners of war and later convicts awaiting transportation to Australia: it was along this stretch of river that old ships of the line were moored as they became redundant and were used as prisons. It was then a much larger, bleaker and a more out-of-the-way place only passed by watermen and sailors. Deadman's Island is the name that was given to the desolate stretch of marshland. Now littered with the bones of old barges too, it was rather apt!

They had tacked along the island, and then with a look of astonishment from the mate, the skipper asked for the engine to be started, while he handed the jib. It was approaching high water and the ebb would soon be running.

'No point in banging on against the ebb, we'll be comfortable and progress will be good', quipped the skipper, adding, 'the fuel tank is full up!'

At this point not another vessel had been sighted on the move, other than a motor boat coming into their creek and some dinghies taking part in a Brass Monkey race under the hills of the old fishing village, north of their home moorings, where a number of sailing clubs were based.

With the jib stowed and engine running they began motor sailing almost hard on the wind up a longish stretch called Saltpan Reach. It was a strange name, probably relating to as far back as Roman times, when salt was produced by boiling salt water in huge saltpans in the marshes fringing the river. This activity continued until relatively recent times. Much Roman pottery and pieces of brick have been found in these marshes, indicating a land above the tides and a working habitation. That was to the south side of the river.

... hot soup with fresh cheese-crusted bread ...

'The salt-making industry continued until fairly recent times too', the skipper said, 'there were quite extensive, almost industrial-size pans on the Grain shores near Cockle Hard, you know, that's the shingle and shell beach we've anchored off of sometimes.' He'd pointed across to the north bank of the river as he'd spoken.

'When was that …?' the mate piped up, her voice trailing away as the question was formed.

'Oh, err, during the 1600s I think. And, it continued into the early 1800s too. Doesn't seem possible now does it – what with that huge port over there!'

'It's thought that the Romans made salt on both sides of the river. Evidence, though, has been found in the marshes above Stangate – as you know.'

No further comment was made by the mate so the skipper settled to helm, keeping his thoughts to himself.

The hazy sunshine that helped to keep the cold at bay was becoming weaker and the mate went below to heat up some soup. While sipping hot soup with fresh cheese-crusted bread to chew on, the skipper worked the boat over to the shallows to keep out of the worst of the tide. As he did so he talked to his mate about the ghostly hulks that rose up in the marshes as they passed by.

'You know,' he said, pausing, 'when I was a boy that one over there used to be berthed at the same place as we were.' (The skipper had lived on a barge as a boy and often reminisced in this fashion when out on the water.)

He continued, 'She's the *Gladys* of Dover, a fairly big barge. Her rails were painted white – look, you can still see signs of it.' Pointing, he continued, 'She's falling to pieces now – the port bow has come adrift from the stem, decks are sagging too. Soon be like that other one over there', indicating a hulk with her stem and stern posts jutting, still upright, out of the water; her ribs, and other debris awash, were being caressed by the gentle waves. Some years back this hulk lay behind a protective finger of marsh. Unfortunately, wave action and the ever increase in tidal levels had caused huge changes in this locality in a relatively short period of time.

The mate said, 'How long has she been here?'

After a moment to concentrate on where they were going, the skipper said, 'The barge was re-rigged by a young man, my mother told me, and was sailed for a couple of years out of Whitewall Creek, then a wide tidal inlet up river.' The skipper, pausing again to correct his heading, continued, 'She had an unfortunate accident, ramming a ship, and was wrecked on those sand flats stretching out from the old fort back there. The wreck was put up in the marshes afterwards and there she has sat ever since.'

The mate, often having to listen to these rambles, said, 'Okay, okay, but when was that?'

'Ah well, let me see,' said the skipper, 'It was some forty-five – no nearly fifty years ago, it was around 1960. She used to move about a bit on the high spring tides. I remember visiting her as a lad and seeing the marks where she had lifted and settled back down in a slightly different place. It wasn't long before the river authority came along and cut a hole in her port bow – I doubt she lifted again after that.'

He went on, 'She had two propellers, and engines I assume too, when she was trading as a motor barge. She had a wheel house. This arrangement was kept when she sailed as a yacht, I believe.' Looking up at the sky, as if needing something blank to look at while in thought, the skipper looked back at his mate and said, 'I remember raiding her for some gear many years ago – barge people did that. Recycling is not a new phenomenon designed by yuppies … it was for some cleats!'

As they left the hulks behind, a curlew rose up letting out its eerie call, a sentinel for the ghosts of men and barges.

'What about that other one up on top of the marsh?' asked the mate.

Above: The *Gladys* as she looked some years ago, when the skipper and his son paid her a visit, in the marsh wilderness of Deadman's Island.

Right: The *Gladys* viewed from the spritsail barge *May Flower,* the skipper's childhood home, when both were berthed in Whitewall Creek, near Frindsbury, on the River Medway during the late 1950s. She was being fitted out as a yacht barge at that time. (Courtesy of Gwendoline D. Ardley)

... a curlew rose up, letting out its eerie call ...

The skipper said that he would tell her about that one another time, as it too had featured in the skipper's early life.

Passing the wide open mouth of Stangate creek, which had some old buildings dating from the second world war still standing in the marshes on one bank, they spotted a smack leaving her anchorage and setting sail. She had a deep double-reefed main and a spitfire jib set, and she was last seen heading out towards the river's entrance as they cleared round Sharp Ness point. The rest of the passage was quiet. On the way, two motorboats passed them and an outward-bound lorry ferry rounded Folly point as they passed by.

They sailed the last leg from Gillingham, through Short Reach, where another sail glided by them, to Upnor. By mid-afternoon, some two hours after high water, they berthed, mooring on the outer side of a yacht club pontoon. The skipper had tried to seek permission the previous day, but failed to do more than leave a message. The mate went ashore to the clubhouse to enquire if it was all right to stay. All met said, 'Yes – nice to see you. Do come up into the club later.'

The heater had been flashed up before arriving, so the cabin had begun to build a level of warmth, little by little! Soon after arrival, as the skipper was clearing up on deck, a highly flavoured coffee was thrust into his hands by his beaming mate.

On the way through the moorings they had passed by a boat with people aboard. Just before dark, these people came ashore and nattered a while – saying that they hadn't had a New Year visitor for ages. Finding out from where the little yacht had sailed, the wife in particular thought they were stark-raving bonkers. They also invited the two visitors to join them, up in the club, later in the evening. The club sat on a rise above the river, on a bend with views across its moorings and down two reaches – a wonderful spot.

At this point the mate enveloped herself in two sleeping bags and buried herself with a book; the radio also provided entertainment, Radio 4 being brilliant when afloat, with time to delve into its delights

During this period, the skipper busied himself with the preparation of dinner, having considered the chances of getting any food ashore as being probably slight to nil (although the commodore of the yacht club later assured them that they could have joined in the celebrations in the warmth – such hospitality). For dinner the skipper had prepared a *Carbonnade de Boeuf*, browning the meat and onions before adding herbs and a generous slurp of red wine. This then sat maturing for their later delight.

As darkness crept over them, the skipper and his mate slid into their bunks ... his enquiring look was met with a twinkling, 'No chance!' The mate felt the cold ... the skipper knew for certain that a total of five layers lay in the way, so with a gentle kiss only, they rested and slept for several hours, gathering themselves together some time around 8 in the evening.

The shuttered cabin had fortunately retained a great deal of its previous warmth, so it wasn't teeth-clatteringly cold, but the heater was quickly relit. The heater, an old-fashioned paraffin unit and in fact pretty efficient, soon had the cabin up to a warm fug.

Dinner was then organised. They tucked into crab canapés and smoked oysters, washed down with an amontillado sherry, followed by the beef served with new potatoes and new baby carrots, which had poached gently atop the *Carbonnade*, until of a succulent texture. This they washed down with the remains of the pretty decent bottle of claret, beneath the seductive glow of their flickering oil lamps. The skipper had cut a piece of Stilton to bring with him – but it had, unfortunately, been left on the sideboard at home. He felt quite rueful about this and said so, rubbing his chin in regret. The mate felt for him, knowing his partiality for that delicacy.

Having cleared up the debris of dinner, and after a wash and brush up ... a change into a dark skirt for her and clean trousers for him, they coated up and made their way to the club, where they were welcomed by the commodore – who was still at her table finishing dinner. Settling down with a glass of something and talking idly, they noticed a tidal flow of people, washing back and forth, going out to the loo – they presumed – and coming back having a long gawk, whilst other faces were seen peering round the bar pillar. News had spread that they had visitors from across the Thames. Several less than sober enquiries were made as to where they had come from!

After a few prompts, the skipper and his mate joined the merry throng on the floor and danced into the New Year. Immediately after 'Auld Lang Syne', the commodore presented them with a serviette, signed and dated, as required by the crew's club! After thanking those around them, they took their leave and by the not unreasonable time of thirty minutes past midnight, in a new year, they were tucked up in their bunk, heading for far-off lands, or waters, in the land of Nod, as warm as toast. The yacht, gently moving on the river's nearly oily-smooth surface, lulled them into sleep. It had been a wonderful day and the sky, although full of stars, did not tempt the skipper and his mate to sit out and enjoy the sight with a nightcap.

The alarm sounded all too soon: it was still before 6 in the morning, and clearing the pontoon they motored away in an absolute calm. The sky showed some breaks in high cloud; however, lower-level clouds could be seen scurrying by. They hurried down river knowing that the breeze would fill in – the kettle began singing and cups of steaming coffee were made. The ebb was in full flow, coupled with the strident efforts of the iron topsail, they were making excellent progress. No other movements were evident!

Off Oakham Ness, as they rounded a jetty, a gentle westerly breeze from astern was felt. Soon after rounding Sharp Ness into Saltpan Reach, they passed along a stretch of marsh, Burntwick Island, a strangely named land, possibly with connection to its past use for salt making. They set sail. The mains'l still had its first reef tucked in, and with the jib, they could feel the sails pushing them along nicely. Their log recorded the time as 7am, and with dual accord the engine was shut down. The yacht's speed soon began to overhaul that of the earlier passage.

It was going to be a grey dawn; the mate produced some more coffee, with a liberal dash of something nice this time. Soon they cleared the inside of the buoy sitting off the old fort. Still no other movement on the water had been seen – this was a solitary passage indeed. The seabirds were still roosting, for their usual daytime noises were noticeably absent. The lightness of day had taken an unusual time to grow; to the east a line on the horizon promised perhaps an improvement. The breeze had in the meantime picked up to a decent breeze, and the yacht was moving well.

Leaving the little river behind, they settled onto a northerly course to take them directly across the London River. By now the little yacht had really begun to pick up her skirts, and a fast passage was enjoyed. Away to starboard, the ghostly masts of the *Richard Montgomery* could be seen clearly in the weak dawn sky. The mate then the skipper following suit, shivering at the thought of the wreck. It looked eerie: it contained a few-thousand tons of ammunition – a long-term present from Britain's American cousins! The ship had been wrecked on the sand bank in August of 1944 and had sat on the edge of the shipping channel ever since, her hull and cargo slowly decaying.

'This is fun' said the mate, adding, 'when we get over the other side I'll make some more coffee.' The mate wasn't to know, but the final part of the passage was made so quickly, there wasn't time for this.

The skipper, with a nod, agreed with these comments, looking at the time and where they were, he said, 'Another ten minutes will see us clear of the London River channel.'

They tacked in towards the shallows and worked up towards the pier that runs out from the shore, for a mile or so, soon passing a buoy marking the low-tide passage between the sand banks. Then, just for the hell of it, as an aid to keep them warm, they continued tacking up the channel, one board after another, sending the warmth generated by physical activity coursing through their extremities.

The familiar scrunching sound made when the boat's clinker planking plunged into the short little seas sending up an occasional shower of spray was now no longer evident. The yacht was enjoying her sail, cutting through the flat water with a good

The sun is caught over the top of a traditional sprig of Christmas tree mounted on the ensign staff, during the twelve days of Christmas.

breeze to push her along. Both of her crew were relishing this last little bit enormously too: the end of their passage was in sight.

Reaching a gutway leading through the sands north-westwards to an old fishing village, marked by a solitary grimy buoy trailing black weed, they were able to fetch up the last leg to the marshy point off the entrance to their own creek. On their way they counted twenty-four seals on the sands, basking in their usual spot, their bellies turned towards the fickle warmth: a thin ray of sunshine had appeared that dappled the early flood.

'Look … what a wonderful sight … seals, sun and sand … look!' the mate had chirped excitedly, grinning from ear to ear!

On the approach to some fishing boat moorings, off the entrance to their creek, the mate took over the helm, sailing on up the gutway. The skipper went forward to ready the mains'l for lowering when clear of the fishing vessels moored in the gut; the mate tacked round. The skipper dropped and stowed the mains'l while they gently ghosted back over the tide, under jib, to a mooring buoy – all accomplished to perfection and a great way to end the passage.

Their arrival, for no one of the human species was to be seen, was witnessed only by the myriad of wildfowl feeding on the mud-flats. Their log recorded the time as just after 10.

Watching a host of birds, a mixture of plovers, knots, dunlin, redshank and oyster catchers skittering and darting about, poking amongst the shells and weed covered debris along the channel, the skipper with a coffee in his hand said to his mate, 'That was a scintillating sail, something to savour, it was grand, just grand!'

Looking at the mate, with a half grin or look of enquiry, he said, 'Do you think we'll do it again?'

'Probably not,' was her initial response, then a more thoughtful and drawn out, 'I'd … have to think about it!'

2
A Reflective Afternoon in February

January had been a poor month for sailing, by the skipper's standards. A few days had been half-decent but they were during a week of neap tides, which had then precluded any chance of sailing. The skipper had, though, got out for a sail on the last day of Christmas, some hours before the twelfth night.

The skipper bemoaned the fact to anyone who had cared to listen, but he had gained little sympathy from friends or family. Other boaters in his club who kept their vessels afloat felt the same way too. Those that had laid up their craft just grinned at the glum faces!

February dawned splendidly, but work prevented the skipper from getting afloat on that day. He had chaffed a bit, but as his wife had kept saying, 'Life does not revolve around sailing.' The next day the skipper had taken a friend for a sail around the open waters along the shore to the east of his estuary island moorings.

The skipper had had, too, a grand sail up the creek, up to a barrier that barred access for most vessels to the waters beyond, sailing up and back on a mainly northerly wind that at times stole towards the west, necessitating the need to slip a couple of short tacks in when going up the narrow channel, adding to the excitement in a breeze that had been a little more than moderate. The efforts of tacking had helped to keep the cold at bay.

It was a day or so later that the conditions described had caught the skipper's imagination as he had set off from his mooring. The breeze of a gentle nature had been forecasted to be a north north-east, force three, but was a southerly force two to three instead. He didn't grumble. Clearing his berth he had quickly hoisted the sails and silencing the trusty diesel beneath his feet. He was then blissfully sailing. At the bow of the yacht, the stem cut silently through the water, as if gliding, neither a gurgle nor any other sound had lifted to the skipper's ear.

Grinning to himself, the skipper said, 'I don't suppose we'll get too far today.' It was to no one in particular, except perhaps the boat. He believed in boats' having souls, so why not talk to them too. Then almost whispering, as he looked aloft, he said, 'With this light southerly, it'll be eminently sensible to let the boat go with the tide and turn for home before high water. We'll take an easy look at all the wild life on the way and get back before the tide ebbs away too far.'

'The old Salvation Army jetty would be an achievement with this wind', he had added after a long pause. With that he'd sat back with his mug of tea, looking around his little world. A smug and satisfied look creased his face.

The water shimmered under the warm sun. The topsides of the little clinker yacht were reflected perfectly on the mirror surface of the incoming flood, the sails were too. In that reflection, an onlooker would have seen that the intenseness of the blue, had given a darker hue to their colours of cream and tan. So, on a gentle beam reach, the

Hadleigh Ray with the stumps of the abandoned Salvation Army wharf (General Booth's Wharf) standing upright, in a soldierly manner: they once had a proud purpose. A flight of brent geese characterises this lonely place, from late September to early May, and the wharf is virtually the only visible remnants of this area's once rich industrial past.

skipper and his yacht had seemed to move effortlessly over the tide, passing berths, some empty, and others the skipper had noticed had boats that were still fast on the mud. He said, speaking into the fickle breeze, 'If those boats were used regularly, then they'd probably be afloat now.'

Briefly, the skipper thought, the breeze had faltered, but looking aloft at the burgee on its stick, it had flapped lazily again, as if to order, to the southerly breeze. Down at deck level, shielded by the moorings, it was quiet. The ensign, a dash of bright red in the sharp sunlight, hung listlessly from its staff, swinging to and fro; a gentle swell was coming up the creek with the tide. Ships were passing along the channel out in the Thames, and in such conditions their wash set in motion rollers that hit one bank, bounced off and went back and forth until their energy was spent. The rollers swung the burgee about, interrupting its gentle flutter to the wind. The sails too, the mainsail in particular, were shaken by the gentle roll, caressing the air along the leach, before it had obeyed the light breeze with a thwack, lifting the sheet, and rattled the horse slider, its back-and-forth gyrations creating an irksome squeal. Beyond the moorings, at the entrance to the creek, the skipper had seen that the breeze was sufficient to ruffle the water's surface.

The previous day they had had a covering of snow, enough to bury a fizzy drink can. Driving to the creek the island had been clear, but the hills to the north were still covered in white. It was cold, no more than a few degrees; frost still lay on the poop deck, but in the sun it felt warm. The skipper, clad in several layers and a thermal coat, had started to overheat. He had released some of this excess by removing his hat, but

Keep that hat on or you'll get cold

had immediately heard the absent mate's voice, 'Keep that hat on or you'll get cold.' So it had been 'obediently' replaced!

Leaving the creek the skipper had noticed that the early warmth that had held, and the placid nature of the sluggish tide had seemed to encourage a huge level of wildfowl and bird activity. Just beyond their moorings, over the shallow flats, a number of little grebes were swimming. They were only seen spasmodically: they dive regularly for food, spending long periods underwater. Their larger cousins had been seen regularly during the winter, but not these. 'Ah,' thought the skipper, 'these little mignons of life are such a joy!'

A passing work boat heading into the creek had sent its wash curving and curling towards the clinker yacht. Her bow came gently up, as the stern followed it downwards, and the skipper felt his boat's curtsey, as if nodding to a fellow traveller. Then, from along the waterline, a gentle swish was heard as the boat's plank lands caressed the wash ripples.

The gentle wash had diminished as it travelled; finally the remnants lapped along the banks to starboard and were swallowed too amongst swathes of cord grass away to the port side. There the skipper saw a solitary curlew, standing erect, on a hummock of marsh, its feet in the water. It lifted off, releasing the familiar eerie cry, piercing to the ear. Its call was a precursor: it announced a few more cutting remarks from other curlews scattered across the marshes.

On the point, nearly awash now, a chattering mass of birds, dunlin, oystercatchers and knots, amongst others, were raucously squabbling for an ever-diminishing area of bare clay. 'It wouldn't take much to get that lot aloft!' the skipper said, speaking to himself.

... a chattering mass of birds squabbling for an ever-diminishing area of bare clay ...

Progress had been slow, at first, but once clear of the creek's entrance and the drag of the flood tide, the ground speed had been a little faster. Clearing the point of marsh that the skipper had been looking at, he now had an uninterrupted view all around him. The sky was clear with not a cloud to blemish its many shades. Above him the sky was a deep blue, intense in its depth. Over the mainland it lightened towards the horizon, but to the southwest, in the direction of the afternoon sun, it was white, almost incandescent in its brightness, the light too dazzling in fact to look at for more than a moment. It was an amazing sight.

Away in the distance, out in the main channel of the River Thames, two giant roll on/roll off ships had passed each other. The duet of wash waves would not take long to reach them. The skipper, an old seafarer himself, had seen over a period of time the ferocity of some of these waves. They were, in his opinion, wreaking havoc with the marsh edges in that local environment.

A cacophony of noise reached his ears, and looking towards the point from where it had emanated the skipper saw, as if to order, a stretch of marsh disappear and reappear as waves washed and boiled across it, scouring the soft layers and creating muddy swirls. The birds, a cloud almost black with its density, had swirled upwards, different species breaking off in, it had seemed, predestined directions. The knot especially, as if working with a conductor, wheeled and spiralled in a sinuous flow. It was a magnificent!

His yacht moving slowly, the skipper had time to watch as wave after wave of birds tried to alight again, but the wash and the imperceptible rise in tide, and the broken surface tension, had reduced their perch. Groups alighted further into the marsh and on an area of beach. Others had flown off. This time the boat did not curtsey either: it had risen up and scrunched and crashed through a series of wash waves. There was none of the usual gentle swish from the hull planking, but a regular hard slap and sloshing that rang hollow from inside the cabin. Eventually it passed and the boat was left bobbing to the last of them as a relative calm was restored to the tidal flow. During the boat's gyrations, the skipper too had held on, as the boat danced to the tune of the wash. The sails had slatted back and forth, all power driven from them: the wind was of insufficient strength to assert its authority. Then, it had driven the boat onwards again.

Settling down after the wash, the skipper had set the bow towards the funnelling passage that ran through a myriad of moorings between the mainland and the island upon which the boat was moored. As he went he gazed across the water to the old fishing town that sat along the shore. Then ran his eyes further east, to a club based on an old 'plastic' naval mine hunter. The skipper saw that a number of dinghies were racing round the cans. 'Part of a winter series for hardy sailors!' he thought. A number of motor boats too were seen in the distance chugging around in seemingly aimless circles, yet surely appreciating the moment; but alas, of other sailing cruisers, none were seen by the skipper.

The sail, moving with the tide along the marsh edge, was serene. The skipper had looked at flotsam as he passed by, mostly wind-blown debris from the land mixed in with dead and decaying plant-life. Over in the marsh a skein of brent geese had risen up in a mass, as if one, flying off towards the low land beneath the hills of Hadleigh Downs. The eel grass, that succulent mudflat plant, had long gone, and fresh young shoots of winter cereals and grasses made a good alternative to their diet.

With time to look around, the skipper began to muse about the time before his own, when this little delta was the home for smacks and other fishing craft. Barges too came and went, up into the creek where the skipper's boat was moored. The barges went beyond the creek too, up to the Salvation Army wharf. They had brought rubbish down from the Salvation Army's own wharf at Battersea, taking bricks away. Other barges would have sailed further inland, up to a wharf above an old causeway which provided a low-tide crossing onto Canvey Island before the days

Long ago a loaded barge, the *Mira*, wended its way eastwards before working across the shallows to head up the London River. She was one of many that would have made this passage from the wharves around the skipper's sailing locale. (Courtesy of the Salvation Army)

of a bridge, and just a few years before the second world war conflict barges would load hay cargoes whilst lying on the hard: feed was still needed for London's horse population.

Many years before, his mate had bought him a watercolour painting. It showed some smacks, their sails furled, sitting off the end of the island; beyond, a barge or two were brought up in the distance. In the middle ground were the marshes of the point; on these wild fowlers were out after wild duck or widgeon, an activity that continues to take place locally. The painting now hung, with affection, in his home.

The skipper had found records of his father's barge, the *May Flower*, before his father had purchased her, trading into Canvey and Benfleet to load hay during the 1890s. On Canvey Island, hay had been a noted crop a century or so ago.

In his mind the skipper saw the barge, not deeply laden – for hay was a light cargo – but the stack was some way up the mainmast, held up by stack irons, thick iron posts that slotted into the low rails ...

The mate up on the stack was shouting directions to the skipper, who was watching his way by the barges wake. 'Moored smack two points on the port bow,' drifted across the water from the mate up on the stack. Watching, the skipper had seen the bargeman peg the wheel and amble over to port where he hung on the leeward wang, to peer round the stack for a look himself.

'He's alright, jus' keep yer eye on 'er an' I'll work uz up abit.' For a barge loaded with a stack tended to suffer from a much greater degree of leeway.

A hay barge, the *Eva Annie*, loaded with a stack of hay and probably some straw too. These are cargoes were taken from both Canvey Island and South Benfleet up to London, during the age of horse transport in the capital. The *Eva Annie* was hulked off Leigh-on-Sea during the 1930s and her stem can be seen out on the mud flats. (Courtesy of B. Pearce)

Watching as the point fell slowly into the distance behind him, the skipper said, 'He'll be able to weather the point soon,' then he added, 'be a fair wind for London this afternoon too.'

In the distance a deeply laden barge, probably loaded with bricks, had set sail too. She had been waiting for the tide in the Ray Channel to take a short cut across the shallows off the marshy point of Canvey Island.

'Must have dropped down earlier,' thought the skipper, 'from the wharf.' to wait for the tide, rather than tack slowly down towards the pier at Southend, 'It's not far, but a heck of a lot of work and bricks won't rot.'

'Them old sailormen knew how to work the tides!' the skipper unintentionally spoke aloud.

With a start, as if waking suddenly, he realised that the barge wasn't there at all!

The skipper, in the reflective mood that had shrouded him, continued to sail along the edge of the marshes that fringed the western end of a bird reserve. Looking about, after he had nipped below to turn off a singing kettle and add water to a mug for a coffee, he saw a large number of avocets rise up, wheel around above an unseen semi-tidal pool behind a low old sea wall. Away on the other side of the creek, some others had lifted off the edge of a mud bank on an island of marsh, known as Marks Marsh, and he watched as they flew low over the water towards the reserve. The slits on a hide were all open and looking through his binoculars the skipper saw a row of heads, little round blobs of a pale hue with hats on, looking intently through their viewing aids, studying the bird-life. Mallards, teal and shelduck occasionally took flight too, disturbed by something or nothing. The skipper sighing had said, quietly to himself, 'Sailing past this stretch of marsh is always a joy.'

A spritsail barge being loaded with bricks. The wharf was a Salvation Army wharf, like that in Hadleigh Ray, during the early part of the twentieth century. Note the workman, below in the hold, looking towards the camera. (Courtesy of the Salvation Army)

In the marshes, the skipper had noticed, too, a hint of fresh life amongst the brown, ragged and broken stalks of the previous year's plant growth. Fronds of cord grass that always seemed to have a green look had looked fresher too. This plant did not die back entirely, for only the flowerhead withered. It was an invasive plant, a cross between the English native grass and an American interloper; it was progressively covering any mudflat that dared to rise above the point at which it would be uncovered long enough during a neap tide for their seeds to germinate. In the skipper's locality areas that he had sailed over not such a long time ago had been 'put out of bounds' by this invasion. It throttled and exterminated other plants, but provided a sound base for silt to settle and rise ever upwards. The grass has an innate ability to thrive anywhere between neap and spring high tide lines. Unfortunately, it is here to stay!

Reaching the gnarled remains of an old jetty, which was once used to export bricks mainly manufactured on lands owned by the Salvation Army, the skipper once again lapsed into a reverie on the past ...

His eyes saw a wharf busy with activity. Two spritsail barges sat alongside. Men could be seen transferring bricks from trucks onto pallets. The trucks sat behind a busy-looking engine on the line that disappeared beyond the sea wall. A crane was being used to load bricks into one barge. The bricks were being swung out over the barge to disappear down into the hold. Men were hard at work down in the hold stacking thousands of bricks, sweating and chaffing at one another. The skipper had assumed that a scattering of concrete blocks, in the marsh, was the base of that crane, but later found that they were for a warehouse.

A foreman could be heard clearly across the water, 'Come on, look lively with that last pallet, this barge has to be away on the tide.' The skipper smiled: he understood too!

The other barge was unloading a hold full of London's waste, a stewing mixture of horse dung, hay and straw, broken crockery mixed with goodness knows what – the detritus of thousands of households. Some would be burnt in the kilns; the rest would be ploughed into the clay soil, enriching it with fresh nutrients.

The skipper coughed, 'Goodness me,' Then he gasped, 'what a stench!' as he sailed past the wharf.

... mind you stack 'em bricks proper!

Looking up, the skipper thought he'd heard a shout from across the water. Then the master of the barge being loaded with bricks, hollered down into the hold, 'Look 'ere, you mind you stack 'em bricks up under the decks proper,' pausing, as he shaded his eyes against the sun's glare, for a quizzical look below, 'I's don' want them t' shift on the way up the Lon'on River.'

Allowing his gaze to wander across to the hills beyond the sea wall, the skipper returned to the present time, but he had still marvelled at the industriousness of General Booth and his followers. The land beyond had been bought up by the Salvation Army over a century ago and used, amongst other things, as a colony to wean inebriates from alcohol. To sign the pledge was a ticket to work and good accommodation. It was a place, too, to become a good soldier of Christ and help spread the gospel, at home and abroad. The colony had run farms and, for a number of years, brickworks as well. The brickworks have long been dismantled and little can now be found where they were sited. The brickworks and wharf were constructed and bricks were being shipped out in not much more than a year after the arrival of the Salvation Army. The skipper had always been intrigued by this industry: it was an industry that he had lived close to in Kent, when a boy, and had wanted to know more about it. The land was still farmed and the Salvation Army now trained adults with learning difficulties for a number of occupations.

Waking from his reverie and looking at the time, as he had passed a line of red buoys, the skipper suddenly realised that he had left the old wharf well astern and he was nearly up to the moorings that belonged to another yacht club. He had reluctantly realised that he had to turn the boat for home, saying, 'It's near the top of the flood, I need to make sure of beating the ebb.' He chuckled because he knew that he had his trusty diesel, which sat silently beneath his feet, to fall back on – if needed.

The skipper often sailed right up through the moorings beyond, to turn off the yacht club and sail back. It was grand sailing with a northerly or southerly wind during the

A stumpy spritsail barge alongside General Booth's Wharf during the brick making era on the Salvation Army colony. (Coutesy of the Salvation Army)

colder months of the year. Sailing in that manner allowed time for an eye to wander, to explore and probe the landscape, to see what would normally have passed by with perhaps just a flicker, or flash, and then be gone. Sailing so close to marsh and land, with its strange mixture of intertwined habitats, was bewitching. These creeks, marshes and the lowlands that fringed them were, thought the skipper, neither land nor sea. It was that mixture that made the magic.

He marvelled, briefly remembering that his mum and dad had sailed their barge this way over fifty years before, on a passage up to Benfleet, where they lay for some weeks. The skipper reckoned that that voyage was the last time a full-sized barge had made a passage up the creek, purely under sail, though a little farm barge rebuilt during the 1980s, the *Cygnet*, had sailed up in recent times.

With those thoughts the skipper, with an almost absent mind, wended his way back through an area of moorings to the north of his home creek. Looking across the water towards the entrance to his creek the skipper's eye was caught by a disturbance on the water's surface. A seal had popped its dog-like head up and swam lazily, well clear, but alongside the boat, looking intently, before it gently submerged beneath the languid surface to fish over the shallows as the tide ran out of the marshes. The seal left a disturbed trail as it headed away. 'Happy hunting!' said the skipper.

Continuing to sail on past the point, the skipper put a slip line on the tiller before going forward to stow the mains'l and rig his fenders. The boat continued more or less on the skipper's desired course. Returning to his station aft and slipping the tiller line off, he allowed the tiller to float in his hand as the boat forged slowly over the ebb towards the creek entrance. A gentle rustle reached up from the stem.

As he passed the marshes at the eastern point of the island he looked at them closely, for it seemed that they crept back westwards every time he passed this way. It seemed

The spritsail barge *May Flower* alongside at a berth that used to be sited just below the old road bridge across Benfleet Creek. This is now the site of a barrier, part of the Thames flood defence system. (Courtesy of Gwendoline D. Ardley)

especially so then, for they had recently a bout of heavy easterly winds that sent heavy bruising waves crashing onto the point. The waves had ripped at the decaying vegetative life and scoured the soft ground to mould the harder clay beneath in smooth undulating curves. 'Gosh,' the skipper said, 'it looks as if those recent easterlies have done their destructive work again.'

He grimaced and added, 'One day, there'll be no marsh left: the mud bank will be under the sea wall.'

Entering the creek the skipper controlled their speed with the jib sheet, allowing the boat to lose and gain speed at his command. On the approach to his mooring the skipper left the tiller to fend for itself, while he had walked forward to run the genoa down onto the deck. The boat, with way on, continued to stem the ebb. Nonchalantly returning to the tiller and shading his eyes, because he had to squint into the bright light of the sun drenched sky, he watched for the right moment. Then, with a decisive movement he put the tiller over and the little clinker yacht, with her long keel guiding her, slid sweetly into her berth. Nothing more than a gentle pull on the stern line was needed to bring the boat to a gentle stop.

'Ah!' The skipper said – or had it been a deep sigh? – to no one in particular, but it might have been to anyone who had passed over these waters, for he had communed with some of their spirits. Old salts from bygone eras were adamant that the souls of sailors were as one with the mighty albatross. Those birds patrolled the ocean deserts and were revered: the souls of sailors never die. The skipper therefore knew, well he felt it deeply, that sailors' souls lingered, forever, over the marshes, the tidal waters, rivers and the estuaries too, and they would have understood …

Then in an almost reverential whisper, so as not to disturb those about him, the skipper repeated, 'Ah … What a glorious, glorious sail I've enjoyed!'

3

A Spring Sail

Easter comes later some years than others: it can be set well into the early part of April. The mate always told the skipper that this was largely to do with the moon's phases and he demurred to her more qualified knowledge on such things. It could of course be useful, because the skipper and his mate often got away for a sail at that time of the year. The days were longer and a little warmer, especially if spring had come early and winter had not dawdled on as it could to blur the distinction between the two.

The weather was settled and a high-pressure system dominated southern England following a late Easter. It was warm by day – though chilly at night – and fine and dry. The forecast had talked about light to moderate north to northeasterly winds. It boded well and the mate and skipper quickly decided to get their things together and slip away across to the River Medway for a few quiet nights.

Leaving their creek with the wind coming nicely from a more northerly direction, they set the sails. In the marshes a gaggle of geese foraged in amongst the grass beds for food. Both remarked about the numbers of brent-geese that were still in residence. The skipper said, 'It may be un-seasonally warm here in eastern England, but in their breeding lands it could be very different for those geese.' The skipper always wondered, with a certain level of awe, how the world's bird-life knew when to go. They had something, the skipper believed, that we mere humans had somehow lost during our evolution.

The point of marshes round which they sailed still supported a myriad of waders of numerous descriptions jostling for a position: the wintering birds had not yet departed. Some knot rose up and completed a few twirls before alighting again. The skipper brought the boat round with the wind nicely on the port quarter for a run across to the North Kent shore; there they crept along the shallow edge of the Nore Swatch, skirting a set of firing-range buoys and slipping inside the outer edge: the red warning flags were not hoisted. The skipper chuckled. The mate looked at him with that 'Oh no!' expression, as he said, 'All our troops are spread round the world at our government's behest – no one is left to fire their guns on the home ranges!'

A couple of other yachts could be seen coming across the Thames from the end of Southend Pier. 'I wonder where they're bound,' the skipper said to the mate. As if to answer his own thoughts, he said, 'I expect it'll be Queenborough.' They themselves were bound for the quiet and solitude of Stangate Creek.

The mate said, 'Do you remember Queenborough before the floating jetty was built?' The mate knew only too well that her crewmate had known that little harbour for some forty years at the time, so she continued, 'I was remembering the days when we had to leave the dinghy moored to the one of the few rings set into the side of the old hard. Sometimes we had to anchor the dinghy half way up. You made me carry it up when we first went sailing ...'

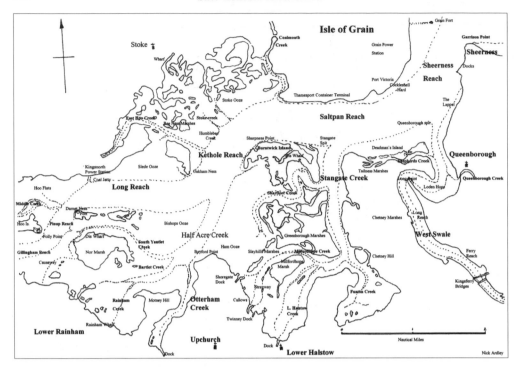

Chartlet: the outer reaches of the River Medway, and the West Swale. Numerous creeks are detailed too.

The skipper said, smiling, 'Well … I was a bit naïve then and, well … sorry!' as he gave her a squeeze and a hug with his free arm.

The mate, smiling at the skipper for this unexpected apology for something that had happened such a long time ago, then continued, 'When our boy was younger he used to look after the dinghy for some extra pocket money. Then there was that spate of bullyboy tactics from some local lads. Do you remember? They'd say, "look 'ere, we'll look after yer boat missus – it'll only cost yer fifty pee." I seemed to remember I asked them what school they went to and if anything happened to the boat I said, "I'll be round on Monday morning to see your head teacher: I'm a teacher too!" It worked – 'cos stupidly they'd told me what school they went to.'

'You did, with that teacher's wag too!' the skipper chuckled in satisfaction.

'They left it alone though, didn't they?' the mate added quickly.

Going down the Nore Swatch, the wind seemed as if at had gained some east in it, so the skipper hauled the sheets in a little. However, the mate, at the helm, was soon bringing the boat's heading round towards the entrance to the River Medway. Heading across the Grain flats they eased the sheets again. The old grey fort, as if still guarding the Grain Peninsula, was soon passed close by.

Passing the fort the skipper took over for a trick. Looking about him, he noticed, as they passed the outfall from the power station, a couple of common terns, early arrivals from their wintering grounds. Soon their distinctive call would be heard in all the creeks hereabout again. The sight of those birds, hovering heads down, eyes fixed on their prey, then diving for food, was one of the delights that fascinated the skipper – and the mate for that matter. But he, in particular, could sit for ages just watching them feeding at the turn of the tide up a mud creek.

Remembering that he had been having a conversation with his mate about the old hard at Queenborough, the skipper reminded her about the time the dinghy had been

... look after the dinghy for some extra pocket money ...

cast adrift. It had, fortunately fetched up along the edge of the mud, beaching itself as the tide receded. The skipper had had to wade through the soft mud to retrieve it!

On another occasion while ashore, when using the new floating jetty, their dinghy had been sunk by a group of louts. Nothing had been lost, because the skipper for many years had lashed all the loose items such as rudder and centreboard to a thwart. The oars, too, had been clipped in with bungee cords – which on that occasion was very fortunate!

The mate said, 'It was that sort of behaviour that has put a lot of yachtsmen off from using this quaint little waterside town. It's such a shame too, because the High Street is fascinating and the old tidal quay round the back just oozes history, with the backs of the houses showing that they're still very obviously used by watermen and fishermen.'

Some years ago when visiting Leeds Castle in the heart of the Kent Weald, they had learnt a little about this ancient town and its past importance in the defence of the realm and its 'ownership' by Queen Phillipa, the wife of Edward III. On a subsequent stay at the picturesque town of Rye, up a similar sleepy creek, they had found a print of Queenborough High Street dated from 1830. It was instantly recognisable. The print now hung at their home to remind them of the sleepy little hollow.

By now they had passed the towering monolith of the oil-fired power station and were crabbing across towards the shoe of Deadman's Island. Glancing behind him over the starboard quarter, the skipper said, 'That place should be shut down. We should not be burning oil for power – another sensible and clean generating system should have been built on the nuclear site at Bradwell. Yes I know – we have to bury the spent fuel underground – but, being simplistic, that's where man mines it from after all!'

'Whoops!' said the mate, thinking that her skipper was about to race off on one of his hobbyhorses, she followed up with, 'Now – I'll make you a cup of tea.'

The mate, looking up through the hatch, saw that they were now comfortably close, reaching along past the island. She was about to speak, having suddenly remembered that the skipper had said that he would tell her about one of the two barge hulks that could be seen up in the marshes beyond. It was barely an hour after high water so her hull, sitting forlornly high up in the marsh, was clearly visible. Before she had a chance to speak the kettle sang its song from below, and she bobbed back down to make the tea. The skipper soon had a mug in his hand.

On the edge of the marshes of Deadman's Island, the once lovely spritsail barge *Ernest Piper* languishes, where she had come to rest after drifting around Shepherd's Creek. Her bow has broken off and dropped into the creek; her stern has completely disintegrated apart from her bottom structure. Inside, the remnants of a home can still be found.

Sipping his tea, the skipper remembered the mate's unspoken enquiry of earlier and also the sail that they'd had up past the very same spot earlier in the year, on a winter passage, to a yacht club higher up the river.

The boat was sailing along nicely over the tide; the dinghy too was giving off her clinker scrunching noise as they both cut through a powerboat's wash waves that intermittently curved across the channel towards them, overtaking them and breaking along the edges of the marsh, causing yet more crumbly clay to tumble away in the wash. The skipper's thoughts returned to the mate's silent request for information about the hulk up in the marsh.

He started, saying, 'Mum and Dad knew the owners of that barge. It's the hulk of the *Ernest Piper,* and she was berthed for a number of years at Abbots Court Dock, which is nearly a kilometre to the east of Hoo. The wharf must have been similar to the one that is now derelict up Benfleet Creek; it was reached by a track on the other side of the sea wall. I don't know how long she was berthed there. Our barge lay alongside her wharf for part of a summer while the *Ernest Piper* was away on a cruise. It was part of a summer, while the *Ernest Piper* was away on a cruise, when my mother stitched up a new mainsail. The sail was laid out in a field of stubble.'

Then he said, 'Of course you know that!'

Then the skipper added the information that he was sure the mate did not know about: 'The *Ernest Piper* was later sold and refitted for sailing. One day round the Swale her windlass bitt heads failed and she drove up during an easterly gale up onto the old coal wharf near the entrance to Milton Creek. The damage was at the time considered too great and she was stripped of her gear and hulked in Shepherds Creek.'

'The old girl used to drift about a bit, just like the *Gladys* had some years earlier. Her shattered shell is that other one to the west. Eventually the *Ernest Piper* floated up onto the top of the marshes and there she has sat ever since.'

'Her bow hung over the edge and, with no support, it dropped off!'

The skipper for a fleeting moment had paused. The mate, looking his way, had felt he looked somewhat thoughtful, as if lost in another time.

Then he said, 'You must remember, I took the dinghy up into the creek some years back with the boy. We looked over the wrecks. It was sad because inside the poor *Ernest Piper* was the detritus of a family home. I saw broken panel bulkheads, upturned sinks and children's toys. It was poignant: I could feel it, *here*', tapping his chest. 'I'd been on that barge as a child. I'd walked the alleyway, the remains of which I had looked down upon. It had, after all, been someone's home. It was strange; it felt as if we were, somehow, trespassing …'

'It was some years ago, too, I remember, when we were at anchor in the South Deep, along the Swale. I poked around the hulks alongside the old brickworks and found a brass hook in the remains of a ditty box against the rotted fo'c'sle bulkhead of one of them. Now those had been sunk for fifty years and it was as if someone's possessions had been left ready for use!' The old hook attached to a cast plate was still in use in the skipper's workshop at home.

'I expect those barge remains will still be up in the marshes long after we've given up sailing. Few will know anything about them, especially the more intimate human side of their history,' the skipper added finally.

By the time the skipper had finished his story, they had turned into the entrance to Stangate and were virtually on a run southwards, leaving the eastern shore well to port to ensure they did not stray over the shallows and an area of littered wreckage along the mud-flats.

The wind was at a slant off the eastern bank. 'It'll be nice and quiet in the shallows to the north of Chetney Hill', said the skipper; so it was agreed that that was to be their destination. The skipper talked quietly to the mate about their plans and then said, 'Round up while I stow the mainsail and we'll run down to the spot we want to anchor.' Their speed had slowed somewhat after reducing sail, giving them time to look around at the other craft that were out enjoying the spring weather. One was a

… helped the mate stow their genoa along the guard rail …

pretty cutter of some fifteen metres; it was large against the normal visitors here, apart
from the spritsail barges, but just as welcome. Another yacht or two was anchored
along the western edge opposite where they themselves were bound. It was generally
shallow in their chosen spot, but during neap tides plenty of water depth was available
for their boat's shoal-draft underwater features.

Nearer the anchorage, the skipper went forward to be ready to let the anchor go.
At the chosen depth the mate rounded up and came forward to dowse the genoa, as
the skipper paid out the cable, snubbing and checking it as it went. When happy he
helped the mate stow their genoa along the guardrail.

The mate said, 'This'll do us for tonight, nice and snug. I'll put the kettle on and
do you want the anchor ball?' She passed it up to him – knowing the answer – as she
spoke. While the tea was being made, the skipper finished tidying up and hoisted the
'at anchor' ball.

Sitting over a mug of tea, the skipper's eye caught a movement in the skyline of
the walled shore. A bird, a hawk, was seen hovering; it had maintained an absolute
stationary height, above the rough grassland that covered the sea wall. Then with
amazing speed the bird had swooped into the rough to gather up its prey.

'Tea for that bird's brood – I'll be bound', said the skipper quaffing his own morsel
too.

'It'll be an early brood – if it is – probably be for itself', retorted the mate.

During the afternoon the skipper took his little lugsail dinghy up into Funton Creek.
He had looked across at a dark smudge on the distant foreshore to the east. There lay,
amongst a veritable collection of hulks, the rotting remains of a famous spritsail barge,
the *Veronica*, built on the Thames a hundred years before. Nearby to the south lay
another, the *Sirdar*, only slightly older than the *Veronica*. The *Sirdar* had been owned
by the famous local company London & Rochester Trading Co., commonly known as
London & Rochester, which had run a huge fleet of spritsail barges and then latterly
coasters. The company had been sold on and was now part of a much larger concern
divorced from the locale now, but leaving and lasting historical legacy.

The *Veronica* had been built for the same firm that had owned the skipper's dad's
barge. By the end of 1932 she had been purchased by the barge-owning family F.T.
Everard. They had progressed slowly into coasters and then had much larger deep-sea
freighters. 'One of these days,' the skipper said, speaking into the breeze which he felt
would carry his words across the now uncovered mud-flats, 'I'll take the trouble and
pay my respects to you both!'

Later over supper, a warming casserole of chicken cooked in cider and poached
vegetables, they discussed the next couple of days. The skipper wanted to poke up
into Colemouth Creek to the east of Stoke Marshes. They had not before investigated
that little stretch of water. Afterwards they would head for Chatham via a sail up to
Rochester Bridge. The skipper wanted to check up on a few spritsail barge hulks. 'The
next day,' said the skipper, 'we'll drop down to Upnor for a quiet walk ashore, perhaps
a meal too.' Then, continuing after getting a nod of affirmation from the mate, 'After
that we could drop down to Queenborough, and then run for home on the following
day. It's only a sketch. We'll do what we can: there's always another time!'

'All sounds good to me and it'll be nice to visit Queenborough. We didn't go there
very often last year. As you know, I do like the High Street, it's such a gem.'

The skipper had pointed out, earlier, that if the weather looked as if it were about
to change, then from wherever they had got to home was reachable on a tide. They sat
ruminating and nattering together, with the glow of the oil lamps casting its seductive
glow around the varnish work of the cabin. The skipper looked across at his mate,
who at that moment sat smiling across at him, and said, 'Shall I put the kettle on?'
He didn't expect an answer, and so went ahead. The mate had continued to smile as

she stowed her closed book, not wanting to ask for the harsher electric light: it would have broken the spell.

Taking their coffee outside, the last of the day's light was dwindling away to the west. The orange of the sun had turned by then to a paler version, casting a glow up into the clear blue sky. From the east the sky was darkening slowly; soon it would be night. It was quiet. There was hardly a breath, not enough to stir their burgee; it was a night to treasure. The stars were beginning to show their presence over towards the east. Along the creek edge, not far away, with the tide on the flood there was a gentle sound of hissing and lapping along the mud line. The skipper noticed that a few waders were using the last of the light, reflected on the water, to feed.

Breaking the spell, the skipper said, 'More coffee?' But the mate said, with a stifled yawn, 'I'll have extras tomorrow.' Taking a final look around too, the skipper hecked that their riding light was twinkling from the forestay, sending its warning glow outwards. The evening had come on and early and they went below to turn in, to sleep the sleep needed after a good day's sailing and a generous dose of fresh air.

On the morrow, they awoke fairly late. The mate had woken in the night and dragged the skipper moaning and groaning out to the cockpit to look around them. It had been an absolute delight: an utterly clear sky, still with no discernable breeze. A hint of frost glinted along the side decks. They'd had a hot toddy to drink too!

With the tide making now and with some three hours to high water they hauled in the anchor and set off under main and the genoa, both pulling nicely on a light to moderate north to northeasterly breeze. With the wind on the starboard quarter, they moved nicely over the tide towards the river beyond. Passing the entrance to Sharfleet, the mate said, 'Yes I know you've said before, but what was that wreck over there?'

'Well,' said the skipper, pausing awhile before going on, 'it was as far as I know a dockyard water barge. It was moored in Stangate to allow minesweepers and others to fill up with fresh water. It's been here for an age, since soon after the Second World

A port hand buoy. The West Bulwark, it marks one end of a once proud ship, HMS *Bulwark*, blown to pieces whilst ammunition was being loaded in 1914. At low water her remains are only a few metres below the oily-looking surface.

War, I think.' It was one of the more sketchy answers he knew he had given to his mate. But it sounded convincing ... The skipper could remember the mooring buoys down Stangate and knew that they were also sited in Sharfleet too. Most of the moorings had been lifted by the early 1960s, leaving the area to be enjoyed by small craft sailors and the like.

Now out in the river and sailing along quickly with the tide under them, the skipper said 'Look, we'll skip the run up into Colemouth Creek today. It'll be easier later in the week, on the way back down river.' The mate was not taken aback; this was typical of their cruising plans. If it didn't suit, then it was done another time. The skipper recounted reading that small craft could still make a tidal passage through to the River Thames until around the start of the First World War.

Passing two wreck buoys, the skipper recounted the story about the battleship HMS *Bulwark* that had blown up while storing up with ammunition during 1914, with the loss of over seven hundred lives. Most of the ship's crew, and those of the barges and lighters alongside, perished. Her remains, a mound, had little more than a few metres over them at low water and it often had an oily, shallow look to it. The place was a favourite spot for day fishing boats to fish near, or over.

'Did you know,' said the skipper, 'over there near the dilapidated, rusting, old Berry Wiggins jetty, amongst Bee Ness marshes, up the evocatively named Humblebee Creek, are the remains of a German First World War submarine? It broke away from its tow and there it has sat since soon after the end of that war. Alongside it is the sunken hulk of a barge. Another barge, the *Plover,* had got up on top of the submarine on a spring tide and got stuck. She sat, balanced, with her ends hanging over the edge. The barge's owner had an old barge, the *Swale*, he could waste – she had been stripped of her gear and was essentially a hulk; this was taken down river and floated under the stranded barge to support it. The stranded barge got off, but the rescuer, not being wanted, was left to end her days alongside the submarine!

'One of these days I'll potter up the creek and take a look, their remains won't last for ever.

'Or any of the others that lie scattered around the Stoke Saltings either.'

'Didn't we sail around that area some years ago?' the mate asked.

'Yes, we did', said the skipper. 'Very briefly up into Colemouth creek it was.'

They both then returned contentedly to concentrate on their tasks, the skipper to the needs of the helm and the mate to her book.

The skipper mused to himself, remembering the days before the power station in Long Reach had been built. An anchorage for powder barges was located in the vicinity of the coal jetty. His father had used the anchorage too. A short stubby jetty had come out from just south of the present structure. Perhaps, one day it'll be dismantled and the river returned to its full width again. The skipper hoped so: he was against the burning of fossil fuels for electricity. Little chance of that at the moment: a new plant is in the planning. Perhaps Greenpeace could stop it – a protest had taken place recently!

The mate had been sitting quietly for a while and was enjoying a period of relaxed reading of her present novel, while the opportunity existed. This lasted round past Gillingham and on towards Hoo. Later, passing Upnor the skipper said, 'You know, this reach has never been the same since the old *Arethusa* was towed away to New York, refitted, rigged and given its original name of *Peking*. She's a museum ship now.'

Sailing down Upnor Reach and into Chatham Reach, the skipper always looked towards his old home area of Frindsbury and the remains of what was now left of Whitewall Creek. The creek had been his home for the first eleven years of his life. It has been told about in a story about a barge and a family. The skipper's heart

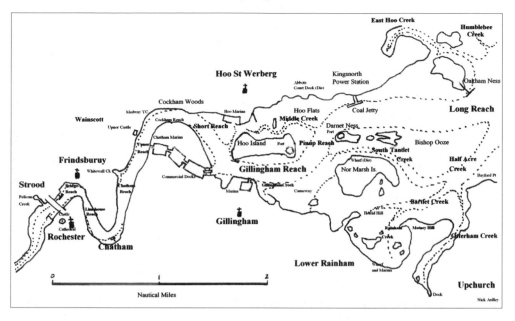

Chartlet of the upper reaches of River Medway and its creeks.

always took a leap as his thoughts wandered back into the past, and that day was no exception!

They were now bound for Strood so that the skipper could look at the remains of his old sailing home, a spritsail barge. They had done this for a number of years from time to time, but in recent years, reclaimed land had been seen creeping towards her remains. It was thought that perhaps little was now visible and the skipper wanted one last look, before allowing her to become just a memory.

The upper reaches of the rivers, from Gillingham to Chatham, had suffered the greatest changes over the decades. But although the trot of ship moorings had long gone, they had been replaced by banked rows of yacht moorings, stifling the waters beyond the deeper channel, restricting sailing space. The old naval dockyard No.1 basin had become a marina at the Chatham end, with the Gillingham basin, No.3, remaining as a viable commercial port. Most of the old buildings had gone. Housing now predominated on what was St Mary's Island, from Short Reach along Cockham Reach to Upnor Reach. It was a multi-coloured conglomeration of beehives, at high water, barely a metre or two above the river level. It was the skipper's view that it could have been maintained as a green and pleasant park, a lung, much as it had been used by naval men for generations, but alas ...

Below Frindsbury, the huge expanse of mud and marsh that had predominated in the environment had been reclaimed, concreted over and covered with industrial sheds. Ballast, dragged from the seabed, arguably accentuating the demise of coastal beaches, now came in by the shipload, day in and day out, thousands of tons each time. Before those changes occurred, that amazing area of marshland had allowed a myriad of sea bird-life to co-exist with man, right in the middle of Kent's largest area of housing.

The nearest stretch of marsh now lay some miles down river. For the skipper that was one of the saddest elements of sailing back into the waters of his youth.

Conscious that the mate was looking at him, the skipper said, 'Coffee?' This was to avoid relating the thoughts he had been tossing around in his mind.

In Chatham Reach, passing the old dockyard, which now is an evocative museum for old ships, the skipper remembered again the days of his childhood when he'd lived opposite, in Whitewall Creek, on an old spritsail barge.

The mate, looking at the skipper, said, 'Yes okay. I felt you saying so much, just now, but yet you said nothing.'

'It was in my heart,' said the skipper wistfully, tapping his chest. 'I was thinking about and remembering this area, the playground and home of my childhood days.'

They sailed slowly, against the ebb to Rochester Bridge, a navigational hazard since the Roman Era, then turned back down river to tack, initially, northwards along the Strood shore.

They left Rochester behind – well the bridge anyway, Rochester would be abeam for quite sometime for the river wound around it. The mate talked about Vikings and old chapels.

'You know,' she said, 'There was a battle here, probably one of many, but the Vikings came up river and raided Rochester just before they were finally beaten and subdued by poor old King Harold.' (It was in fact in 885 and about the time the Vikings [Danes] settled for a part of the English lands and ruled it under Danelaw.)

Continuing, she said, 'On the eastern side of the bridge is an old chapel. It sat near the end of the medieval bridge. Built in 1393 (the information I read said) and it was used for the good of travellers. Over the centuries it fell into various uses, finally becoming derelict by the mid-1930s. It's been refurbished now.'

'Be a good place to visit some time,' she added, finishing the subject.

Downstream of an old riverside public house they saw that the remains of the skipper's childhood home had gone forever. There was no sign at all along the foreshore. A wharf had been built on the spot. It had a number of vessels, lighters being converted to houseboats, sat alongside. Up on the wharf a pile of debris were seen with pieces of wood protruding.

Spotting the pile, the skipper looked intently, then, choking back his emotion, he said, 'Bloody hell! That pile of mud and tangled broken wood must be the remains of my old home ...'

They had turned below Rochester Bridge. Next to the Bridge Commissioner's house is an ancient chapel said to date from 1393. The chapel is to the left.

The mate instinctively gave her skipper a hug. It seemed full of tenderness. Nothing was said, but she thought of his book about his childhood.

Many other hulks had been placed in the old Strood Dock and canal entrance; the two old spritsail barges, seen before on numerous occasions, were disintegrating. It seemed that the whole area was going to be reclaimed. 'Why?' thought the skipper, 'The river bank should be moving landwards not seawards, sea levels are rising. What they're doing will only worsen the problem locally, bit by bit. All those little bits add up to a much bigger effect ...'

'Easy!' he said aloud, unintentionally, for the mate had heard! 'Nothing!' he quipped quickly, to a question from the mate, for she had listened too often to her skipper's warbles on his pet subjects! But the skipper had not finished yet.

'Look at that wharf over there just upstream from that old slipway. The bow of an old spritsail barge, hulked when the wharf had been built, has come into view. That site was the lower barge yard owned by Curels, a local and respected barge builder up to his death towards the end of the 1890s. It was taken over by Gill's, which became London & Rochester Trading Co. and finally Crescent Shipping. The company has been sold away from the river now.'

The mate merely nodded as the breeze caught their sails and the skipper, who was at the helm, had to concentrate with sailing in the shifty conditions being experienced. On the Rochester side some of the wharves seemed to have been cleared and some new piling operations were in progress.

'Must be renewing those wharves,' the mate said. 'It'll be a mass of housing,' she added pointedly.

The skipper said, looking rueful, 'It'll be such a shame if that is the case. We know some housing is planned for this area, the old boy we spoke to last year told us – don't you remember?'

'Yes,' said the mate, quickly: she felt that the skipper had more to impart.

A long-lost spritsail barge reappears, many years after her hulk was buried during land reclamation, as the action of vessel wash and the ever-increasing tidal height erodes what man had stolen. An old barge sprit can be seen along the bank. This redundant industrial area on the fringes of Strood (in the parish of Frindsbury) was under development by 2008 and was previously a barge yard owned by the London & Rochester Trading Co. Ltd, which later became Crescent Shipping.

'It would be nice to think that some of the frontage could be transformed into a park for the people of this city. It could be a beautiful spot with access right down to the water and ... I don't suppose that's been possible here for a couple of centuries.

'A pontoon too, for visiting yachts, would be a grand idea – It'll be way beyond the thoughts of the city's planners though! You remember those Dutch and German flagged boats last year that came up here? At the time it seemed as if they were looking for somewhere to moor and to get ashore for a look at Rochester – sad, wasn't it?'

Finally the skipper said, 'Shall we pick up a mooring off Chatham, or potter down to Upnor?'

The mate thought for a moment and then said, 'We usually come here in the summer. Let's keep it that way. We're not planning to go into Rochester, so no, let's drop back down to Upnor. Be nice to go ashore this evening for a walk – it'll be warm in a pub!'

So, leaving the little wooded oasis that surrounded the old dockyard church and the comfortable little row of moorings behind them, they continued down river. By now motoring as they headed the light breeze, they looked at the offices originally built for Lloyds of London and how the building had been sympathetically designed to fit in with the world's longest rope house along the eastern side of Chatham Reach.

Later after returning aboard from a visit to the local yacht club, one of whose moorings they had picked up, they sat out in the cockpit for a while. St Mary's Island was a blaze of light; people could be seen moving around inside un-curtained rooms. Lives were being lived alongside the languid river that flowed past them, they probably only marginally aware of its existence. The skipper said, 'I wonder how many people really appreciate this little river? A river threads through their city and lives too, flowing back and forth around them and yet ...'

The next morning the forecast from the local radio station spoke of an end to the fine settled spell in a couple of days, with a westerly coming in by the weekend, bringing the chance of rain, but for the time being was still from the north-northeast. 'Well,' said the skipper, 'That's that. I suggest that we go to Queenborough today and head home on the morrow.' The mate readily agreed with that proposal. It had been a pleasant few days and one more night would put the shine on the binnacle!

They had reached the last of their bacon too and fresh stores would be a bonus! So, as soon as they had breakfasted, their clinker sloop was readied for a gentle sail down river. The mate said, 'Let's go through the cut inside Hoo Island.'

'That's Middle Creek', said the skipper.

'Okay, whatever', the mate quipped.

The tide was on the flood so, with the boat pointing in the required direction, they set the sails allowing them to be caressed by the pleasant little breeze. Casting the mooring overboard the skipper proceeded tidying up around the decks. The mate hauled in the sheets of the two sails and nosed clear of the line of moorings to reach down inside the line of moored yachts. It was blissful sailing. A number of walkers on the beach stopped and watched their departure. Their voiced comments of appreciation drifted across the narrow stretch of water. It's a wonder, but so many people do not realise the power of the water surface to carry the human voice – clearly! But the sentiments were appreciated.

'Do you remember,' the skipper had started to say, but stopped as gave the mate a bit of advice. Continuing, he reminded the mate about a barge that they had come across some years previously, stranded on the beach adjacent to a dinghy racing club underneath the wooded slopes here. The barge, the *Glencoe*, had stranded on the

The stranded hulk of the *Glencoe*, a spritsail barge, built in 1905 above Rochester Bridge at the waterside village of Borstal. Incidentally, Borstal gave its name to the penal institutions for young offenders. The cabin from the *Glencoe* was removed, refurbished and reconstructed as an exhibit for the National Maritime Museum at Greenwich, London. The barge was later broken up on this beach at Upnor. No sign of her existence now remains.

beach whilst being moved from another place. The poor old thing had been broken up shortly after and removed in its entirety. She was now just a memory and a name in a book or two. He told her all of this while they gently passed through a mass of moorings along the edge of the Hoo mud-flats.

The breeze carried them nicely over the tide. The skipper took over as they approached the withies marking the gutway up into Hoo Marina. Seemingly heading for the ragstone-clad seawall protecting Hoo Island, the skipper located his marker and turned to jiggle round a submerged point and they settled down to follow a line of moorings and then a well-marked passage. Sailing barges and coasters still use this passage to reach a wharf. The skipper used a few moments to look across the water towards a partially submerged old spritsail barge, the *Remercie*. He had known her from his youth, when she traded as a motor barge. She had appeared here the previous year, ostensibly for major repairs, but had now become another loss to the ever smaller numbers of spritsail barges remaining. Some years ago they had seen that barge, rigged, at Faversham.

Coming out towards the river again, the mate said, 'There seems to be more of those dumped hulks under the northern end of Folly Point.'

The skipper responded with, 'Yes, I think you're right. I can only assume that they are being used to protect that end of the island from erosion.'

'Had a bit of a problem round the other side, haven't they?' Some old lighters had been placed in position to act as groynes to try and stop the erosion that was continually taking place. The skipper said, 'I wonder if the old fort will eventually be threatened? Look, the banks are definitely washing away.'

Crossing the tideway of the Medway the skipper headed for a gap to the south of the other old fort on Darnet Ness. He said, 'Let's reach through the South Yantlet. Its not a problem with this northerly.'

Folly Point, on Hoo Island, sketched by the author, as he and the mate slipped past one lazy day.

Over to the south was a huge area of flooded farmland, Nor Marsh. It was connected to the mainland by a strayway, the remains of which still trailed across the mud-flats and could be seen from the river when the tide was down. The island, used for grazing, had been abandoned after the floods of 1953, as had many other low-lying areas flooded at that time – all now the haunt of bird-life.

'Did you know,' said the skipper, 'in the book we have at home, about this river, written by Robert Simper, (*River Medway and the Swale*) Simper says that a waterman's public house used to stand on the Ness years ago?' pausing as he thought about it, 'Doesn't seem probable in this age now, does it?'

'Of course,' he went on, 'the river must have supported a huge number of river workers – watermen they were called – and, of course, there was nowhere between Sheerness and Gillingham that could be reached at all states of the tide either.'

Looking, from time to time, down the curve of the channel and its snake of buoys that ran in the shape of a banana, the skipper kept the boat in the deep water. It hadn't stopped his flow – though most of it went round his own mind – leaving the mate alone!

In a recent book (*Sea Charts of the British Isles,* by John Blake, published by Conway) the skipper had been given, further fascinating small bits of detail had been discovered about this area too – which he homed in on. A section of a chart of 1802, *A Survey of the River Thames and the River Medway,* published by David Steel and held in the National Archives (PRO: MPH1/578), shows that a farm existed on Nor Marsh, aptly called Normarsh Farm. Bishops Marsh to the north, running back from Darnet Ness, was an extensive area of land with a high knoll called 'The Mount' – now this and most of the marshes have disappeared.

The channels of the South Yantlet, and Half Acre Creek (not named) are shown to be wide and deep, providing a decent secondary route through into Gillingham

And through the South Yantlet, past the ancient island, Nor Marsh and its crumbling wharf, then out into Half Acre Creek and 'overland' into Sharfleet.

Reach: the outlet between Darnet Ness and Nor Marsh was as wide as that of the main Medway stream and a shoal to the north of the Ness.

'Fascinating stuff – especially when you join all these titbits up,' the skipper had said to himself, before going on.

'I've read somewhere too – I think it was in Simper's book – about the Medway, that an oyster fishery existed down the end of this channel near Bartlett Creek too. I believe it had finished, or died out, by about the 1920s.'

'Our wharf at Callows – when I was a boy – had to have clearance from the fishery company too,' he added as an aside, 'when we rebuilt it.'

'Mud and blue clay was dug out around here during the Victorian and Edwardian eras. A huge amount of marshland disappeared into bricks.'

The 1802 survey chart bears all this out!

Hauling the sheets a little the skipper cut across the bottom of the Bishop Ooze, and then barely perceptibly changing the direction of the boat, he headed across the deep wide water of Half Acre Creek. Years ago, it was here that an old barge hulk had been found drifting, after floating free of its sea wall grave. The skipper pointed the bow of the boat, towards a beacon, to the south of which was the back entrance to Sharfleet Creek. The passage would not have been possible in 1802: a solid ridge of marsh existed here.

The skipper, taking a mug of coffee from the mate, looked north to the Stoke Marshes and its torturous creek. Some waterside moorings could be seen lit up by the spring sunshine reminding him of something, he said, 'The *Medway Queen*, the old paddle steamer, is over there. The Preservation Society has had a lottery grant recently; maybe you'll eventually see her out on the river too. I used to see her when I was a boy on the barge.

'That old steamer pulled a huge number of men off the beaches at Dunkirk during that infamous retreat from mainland Europe in 1940. She is not as big as the *Waverley*, but I believe the vessel is important enough to save. Our country has neglected its maritime heritage for too long. A restored vessel, kept in use, could just be kept going for ever if repairs were carried out as and when needed.'

Pointing across towards the twisted and tangled morass of steel girders and broken pipes that was now Bee Ness Jetty, the skipper told the mate that to the west of the jetty was another little creek that they had not visited, other than a nose up some years ago. The skipper said, 'We'll do those creeks and Colemouth Creek another time, I promise.

'We'll look for the submarine and barge hulks I told you about.' he added, with some finality: he had to concentrate as they had reached a beacon!

The skipper glanced eastwards, looking for another, and passed the beacon well to starboard. It appeared to be standing to attention out in the middle of nowhere, for no good reason other than that it was there! It was in fact one of three that were sited in a line, running east and west, more or less, from the Hoo mud-flats to the marshes on the south side of Sharfleet Creek. They were, as far as the skipper knew, a remnant of the naval presence on the river, being used for navigation exercises. Others sat out in the estuary still – one out on the Barrow Sands had recently collapsed and was now a navigational hazard, where it had formally, but unintentionally, marked a swatch through the sand banks!

They now crept slowly into Sharfleet. They were still sailing against the last of the flood, and the wind eased somewhat while the skipper had been regaling the mate over the last mile or so.

Now close into the marsh banks, the early spring growth, the first signs of the coming succulent stems of glasswort were poking upwards, and also cord grass was seen to be back to life. The sunshine that had come that week would further encourage their growth. There weren't any flowering plants yet, the magic of the saltings was a month or so away. Tufts of sea pusalane, whose flowers were yet to come, hung grey-green along the clay edges. Many of the marsh birds were actively squabbling, protecting chosen nesting sites from interlopers. The breeding season was but a whiskcr away.

After working through Sharfleet and out into Stangate, where the ebb set in, they had a quiet sail down the main river. Sailing along the southern shore beside Deadman's Island, the skipper remembered the old swim-head barge he had looked over years before during his youth. It was reputed to have been built some years before the Battle of Trafalgar, 'I expect she's still there, though she'll be no more than a few marsh-covered rib stumps,' he said to himself quietly. The barge was thought to be of a type historically known as a Chapman chalk barge, and was in many respects was a treasure, as much in the skippers' view, as more well-known national maritime icons.

Finally they made a slow passage into the West Swale to pick a mooring up off the town of Queenborough, but not before the mate had loosed a few of her usual long sighs, whilst wondering when her skipper would remember the engine password ... Finally, the last little leg in was completed under power: the breeze was insufficient to butt the ebb!

Over dinner at a little restaurant, beyond the High Street, further than most yachtsmen tend to go, they enjoyed a good meal. The mate said, 'It's been a great few days, perhaps a little chilly at night,' a smile lit up her face and it radiated around. Then she continued, 'but even that has its compensations.'

'The sail from Upnor today was wonderful, all your stories lit up the area, giving all that emptiness life and vitality. This river has so much history and yet vast areas of it look untouched by man. But man has in fact shaped this whole environment!'

The skipper looked across at his mate and smiled too, for he was a lucky man indeed: it was not every sailor that had a mate and a wife in one!

'Comc on you silly old boy,' the mate said, 'tomorrow it's homewards for us. Come on, finish that glass of wine, we'll have a nightcap in the cockpit and just remember awhile.'

4
Early Morning

It was early on the flood. Dawn had broken over the fleet with a golden sun rising above the low hills in the far distance, sending its light and warmth unobstructed across the sunken fields, colouring the water outside the sea wall with a glowing luminance. It was still relatively early, but all the signs indicated a fine summer's day ahead. The sun was quickly warming the cockpit of a little yacht sitting quietly at anchor; already the dew had all but evaporated and her varnish work glowed in the light. Ripples caused by the tide crossing the shallows flickered and glinted. Dappled reflections of the yacht's hull and rigging looked back too, the skipper had noted, as he moved forward to lower the riding light – its job for another night done.

The skipper sat for a few moments on the fore cabin top enjoying the sights and sounds of birds squabbling and foraging on the last of the shell beds that were being quickly covered by the tide: shell beds abounded here, littering the creek bottom with a profusion of contrasting dark patches against the brown-coloured mud terrain. The shells continued up the shallow sloping bank, to a point determined by nature in conjunction with the tidal conditions in this area, towards the island opposite the sea-wall shore. It was this island that made the channel such a good anchorage. 'It's funny,' thought the skipper, 'how nature provides these things too.' Lingering a few more moments, watching the tide flowing over the shallows, the skipper stirred himself and took the lamp aft, carefully extinguishing the light and stowing it away.

A gentle northerly, not more than a zephyr, left occasional cats' paws on the smooth flowing tide. 'What a difference a night makes! Come on, out you get, it's a glorious morning up here', the skipper called to his mate who was still snuggled down in the bunk below decks.

'Never mind that – let's have a coffee', the mate called back from below.

The choppiness that heralded their arrival in this desolate anchorage late in the previous afternoon, setting the little yacht curtseying and rolling, had eased away during the evening, leaving the yacht still and quiet. The unsettling motion had been caused by a moderate northeasterly breeze crossing a fast-flowing spring ebb tide. Sitting in utter tranquillity, the two of them had enjoyed an Irish coffee or two, under a bright, low, nearly full moon, which lit the area around the yacht with a romantic silvery glow. With the moon behind them, stars abounded in the clear sky, a host of twinkling pinpricks of light, varying in intensity from intense blues, yellows to almost white. It was with reluctance that they had both gone below to escape the chilly air.

Shaking himself, the skipper stopped musing and dutifully filled the kettle, putting it on the stove to heat. It was time for their early-morning drink.

The previous night it had been decided that they would take the tide up into one of their favourite little places and stop over at a wayside mooring. Here a shower could be had and good food was dispensed at a pub with an excellent selection of ales.

Above: Quiet and solitude is often enjoyed in the South Deep, a channel to the south of Fowley Island, along the broad central east- and west-running swath of the Swale.

... started to shorten the anchor cable ...

Near the entrance, Conyer Creek hugs the shore line as it runs alongside an overgrown industrial wasteland, which until recent times supported an active brick making industry, latterly Redland Ltd. Here, since the late 1940s, two spritsail barge hulks have sat abandoned against the seawall. In the foreground is the *Landrail*. Beyond her is the *Kestrel*, built in 1896 at Lower Halstow for Eastwood the local brick makers. The rudders on both barges still stand proudly.

There is one sure way to thoroughly disturb a reluctant crew below decks, so the skipper started to shorten the anchor cable, sluicing it down and leaving it on the deck to drain before letting it rattle down into the locker below.

This had had the desired result: the mate came out on deck pulling on her shirt. 'Okay, okay, I've got the message – showers later, after a breakfast alongside', she garbled, with a look of disdain towards the skipper. Her book, reluctantly cast aside, would lie alone for a short while. There would be plenty of time for it later, when moored up and fast aground on the soft ooze that made up the bed of the creek into which they were now bound.

Looking at the chart over coffee, they discussed the short passage and their planned mooring up the creek. After draining the dregs of his coffee, the skipper went forward and hoisted the jib, letting it flap lazily; he pulled in the last of the cable until the anchor was housed at the stem head. The mate took in the slack jib sheet and the yacht forged ahead with sufficient way over the flood to maintain steerage.

The skipper sluiced the deck clear of inky mud and shell and stood watching the shoreline slipping slowly past. The wind being from the northerly quarter allowed a gentle reach up the channel between the marshy island and high sea-walled shore. It would not be long before a more intricate creek channel was to be negotiated. So less of this musing …

At the entrance to the creek there is an old wharf, the only tangible remnants of a huge brick manufacturing site, and it provided a useful visual marker along the blank-looking sea wall, indicating the entrance. There are two ways into this creek: one a torturous channel marked by withies and buoys; the other a shallower swatch called 'The Butterfly', which ran close by the old wharf, but was now a useful alternative, well-buoyed and deep enough to suit an early arrival further up the creek.

The decision earlier, which did not astonish the mate at all, was to go in via the deeper more complicated channel as it was very early on the flood. The wind would be more or less astern, so this was not of concern to the skipper. The mate had hid her feelings, but now her initial lack of astonishment had worn off, exposing her misgivings. She said, 'Isn't it too early on the tide …?' not finishing the question as she knew that they had come this way often enough!

The skipper shrugged his shoulders nonchalantly and grinned back at his mate, saying, 'If we touch, the flood tide will soon lift us off again.'

The yacht was steered tight to the bends to ensure she slid round safely, moving from withy or buoy to the next with consummate ease. Soon, rounding a sharp turn, they were sailing in a straight run past the old wharf – not the time to relax yet. Just beyond the wharf were two old barge hulks, whose stems and transoms stood upright with sea-wall stones mingling with her bank-side side planking. On the outer sides of the two barges their broken and wasted ribs poked eerily above the surface of the water. Down the creek bank, out of sight, attached to sections of fallen side planking, her iron straps pointed outwards, waiting for an unsuspecting yacht. The crew knew of those, having previously explored in a past season, sailing on a balmy afternoon up to the village in their little dinghy. Passing well clear of the barge remains the skipper and the mate sailed serenely onwards, the skipper thinking of bacon sandwiches and coffee, the mate in a world of her own. Behind them, channel buoys gently bobbed and curtsied in the ripples left by their wake, and the near-perfect reflections of withies curled and broke into zigzags too. This was an idyllic early-morning sail.

Maintaining this leisurely progress, they nattered about the tranquillity of this marsh-fringed creek and the bustle of its past life, when bricks, farm produce and other goods were dispatched far and wide. Here, too, spritsail barges were built in large numbers, but now all was slow and sleepy. The tide was still down below the mud edges, so the deep water was easy to follow, allowing this reverie to take place. Along one side of the creek on the salt marsh some sheep were lazily grazing. Some looked up from feeding and, continuing to chew, looked blankly in the crew's direction, letting out their familiar warning bleats, but most took little or no notice of the yacht slowly creeping past them.

A little further on the skipper and the mate watched little egrets foraging along the creek banks amongst sea grass and the little patches of seawater-filled mud holes that pervade the edges betwixt land and sea. Sensing a presence nearby, the egrets stood erect and perfectly still in amongst the cord grass, an eye looking towards the passing boat, as if to say, 'You can't see me' and 'I'm not here!'

Suddenly a flash, with the colours of a rainbow, streaked across the bow and alighted on top of a withy right in front of the yacht, not more than ten metres away. The flash had been a tiny bird; it shook itself, still holding in its beak a glistening silvery fish, which with a quick movement was gone – a decent breakfast indeed. The bird was of course a kingfisher. It looked in their direction and must have decided that this slowly dawning shape moving up with the tide would soon go by: they were not a threat. The bird shook itself again and began preening its feathers; the sun shone on these and the bird's movements gave vivid flashes of its extreme colours, of blues, turquoise and greens. Then, standing erect, plumping itself out in a final shake, the contrasting colour of its russet brown breast glistened as the mate and the skipper passed by.

They left it sitting on the withy, erect and still, ignoring events and probably thinking of the next fish after they had gone. The skipper was able to scribble a thumbnail sketch in the log book as they passed by. It was a moment to store in the memory, to

The skipper's thumbnail of the Kingfisher on the withy from the log book of *Whimbrel*.

... a flash, the colours of a rainbow, streaked across the bow ...

savour in the dim distant future, when sailing could no longer be enjoyed …

Still dazzled by the kingfisher their attention was drawn to their rapidly approaching destination, which was appearing round a bend. So, still thinking wistfully of what they had seen, they concentrated their attentions. The mate took mooring lines forward while the skipper dealt with those aft. Fenders were tied off and all was quickly, with practised ease, made ready. Immediately after passing the visitors' mooring pontoon, they turned into the opposite bank, touching the bow on, briefly, while the tide swung the stern round. Facing the way they had come, the boat fetched slowly back over the tide, to berth neatly alongside a pontoon.

After setting the mooring lines and stowing the jib, they sat in the cockpit to enjoy their breakfast of bacon sandwiches, toast and homemade Seville marmalade, washed down with coffee. The local bird-life had not finished with them either – a family of ducks appeared and any resistance to feed them was quite futile!

The mate was still ecstatic about the sight that they had witnessed and of the composure of the little bird, sitting preening itself, as they had passed slowly by, 'It just ignored us … those colours … It was a wonderful sight,' she bubbled and enthused ecstatically.

It was indeed!

5

A Mystery

Unseen, the dawn slid in early and with it the day came brightly, lit up by a golden sun which glowed warmly upon the regimented lines of moored yachts. The skipper and mate of one of these had stayed in their bunk much later than usual, having eaten the previous evening a good meal ashore at a rather pleasant little restaurant which sat at the top of the little town that straggled back from the waterside. They were in no hurry and felt lazy.

A harsh knock on the cabin top brought the skipper to his senses and he shot out of his bunk, wondering what the —

Peeping through a curtained cabin window, he spied the harbour launch. 'Blast!' he said quietly: the harbour master wanted payment!

Dragging on some clothes and grabbing his wallet the skipper quickly emerged, tousled and un-shaven into the bright sunlight. After exchanging a few pleasantries and paying their mooring fee, he watched the boat pull away smartly.

Some years back, this same boat had come clumsily into their side with a hefty thwack, fortunately only a glancing blow, but catching a cap shroud, which when it freed itself shook the whole rig, sending vibrations through the hull. No lasting damage was done and only a little scuffed varnish had to be attended to later. The boatman, of the time, didn't appear to be concerned nor was an apology given, so the skipper was always wary of this little exercise and liked to be on hand, ready to fend the launch off.

At the mast head a gentle breeze from the south-east fluttered the burgee. Moving into the cockpit, the skipper set the ensign flying – a little late perhaps, but at least it had been taken down the previous evening – it flapped lazily! 'This is a good breeze for a potter,' thought the skipper, grinning. 'Breakfast first, and then let's get under way!' he called to his mate, who had appeared holding two mugs of coffee.

They were bound that day for a little old barging harbour, beyond the marshes, over to the west. It would be lazy.

The previous day they had enjoyed a scintillating sail from Harty ferry, round the inside of the Isle of Sheppey, into this anchorage. It had been all the better because it was achieved without the use of their engine. The mate was quite sure that the skipper had a mental pin number that had to be remembered before the engine could be started, but the truth was they had not needed it yesterday: they negotiated the shallow Swale passage, even though a tack or two had been required, with consummate ease with the help of the steady breeze that had blown.

Referring to this harbour, at Queenborough, as an anchorage was a little misleading at that time, for there was hardly a spot left in which riding to one's own anchor was possible. Moorings abounded on both sides of the water. To the south they ran round a bend westwards to a position opposite a large ship wharf. Off the town's waterfront an

The inshore route: the skipper and mate, bound for Queenborough, feeling their way through the Swale near low water.

old hard ran out to the channel edge where a dozen or so fishing boats moored to a trot of buoys. To the north they ran towards the junction with the river beyond, on one side, stopping short of the remains of an old wooden pier. On the other side, a line of barge or tug moorings followed those for the yachts. A spot to anchor in could be found on that side, if desired, close in to the mud edge off a gully, the entrance to a creek up which few now ventured: it was a haven for hulked spritsail barges and old wooden mooring fenders or painting cats from the days when the river was a vast naval port.

The mate and skipper, ablutions and breakfast over, mused about getting their yacht ready for departure. Neither was in any hurry. After their lazy start, they had followed up with a decent breakfast of grilled bacon and tomatoes, with a fried egg each, bread and home-made marmalade, finishing with a coffee, all consumed at the cockpit table under a pleasantly warm sun. The mate, who prided herself as the yacht's Health & Safety officer, had dispensed sun block. Both, in the initial gloom of the previous morning, had forgotten and subsequently they ended up with red noses. It had become a typical summer's day with clouds moving lazily across the sky blotting the sun from time to time enough to forget the usual rule. They had been caught and the sun had done its harm.

The sky was still clear, as it had been on the previous evening. It boded well for the next few days. Going ashore yesterday evening it had looked a bit threatening, at first. The mate had taken a skirt, in a bag, to change into at the harbour amenities. They had, as a treat, enjoyed a sumptuous meal, then slowly wended their way back to the water front. The clouds had gone, leaving the sky clear. Once the street lamps had been left behind, the sky was filled with an amazing array of stars. Beyond, towards the river, where lights blazed around a container terminal, contaminating the local environment, the sky was lit as if from a weakened sun; the orange glow fading as it crept upwards, blotting a segment of the night's stars.

... breakfast ... at the cockpit table ... under a warm sun

Back on the yacht, the mate had laid back, on a cushion, on the cabin top and warbled about seeing this or that and ... and ... 'There's so many of them and ... can you see that one? Look what's that pattern over there?'

'You can see far more at sea – in fact it's the only place to really see them.' The skipper had commented: he had been a seafarer on big ocean-going ships and seen wondrous sights.

The skipper got the kettle on for a hot toddy; he liked to get his priorities in place. This done they both sat back and luxuriated in the star lit cockpit, reclining, to gaze up at the brilliance and wonders of the sky. The skipper knew a number of the shapes, but neither had ever bothered to delve into the science of stars: the sheer beauty was enough for them.

Before it was suggested that the bunk would be a good idea – who suggested it, they couldn't remember the next day – they had another coffee. It didn't matter, for they were in port and securely fastened to a buoy in good conditions and weren't planning to go far the next day.

Eventually, waking up from their post breakfast reverie, they began to think about departing this quaint little harbour. The skipper loosed the mains'l lashings and the jib was readied; both sails were then hoisted. The mate and skipper discussed their departure. The mate was going to be at the helm this time.

The tide was still running out so giving the boat a sheer. The mate sheeted in the mains'l to get way on the boat. As the skipper let the mooring go, on the windward side, the mate hauling both sheets got the boat clear and sailing, working her through the other moored vessels. The crew of another moored yacht looked in their direction giving a friendly wave as they passed by. The look, of admiration, said it all.

Clearing the moorings, the mate smartly brought the boat round to reach out of the Swale. Clearing the long spit at the entrance, she freed the sheets to almost a run before the wind, westwards, up the river outside.

... old boy ... stood at helm, gave a cheery wave ...

Leaving the Swale at the same time was a little clinker motorboat moving along close inshore. It had the look of an inshore, or river fishing, boat, of the type used by netters working the shallows at the bottom of the tides. They had seen netting along those shallows before. The skipper thought that perhaps that a net was strung out close by so they kept their eyes glued to the waters ahead of them. On the fishing boat was an old boy wearing thigh boots, with a grimy woollen hat pulled down over his ears, which with his beard nearly covered his face. He stood stoically, alone at the helm, and gave a cheery wave as he passed by too. The phut and spluttering of the engine's exhaust bubbling water at the transom was audible to the ear for quite some time.

The two of them watched as the little boat worked its way along the shallows, close to the mud edge, until reaching the entrance to Stangate Creek. The boat then shot off westwards, across the main river, into the distance. What the fisherman was looking for was not at all obvious.

The yacht was bound up the creek that the fisherman had passed by and the crew soon stopped wondering about him as they came round harder on the breeze, for a close reach, into the creek. It was far too early to think about heading towards their destination, the tide being about the bottom of its cycle. They headed off to starboard up a snake of a creek, known as Sharfleet, through a number of anchored yachts, keeping well clear of a long spit of clay, hidden about half tide, but at the time fully in view.

Opposite the spit was a deep bay which could catch the unwary: an extensive mud-flat ran well out into what looked to be deep water after half flood, it then sloped gently upwards to a beach and an old wharf, where all was once a hive of industry. The beach was a morass of broken Victorian glass and pottery, mixed with crumbled clinkered brick, shells and other more normal beach matter. Bird-life ruled this solitary world; man did not often venture ashore here, only perhaps a dog loving boat owner to exercise a mutt or two.

The old wharf in Sharfleet, where once vessels came and went. Now it is all quiet and the domain of the bird world.

'You know, this little creek was used for moorings by the Admiralty during the Second World War. Did you notice how deep it has been? Patrol boats and mine sweepers would have rested here between doing what they had to do. Motor boats would have dashed about, to and fro, taking men ashore for a few hours' local leave – what activity – it's hard to imagine,' the skipper warbled to his mate.

The mate, looking about with a gentle knowing smile of satisfaction, quietly said, 'Now it's tranquil, all the ghosts are at rest and only nature rules. I like it this way.'

Along the marsh edge, the crew could clearly discern the plant-life that abounded. Sea Pursalane growing along the top displayed yellow summer flowers and it flopped, profusely, over the crumbly clay edges of the marsh. In places, they noticed, clumps had fallen down the steep banks. It was unfortunately a common sight around the creeks, due in part to wind-driven waves or the wash from power boating and the ever-increasing rise in sea levels. Along lower flatter areas, below the banks, glasswort grew in abundance, protecting the higher marsh behind. This, with sea grasses such as cord grass, created a protective environment and a base for marsh regeneration. The sun picked out the glasswort, giving the stalks a golden glow, tinged with green. The crew knew that the top of the marsh would be awash with the colours from a myriad of flowering marsh plants, but all of this was out of sight. It was a delight that they had experienced at close hand in many other places that they'd poked their clinker yacht up into, when the tide was near high water.

Rounding the spit they continued to another bend, the skipper keeping well clear, knowing of the shallows beneath the marsh. Coming round this last turn the marsh banks moved rapidly away, leaving an expanse of shallow water and wide open mud-flats merging in the distance. If the tide had been up, they could have made a passage back into the main river across those of mud-flats.

The mate, who was monitoring the depth, gave warning of a rapid reduction. The skipper nonchalantly put their yacht smartly about and they backtracked, having to

tack and reach depending upon the course needed. Rounding a bend they saw their
fishing-boat friend, again. He was again following the mud edges, disappearing up
into the rills and gullies, then reappearing. Coming past them, close under the stern,
the old fisherman eyed them, closely, as he passed by, before heading off to run along
the opposite bank of the creek, looking intently at the shore. Both the skipper and
mate were totally bemused by this activity.

The mate said, 'What the blazes is he looking for?'

The skipper could not think of anything sensible, so didn't respond. He continued
to gaze dreamily over his surroundings. Sailing back out towards the main creek they
passed a bonny little motor cruiser, of the old-fashioned, pre-plastic age type. It was
manned by an old boy and was flying the same ensign as theirs. They exchanged a
cheery wave. Shortly after this, the skipper felt the steering go slack and the yacht
ground slowly to a halt!

The little fishing boat, with its grizzled occupant, soon disappeared from view.
The mate tutted, saying, 'You said you'd have to keep well over here – you're not
concentrating', and tutting again, 'You're daydreaming.' She gave the skipper a
quizzical look.

'Do you want me to take over, so that you can drift in your own little world for a
while longer?' She added for good measure.

The skipper quietly muttered to himself before saying, 'The tide is on the flood,
we'll be off in a moment,' and as if at his command the yacht gathered way, scraping
through a patch of mud and shells and they continued the lazy sail. 'You know, this is
what ditch-crawling is all about,' was another murmured comment heard by the mate
– it had needed and got nil response from the mate.

Reaching the main creek again, they turned to starboard and started reaching down
towards the south. To their amazement, the little fishing boat was seen puttering down
one side of the creek, again close to its edge. It disappeared down a little gutway that
had sufficient water in it at low water to allow a line of yachts to lay afloat for some
distance up its course. A number could be seen, with the mast of a couple more rising
above the curve of a bank, further away in the distance.

'Let's follow it!' the mate said, with a voice that signified her sheer inquisitiveness
too. It was frustrating!

Reaching the bottom of the main channel they hardened right up and shot into a
narrow neck of water beyond. In the near distance, they saw, it curved away to their
starboard. The little fishing boat was disappearing round that curve as they entered
the channel. A couple of short tacks in between a string of anchored yachts, now
turned to the fresh flood, engaged the crew for a short spell, before they were able
bear away round the curve of the channel. The look of disbelief from recumbent lazing
crew was a picture of delight for the skipper and his mate, as with a casual wave they
passed close under the stern of one particular yacht.

Sailing round the bend in the creek they spotted, over the tops of the mud banks, the
little motorboat approaching them, the fisherman still scanning the sides of the banks
and across the mud-flats. Again, he looked closely at the clinker yacht as the two boats
passed. He gave the crew a quizzical look, as if to say, 'Are you following me?' The
mate returned the look with a feminine smile and a nonchalant wave.

'What the blazes is he up to?' the mate had said quietly, knowing only too well how
a voice to travels across the water.

They were the skipper's thoughts too. He was wondering about a seal watch,
knowing that these creeks supported a number of these fine sea mammals during
the summer months. Belly marks were often left on the mud banks from where
the seals slid down them. They had become more noticeable for a number of years
now.

The mate, thinking along similar lines, wondered aloud, 'You know, you keep telling me that the number of Canada geese have risen enormously these last few years – do you think he's looking for them?'

The skipper shrugged his shoulders as he looked closely at the water and closing mud banks – concentrating on manoeuvring the boat in the shallows. Then as the echo sounder indicated a distinct lack of water he put the helm over smartly, spilling the wind from the jib, to bring the yacht round sharply. He had already worked over to one side of the gutway with this manoeuvre in mind, so with the jib pulling the bow round hard, he let the main sheet run out as they did a complete pirouette to run back out of the little creek.

On the way out, they were hailed from a yacht they had passed earlier, on the way in, a question drifted across the water, 'Did you go aground?'

'No!' the skipper shouted back, chuckling, for he knew that once again he had confounded yet another sailor with their sturdy clinker yacht's handiness when sailing in shallow waters.

Clearing the little creek the fishing boat was seen heading back down the main channel, following the shoreline, on the side that the man had not already traversed. It was strange, very strange indeed. They did not follow: it was time for them to start heading up into their lunchtime destination – Lower Halstow.

The skipper and his mate looked at each other; both grinned wryly and shrugged in unison.

Then, as if one, they chorused, 'What a mystery …!'

6

The Old Bargeman

It had been one of those weeks; high pressure had predominated over the south of England, giving the Thames area a prolonged period of hot sunny weather with light breezes. On some of those days a pleasant sea breeze had brought a waft of cooling air, but on the previous two the crew of one yacht, a wooden clinker sloop, had sweltered under an unrelenting sun.

After a lazy early morning passage, with a sluggish tide helping them along, the skipper and the mate, of the sloop, let their anchor splash overboard in another quiet creek to relax, read and perhaps, on the skipper's part, touch up a bit of varnish work. Maybe later, after supper in the comfortable cool of the evening, the skipper would enjoy a little sail in the lugsail tender, using the last of the day's airs.

The sun had climbed ever higher towards its zenith; it was patently obvious to an observer that it was going to be too hot to carry out any varnish work. It was windless and sultry; the heat shimmered around the boat. It was too hot for the cabin, so both the mate and skipper settled down in the shaded cockpit, where they lay back on their cushions, in relative comfort, quietly reading their books.

The skipper, resting his book briefly, looked across the smooth oily-looking surface of the sluggish ebb. His eyes travelled on and ranged the glistening mud-flats which had recently been uncovered by the receding tide, where a myriad of waders were busy scratching and digging for another meal. Moving his eyes further towards the shore, they rested on the broken, crumbling and scattered remains of several spritsail barges that rested deeply sunken into the ooze. One showed her transom: some of the boards were still fastened to her sternpost. It looked, from the skippers viewpoint, as if she were wallowing along, deeply laden, with a heavy estuary swell swilling along her buried decks.

Another, higher up the mud-flats, had been hulked on a firmer bottom: her stem was still intact. It stood erect, proud, with her breast hook still firmly fastened below the stem head that still carried the carcass of a stayfall block. The skipper's keen, knowing eye could see the run of her decks and sheer line from the breast hook, back beyond into vacant space. Some of her frames came up out of a weed-infested moraine of rotted hull parts; these ran back some way, before petering out, aft, into a weed-covered bed. Some way back from the stem, her rusted, yet intact, mast case stood as if ready to receive her long-lost mast. It had fallen probably years beforehand, with her mast waist deck and beams as one piece, to rest on her rotting keelson beneath. There it had sat and would continue to do so for many a year yet.

The skipper's thoughts wandered, his mind abuzz with childhood memories that whirled round and round: he'd known these hulked old ladies then too. That was long before this time, when the skipper of the little clinker yacht had known an old bargeman – well he'd seemed old to the skipper – when he had himself been very

Remains of the spritsail barge *Emily*, sitting near the entrance to Chetney Marsh Creek, along the eastern bank of Stangate Creek.

young. Those thoughts and memories continued to flow: they were, to the skipper, real life and they alighted firmly on the old bargeman ...

The bargeman had started his life nearly two decades before the skipper, a life that was different in many ways, but in others not quite so. The skipper then lived on an old spritsail barge, it being owned and sailed by his mother and father. His father had bought her out of trade, to sail and live on.

As a young lad, the old bargeman lived in a leafy old town that fronted onto a wide swift-flowing tidal river. On the river, craft of all types came and went, day in and day out. The types and numbers were numerous indeed and so thickly did they cover the water, at times, that they were difficult to count. The larger ones in mid-stream, steamers from lands across the oceans loaded with tobacco, spices, hardwood from the tropics, bales of cotton and hundreds of other things, blotted out many of the smaller sailing craft that crept along in the shallows, beneath the shadows of the seemingly continuous line of waterfront warehouses.

It was the ones that crept along those shallows that had drawn the lad to the waterfront: they captured his imagination with their russet sails and miles of rigging. Often they were deeply laden, with water sluicing along their decks from the waves and wash of passing powered craft. As far as he could see they were operated mainly by two men and, as is often the case, a dog of very mixed pedigree, barking and jumping at waves and closely passing craft, but seemingly to help none the less. The sight of these splendid craft left him enthralled.

Whenever he could escape from school or from doing the bid of his mother, about the typically small, Victorian, neatly kept, two-up, two-down, terrace house that he lived in, he would be found paddling along the foreshore when the tide had ebbed away. He would wander the waterfront, dropping down from the paths, when the tide had ebbed, to look round the hulls of those tan-sailed craft high and dry on the unloading berths. He would chat to old skippers and mates of the barges, or on their larger sisters, the third hand. To him, all of this was by far a more preferable past time than the education dispensed by the school he attended: this was an education in itself!

The craft he loved most was, of course, the ubiquitous spritsail barge, which had once numbered in their thousands during their heyday, around the end of Queen Victoria's reign. They were fine craft and were the lorry of their age. They had evolved slowly over some 200 years, from little flat-bottomed river craft with two sails to powerful coasters.

The first 'spritsail barge', as they were to be called, had a single mast with a four-sided main sail set on a 'spreet' or 'sprit'; this had a very high peak. The sprit was a spar set at an angle to the mast, supporting the peak of the sail: its form made it simple to handle. A foresail was set on the forestay and was the normal triangular shape. The hull was more akin to the hull form of the well-known river lighter still seen on the river today. The flat sloping bow was known as a swim head and hence these barges were known as 'Swim Headers' or 'Swimmies'. These craft were tiller-steered.

As time progressed a mizzen was stepped on the rudder head; later a topmast was fitted to the main mast and topsail set. Along with this came a bow sprit with all the additional jibs that could be carried. All these changes improved their sailing ability and the distance that they could cover. In line with these developments, the hulls got larger and more robust. There were two final major changes in their evolution. The first was the advent of the rounded bow, as on a traditional ship, with a stern sweeping up to a curved, or shallow 'S', transom, with refined lines above and below the waterline. The other was the change to wheel-operated steering, allowing the mizzen to be stepped inboard. This also meant some barges could be rigged with a much larger aft sail too. In theory, they were essentially ketch rigged.

The bottoms of the barges were still flat. This was one of their chief features throughout their evolution, allowing them to take the ground to unload and load just about anywhere, from beaches up near Newcastle loading coal, to a rickety quay up a narrow gutway loading farm produce.

By the end of the Victorian Era barges had been built in huge numbers, ranging in size from big coasters with a high freeboard able to load huge cargoes of 200 to 300 tons, to the more traditional river barge which was more likely to be around 100 tons. In between was a huge range of barge sizes, the overall dimensions often not differing greatly, the extra tonnage capacity being catered for in a greater depth of hull by the builder. They all shared the same rig, with minor differences, and in sail area of course! All of this was long before the young lad from the riverside town began to get acquainted with these fine craft.

The young lad collated all the differences he saw and imperceptibly his life began to be shaped by what he had seen. He would try to get hold of books about barges, scouring the local libraries and bookshops, discovering that there weren't many available, but of those he found, he read avidly. He would get aboard a barge when ever possible. He had by now got to know the friendly skippers, where he would ask questions and look carefully over areas in closer detail to make comparisons with what he'd seen on another vessel. Often he would enquire from a skipper or mate why something was done in a particular way on their barge, having recently been aboard another.

A typical response would be, 'Well let's see, yus, the Essex men, they always did do things different,' without giving any particular reason. Later he learnt that the Essex men said the same about their Kentish counterparts. The lad learning only that the men of Essex and Kent did things differently, this was always said with an undertone of, them and us, the skipper being a Man of Kent and hailing from Faversham.

If the young lad was down at the waterside during the final moments of a barge being loaded he would often ask if any help was needed. Barges being nearly always shorthanded, help was not often refused and he would help the mate and the skipper lay down the hatch boards, which with their sailcloth covers battened down kept the cargo dry. Sometimes the covers were simply laid over a stacked cargo to keep the spray off. This was often the case if going round to the River Medway or down outside Sheppey, into the East Swale with a cargo of animal feeds. Often he noticed that as a barge picked up on the tide the decks were almost awash. It amazed the lad when the crew showed no concern with this at all.

During his time getting to know skippers of all sorts of barges, he was taught how to scull the barge boat by friendly mates and set it back up in the davits. He set and stowed the foresail and found out what the bowline was for. The foresail sheet was a loop, often of chain, which ran on a horse, a wooden or steel pole across the width of the deck. One mate told him about poling this sail out, when sailing down wind, by unshackling the strop and setting it out on a boom. While a barge was afloat, he found out how to work the leeboards and what they were for too.

One day a skipper, knowing of his interest, taught him how the mainsail was set and stowed. Equally, how the sail could be controlled by its main brail winch and, with the lowers and uppers hauled in, have it set at any particular point, colloquially known as a few cloths or more. He learnt that the mainsheet had to be hooked onto a traveller which ran on a horse across the aft deck in front of the wheel. The mate pointed out the importance of mousing the mainsheet block hook to stop it from becoming detached. The skipper reiterated the point with a tale about how on one barge he knew, where it had come adrift and flailed around, the crew scattering out of reach, until it had wrapped itself around a mast shroud, causing much fright and angst. This had been told him by an old boy from down South Benfleet way, who had been sailing master aboard a barge being sailed to Leigh from Maldon, by her new private owner and a motley yacht club crowd.

Feeling more confident the lad, with a little hesitance as he addressed the skipper, said, 'What are those long wires and tackles back aft for?' surprising himself with the assurance that had somehow come into his voice: the hours he had spent in the company of these knowledgeable men of the river was at last paying dividends far beyond his young expectations.

So, with both of them walking aft, the skipper pointed aloft and said, 'The sprit is controlled by those long wires and tackles – wangs, or vangs as some bargemen say – that come down aft from the sprit head', pausing to answer a tentative question from the lad before continuing, 'Look they come down to those convenient positions near the wheel to port and starboard.' The lad following the skipper's indications ran his eyes down the wires, to the tackles and on to the cleat positions.

The skipper continued his explanations, saying, 'These wangs with the main sheet are used to control mainsail shape when sailing.' With a grin, full of meaning, he went on, 'You must never take a wang of its cleat completely, let out with a turn on the cleat: if you don't you'll get burnt hands!'

Later the lad learnt a lot more about all of this, but at the time it had all still been a dream.

He would often watch as a crew got their barge clear the wharf. They would get a bit of sail on the barge, a topsail, a bit of main let out with the sheet hooked on its traveller aft ready to be let out fully and sheeted in when clear, in an off shore breeze. Sometimes it was on shore, then they would have to kedge off into deeper water before being able to get away, the mate rowing the kedge anchor out and laying it at the end of the dolly winch line, rowing back to winch the barge out. Sometimes the big sweeps were shipped into huge crutches set on the bow rails and they would row the barge away, working her into a safe place to anchor in deeper water and await a breeze. On occasions a tow from a friendly tug or powered barge would be taken. The one thing the old barge crews always made use of was the tide, for it could help a barge off a wharf, set her down river or give her a lift to shoot up past a buoy. They never bucked a tide unnecessarily.

One day, a friendly old skipper, seeing the lad looking wistfully over the river and the barges turning up stream on the last of the flood, said, 'Are you ready for a sail then lad?' adding with a glance at his mate, 'Jump aboard, the mate'll put you ashore downriver.'

Without a thought for his dear old mum, the lad leapt at the chance and jumped down onto the barge's deck with a look of gratitude towards the skipper. Beaming with pride and thinking of the absolute pleasure he was going to get from the approaching voyage, he asked what he should do.

The skipper sucking on his pipe said in a firm but fatherly tone, 'you jus go forid and do what the mate tells you me lad.'

The wind seemed to be coming in fits and starts, but it had a slant across river, which with its direction suited the skipper nicely. The lad saw the skipper looking aloft, at the bob, then he told the mate to sheet the topsail out to the end of the sprit, and then hoist it up the topmast. Glancing at the lad he added, 'Go on you give 'im a 'and then.'

Once hoisted, the lad saw that it was just catching the breeze, enough he thought to push the barge off: he saw that it was being gently caressed by the breeze, above the rooftops of the waterside buildings, every now and then filling into a graceful curve, causing the bow mooring to stretch taught and flick droplets of water, then relax again as a wind shift shivered the sail, easing the pressure.

The mains'l was dropped to the sprit and left hanging on the main brail; the sheet block was carried aft by the skipper, hooked on and carefully moused to the traveller. The mainsail, being shrouded from the breeze by the wharfside buildings, wouldn't be of much use until clear. The foresail was readied for hoisting. Without stopping the mate, with the lad helping, removed the springs. These were lines that normally stopped the barge from fore and aft movement on the berth.

It was now close to the top of the tide. The skipper, watching a string of lighters being worked across the last of the flood, was waiting until they were clear. He hollered across at the watermen, indicating his intentions, for he reckoned that the tide had gone slack and he wanted to get away. Choosing his moment, he ordered the forward mooring to be let go, as he'd done the aft. The skipper had already dropped the outboard leeboard to give the barge a bite in the water. He fended the stern quarter of the barge as she started to swing and gather way, imperceptibly at first, then with a greater pace. As this happened, he called for the foresail to be hoisted and held to windward, on its bowline, to further aid the swing of the barge.

Once moving clear and with forward motion the mate, aware of what was to come next stood with the bowline in hand, awaiting the skipper's clearly pitched, 'le' go.' As soon as the skipper sang out, the mate flicked the bowline free and the foresail smacked across to the leeward side. The mate set the leeward bowline through the foresail tack cringle and back to a cleat on the forward shroud, ready for another future tack. They were underway, surging forward, but there was no time to rest yet.

The skipper, spinning the wheel, called out, 'gybing,' and round they came. The heavy gear slowly and then with gathering pace creaked and rumbled over to the other side. The heavily laden barge slowly lurched and then steadied with a slight lean to the new leeward side. During this the mate shot across to that new leeward side to loosen the topmast backstay, to prevent it being hit by the sprit as it came over. The other side also had to be tightened, which the lad did at a prompt from the mate – smartly too!

All is now set. The crew look aloft: all is well? It could have been the Old Bargeman. (Nick Ardley collection)

Next the skipper called for the mainsail to be fully set. The lad watched as the mate let the main brail winch run, in the way he had learnt, but it was all so much faster and with purpose. The lad remembered to watch the other brails to ensure that they had run free; he saw the mate watching him.

The mate said, 'As long as those brails are dropped onto the deck properly, they'll always run free.'

Back aft the skipper was busy adjusting the mainsheet and wangs, and the barge was set on course down river. The lad helped the mate to coil down the mooring lines onto the hatches and pick up and hang off loosely, various brails, tack ends etc. While all this was going on he found it difficult to get a moment to look around. When he did he found that they had left his waterfront town well behind. Before he could get set into looking at the world moving past him, the lad was sent aft and under the direction of the skipper helped to set the mizzen.

It was busy out on the river, with craft seemingly coming at you from every direction. The river bends caused the lad a few moments of anxiety, but the old skipper knew the ways of the river and approaching vessels slid down one side or another, following the curves. The lad noticed that they were heading down one side of the river, so had asked the mate why. It was explained that this was done to ensure large vessels especially were passed port to port, explaining that it was the rule of the road. The young lad realising that he would have to look into these aspects too!

He later questioned the mate about why the skipper went across the stream close to bends.

'Well, our ol' skipper don' wan' t' get stuck inside a bend and he uses the outer sides to get a lift and t' shorten the passage, when ever he can.'

'good luck lad, and I'll be seeing you'

The lad nodded: he realised there was a lot to learn and to take his mind off he spent some time looking aloft: in awe at the spread of canvas with, usually, two people in control of it!

The many bends in the river entailed a measure of running downwind, gybing from time to time, and some reaching. They rapidly sailed down towards Gravesend, where the skipper had planned, and promised, to drop the lad ashore. On the approach to this busy waterside town the skipper called for the mains'l to be taken into the sprit. Luffing up, he tacked the barge round, the barge then made up slowly against the tide. It was time for the lad to get ashore: his first voyage was over.

Thanking the old skipper the lad jumped into the dinghy as the mate pulled it up alongside. The mate, to the surprise of the lad, allowed him to scull the boat shorewards to a landing by a barge yard. The boat's way stemmed the tide as it barely kissed the landing. The mate took the oar and gave a hurried wave, as the lad leapt ashore, with a shouted cry of, 'Good luck lad!' and 'I'll be seeing you!' ringing in his ears. The barge boat sheered away. The lad watched as the mate sculled strongly across the tide, back to the barge, sheering the boat alongside, then leapt aboard with the painter, tying it off to a cleat aft, in, it seemed, a sweet continuous movement. The skipper, having sailed up some way, then down, had been heading back up to be off the landing as the boat came back out. As soon as the mate was a board, the skipper brought the barge round to reach away down river again, raising an arm towards the landing, in salute to the young lad. They were bound for a quiet berth off Southend for the night, with an early start the following morning, to make a passage across the Cant to the East Swale and on up into Faversham the next day.

The boy, full of awe and wonder at his good fortune, watched his new-found friends' departure with more than a little sadness, lingering until the barge had turned down another reach in the far-off distance, with the wind, he saw, on her beam; he could feel her heel to it. The next turn (he did not know then) would open up into the Sea Reach and the open waters of the estuary. Reluctantly the lad turned his back on the river and walked up past the waterside shipyards to the station.

On the way to the station he noticed a quaint clock tower above a waterfront building. Later he learnt that this was a ferry landing. Looking at the time he had suddenly become aware of the lateness of the day. The long summer evening and the sail downriver had, it seemed, been timeless, but he knew it hadn't and he grimaced in the knowledge of the roasting that awaited him on his return home.

Walking down his street he could see his mum. Even from a distance he saw her finger beginning to wag, her voice rising to a crescendo as he got closer. Reaching the front door he thought, 'I've had it.' His mother chastised him severely, knowing that his schooling was far more important: his homework had not been done, but to a lad growing up, desiring the life as a mate on a barge, or just a boy, it felt like rough justice indeed. It did not stop him from making many more short river trips, whenever the chance came his way.

A mate of one of the barges said to him one day, 'I've got to give all this up soon, the gel I'm a marryin' wants me ashore "doing a proper job," she says, so the skipper is goin' to be short of hands aboard this barge. She's a big'n, needs a third hand really to operate her proper.'

With a long, drawn-out sigh, the lad said, 'I'd love to ship aboard, but my mum wants me to go to college and that's where I'm going.'

One day, some time later, the lad sat on the hatches of a freshly painted barge, recently converted into a sailing home, talking to the skipper, an old boy retained by the barge's new owner to act as sailing master. The skipper, who was puffing away at a gnarled and battered old pipe, pointed with it – its end, marked with many jaw-clamped teeth marks, dripped an ooze of tobacco juice and saliva – as they nattered, in the direction of an approaching vessel. It was a spritsail barge. She had appeared from round a bend down river and was making her way, on the flood, up past the wharves towards where they sat. She was sailing light – that they could discern at first sighting.

The Curels' barge sails upriver past the Old Bargeman. Having cleared the foot of the Isle of Dogs, she heads towards Deptford Power Station, before having to start tacking up the next reach. (Nick Ardley collection, original by B. Pearce)

As the barge approached, the master of the yacht barge said, 'She's one of Curels' old barges, used to be with Parkers on the Blackwater for many a year too. The Parker family sold her and the rest of the fleet when the old man died, back in the early 1930s. That barge went to the Maldon millers, you know, up by the Fullbridge, Greens they are. They sold her some five year ago – still sailing though 'aint she. Sails are freshly dressed too – see the shine of the oil, cod fish oil that be, in the tanning, but did you notice how old they looked,' he finally added, seemingly, in a grudging tone, 'They seem to know what they're at.'

They continued to watch, the old skipper with a critical eye and with a sailor's squint to block out the sun's glare which was coming sharply across the water, as the old barge reached past them along the opposite shore.

The young lad looked carefully and took it all in, along with the bargeman's words. Looking back at the old boy, he asked, 'Don't you think she'll be sailing for long then?'

The old skipper, looking intently at the barge sailing out on the river, said, 'No, I don't 'spect so, when them sails give up, so will they. It's what usually 'appens, you know,' looking slowly around the decks of his present charge, 'I expect ...' pausing awhile as if reflecting and with a wry grin spreading across his face, 'Yus, 'spect this'll be the same too, you'll see.'

'They'll all be gone before long', he said, and with a final grimace added, 'You mark my words lad.'

With that, the barge disappeared round a bend further up river; they continued to watch her topsail slowly moving above the skyline, until they lost sight of it.

'I wonder where she's going,' said the youngster, looking at his old friend.

The old barge master, looking thoughtfully at the youngster said, 'Only one place left upriver for a barge now. St Katharine Dock is most likely, only two of 'em aboard, did you notice – skipper and a wife is all it takes to handle a barge of that size.' After a moment or two, he added with a sigh, for he knew in his heart that the life he had led since he himself was a boy was ending, 'Maybe it's the future for barges – for a while leastways.'

When the lad finally left school and started at a college to continue his studies, he wasn't sure where he was going, only that he wanted to go afloat and work on a spritsail barge. His mum especially was greatly displeased with this, feeling that only college would provide a proper passage into an adult situation with a future. Often from the front room of the little house could be heard the raised voices of the lad endeavouring to get his view understood, one session ended with him shouting, 'But ... Mum ... in a few years there won't be a single spritsail barge left carrying a cargo', continuing in the same breath, 'If I don't go now, it'll be too late.'

His poor old mum didn't budge from her solidly set view on this matter: her husband had been taken from her by a torpedo during the recently ended world conflict. Her son, for whom she only wanted the best, slunk away wondering what was to become of his dream. An observer would have seen a sad and disconsolate young man, sitting glumly, feeling that the whole world was against him. 'For why ...' he'd thought, 'couldn't I come back to my studies later', and speaking to no one in particular and in a despairing voice, said loudly, 'It's such a simple choice.'

Remembering what a young mate had told him the previous summer, he spent hours away from college mooching down by the river on the look out for a barge needing a crew. Fewer and fewer barges were to be seen on the waterway now. The last few years had seen a huge change on the river; the ubiquitous tan sails were disappearing fast. It was plainly obvious to those around him – he was not happy – he was missing his chance!

Ultimately he ran away and shipped aboard a passing barge which was in need of a third hand, the skipper having once or twice taken him on a trip down river. On board this, the lad was quickly turned into a lean, wiry and strongly built young man, learning his chosen trade to the satisfaction of the skipper. Returning home, many months after running away, his mum upon seeing him could not truly believe that it was the same lad that had left home so abruptly earlier that year. Nothing was said about his studies though!

It was not long before the by now seasoned young sailorman (as the river folk called barge men) was offered a mate's job on a barge running between the River Orwell and the London River, carrying cereals to a mill at the top end of the Ipswich wet dock. This went on for only a short while: the sailing barge was becoming increasingly rare on the water and sailormen were no longer wanted.

Many were by now fitted with engines, with no mizzen, or completely cut down to a stump mast, without sails. It was a sad sight for the young mate – the lad of those few years earlier, who had had such dreams of a life working these craft for countless years ahead: now only the odd sailorman bound down the Swin or up the London River was to be seen.

He mused: in just a few years, the once wondrous sight of a dark smudge on the horizon gradually becoming distinct, a metamorphosis, as a fleet of sailormen came tramping along on the flood, had disappeared. He remembered the words of the old skipper, who had taught him so much when he was a youngster, picking up whatever a bargeman would tell. 'They'll all be gone before long,' and he remembered the grimace too with the final remark, 'you mark my words lad.'

It saddened him, but at least there were a few barges sailing as yachts, and homes too. Eastwoods, the Kent Brick manufactures, The London & Rochester Trading Co. and the Everard family still had their barges kept solely for racing – but for how long? A club had been formed a decade earlier with the express purpose of keeping a barge sailing. They had the old *Arrow*, though she was getting a bit old by then: they just kept her sailing!

It came to pass that the now-experienced bargeman was offered a skipper's job on a motorised ex-sailorman, trading in ballast products (sands and gravels etc.) between the London River and a place up the River Colne called Fingringhoe. By this time, too, he had progressed to owning old barges himself, buying them in partnership with a couple of other young men. They bought up a few old barge hulls as they became redundant, doing a little work and selling them on. They would scavenge old barge yards, buying up as much old gear as they could find. It was all planned for reuse one day. Alongside this, he worked for a while in a local yard, an old barge yard, in fact one of the last to operate.

Some time ago the lad from the London River had moved a long way from his childhood home. He had settled at another smaller waterside town, which lay far up a wide, salty river that narrowed as it approached the town. It was surrounded by undulating farmland, with open fields and clumps of woodland rising up from marsh and low fields hidden behind sea walls. It was a far cry from his early years and here he had put down his roots. The young lad was now a mature young man, moving on in years, though not yet thirty.

A barge used as a sailing home came into the yard for repairs over one summer; she had aboard a pride of children. They seemed, at first sight, a happy band of youngsters. Locals noticed how able they were; they had to be, to do a large number of differing jobs about the barge. They helped, too, to keep the fire for the steam chest burning, feeding it old and scrap timber to ensure a steady supply of steam to cook new planks until they were supple, for their barge home. The children watched as these were walked quickly to the barge and clamped into place, marvelling at the suppleness of steamed timber and the ease at which it was been bent into shape. The youngsters took it all in.

... the skipper awoke with a start ...

The barge had had her repairs carried out over a few months and then she sailed away off to a river on the Kentish shore, to disappear up a creek where her home berth was located.

A young boy aboard the barge never forgot one of the yard workers, the 'lad' about the yard, for he had often dispensed tea and cake from a little old boat moored off the yard, which then was his home ... he told the older of the children tales of being a lad on a sailing barge, becoming a mate and then, later, a skipper of a motor barge. To the children, the boy in particular, he seemed to have been an old bargeman ...

The skipper of the clinker yacht woke with a start. The mate was saying, 'you daft old thing, you were out for the count, I've finished a whole book while you've been dreaming out here in the sunshine. It's a good job we put the shade over the boom after anchoring this morning. Now let's see, would you like a pot of tea? You must be thirsty. From the noises you've been making, chattering away, mumbling and such, one would have thought you'd been hard at work!'

The mate, who was intrigued, had been looking intently at her own mate across the cockpit. She followed up after a pause, 'You were, and it's no use denying it, mumbling and talking to someone in your sleep – what was it all about – who was it – can you remember? Do tell!'

The skipper still felt far away in a different world, but was now a little more alert and remembered the offer of tea, he stuttered, 'That ... that ... would be great', adding as his thoughts fully gathered the time frame that he was actually in, 'I believe there's a scone or two left in the locker, and I'll have some strawberry jam with them too – please.'

'Now that would be nice!'

Strangely the skipper remembered everything that he had, by now he obviously realised, dreamt. The arrival of the tea briefly interrupted his thoughts, but soon after with his mug in hand, he paid a silent salute to the Old Bargeman, mouthing, as he gazed across at the scattered, broken hulls resting in the mud, 'Someday, I'll tell your story.'

7

At Hoo

The passage up the River Medway had been quiet and uneventful. The previous evening's northeasterly had become a light land breeze; soft, warm and soothing. It carried the sweet scents of the land, mixed with the stronger saline scent of the marsh, wafting across the water. The breeze, now a southeasterly, allowed a casual run up the river. They picked up a mooring and checked ashore that they were clear for a night: these moorings belonged to one of the river's prestigious yacht clubs, and it was, after all, jolly good procedure!

The previous day the skipper and his mate had had a glorious sail down from Pyefleet, a little fleet or creek running off the River Colne, which ran between the low-lying marshes of the mainland and Mersea Island. The area is very much the land of the Romans, for they had colonised the area for oyster fishing, which still takes place.

Dawn had broken in the east as their anchor came up to the stem; the ebb had been running awhile and by first light they had cleared Pyefleet, leaving a line of sleeping yachts behind them. Later, as they passed by the Colne Bar, bearing away for the swatchway through the sands, the mate produced grilled bacon sandwiches. The mouthwatering aroma had given them both hunger pangs: this was one of those anticipated enjoyments that went with early starts.

It was slow progress across the swatchway and then towards the Swin, but by the time they had passed the Whitaker Beacon, the young flood could be felt, the sands along the Whitaker spit being swirled up with the change in tidal direction. This helped them on their way. The wind had been a light north to northwesterly when they had left in the early hours but it freshened during the forenoon and became a more northeasterly. The warmth of the sun too had brought an early sea breeze into the estuary. This ensured a good passage and the final period was exciting indeed.

The mate helmed for that last two-hour stretch, taking them to through the entrance to the River Medway and into the West Swale. They had a run from near the Swin Bell straight for the river's entrance with the mains'l out to leeward and their big genoa poled out to windward: it had been one of their finest passages down this stretch of water. Gentle rollers had built up, gradually overtaking the boat, lifting the stern and then the bow, rocking their surging platform up and down. Every now and then a larger roller seemed to hesitate amidships as the boat was bodily lifted, and then she surged forward in the grip of the water's pulling power. By early afternoon they had picked up a river authority buoy and enjoyed a lazy afternoon sitting off the quaint waterside town of Queenborough.

Later they returned to the boat after a supper ashore and sitting in the cockpit, watching the night close in, the mate, talking about the passage, said, 'It was like seal surfing, running almost as fast as the rollers alongside the boat. The rollers finally

The Whitaker Beacon, a solitary sentinel, some seven nautical miles off shore.

breaking and then with a surge, feeling the boat take off, then again to surf with and down the next – it was fantastic!'

Now moored in another of the river's more picturesque locations enjoying afternoon tea and what was left of their supply of teacake, the mate said that they would have to suffer another meal ashore because their fresh produce was down at a low level and in need of some major rejuvenation. Tins were available, but those were for emergencies and good food could be had in this anchorage from a number of decent hostelries. 'Ha – oh what a shame!' the skipper said with more than a little glee: he generally cooked the evening meal!

On the morrow they had planned to go into the little tidal marina at Hoo and sit in the lagoon for a day or two, stock up, make use the facilities to wash their clothing and laze awhile. The skipper had a desire to go exploring round a yard to the east of the marina, to investigate a number of old barge hulks and look at what was happening in this little backwater. The mate, when the skipper was paddling through mud and scrambling over the marshes, often stayed put to enjoy her holiday reading. When they were away for their summer sailing, the mate brought aboard the boat a holdall full of her favourite books and apart from the sailing this was her ultimate pleasure.

The marina had changed hugely since the skipper was a boy on his childhood home, a sailing home, a spritsail barge in fact. His father would anchor the barge on the mud-flats to the west of the concrete barge cordon of the marina and they would, sometimes, spend several weeks laying there. The skipper's earliest childhood memory went back to about 1960. His father had brought the barge into the marina often during the early 1950s, when it was essentially a home for yacht barges. The marina operator had a number of barges himself over those early years too. Now the older part was stuffed full of an eclectic selection of floating homes, ranging from retired continental barges, old tugs, converted lighters, to a few old lightships. Of the humble and ubiquitous Thames spritsail barge, there were now none.

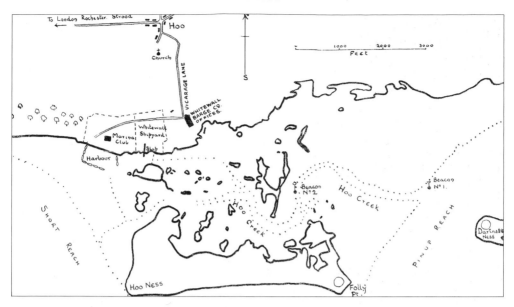

Map of the original marina at Hoo St Werberg on the banks of the River Medway. (Courtesy of Gwendoline D. Ardley)

Sailing past on the previous day, the mate and skipper had both commented on the growth of the collection of vessels moving westwards from the old perimeter. The skipper reminded the mate about how his mother and father had, with the help of their two older children, constructed a new leeboard for their barge on a beach on the foreshore. It had then been floated out to the barge and fitted, before they had sailed upriver to their home moorings in Whitewall Creek.

That evening, ashore, on a visit to the clubhouse, they bumped into the club's commodore, who remembered the skipper and his mate from their visit over a New Year recently. The club's catering was pretty good, but choosing to walk along the shore to one of the inviting public houses for their food, they had drunk up and not dawdled. Wending their way above the foreshore, looking out over the river as they went, the skipper started to reminisce about his childhood hereabouts and of more recent times with his own family. Pointing down to what was left of some bulks of timber along the foreshore, the skipper said that they were the remnants of a barge repair yard. The blocks had in fact still been in use until some forty or so years ago. The mate, humming a tune, had a thought (a premonition perhaps) that the skipper was set upon another of his tales.

Further along they came upon the spot where they had for many years always stopped to look up at the huge figurehead of the *Arethusa*, sitting ashore, by a swimming pool belonging to an outward bound organisation. It had now been enveloped in a shed with a glazed front. Their son had always come to a stop here to giggle up at the figure head: in particular her bare breast. He often said, to his dad, 'Look,' pointing up far above his little form, 'just like Mum's!' His dad always had had a giggle too. Mum had never been amused! The *Arethusa* had been a boys' home, before which it had been a nitrates clipper, called the *Peking*. Some years ago now the ship was sold and is now a museum in the United States of America.

The waterfront here once supported a large barge repair yard, the buildings mingling with those of a mighty cement works which had sat above, in a huge hole carved out of the hillside. The cement works had for years spewed clouds of dust and smoke upon

The *Arethusa* and the spritsail barge *May Flower* at anchor in Upnor Reach, October 1951. Note that the river is clear of the profusion of yacht moorings that now infests hereabouts! (Courtesy of Gwendoline D. Ardley)

the river and surrounding countryside. The leaves on the wooded hills hereabouts had been constantly coated with a grey dust. Housewives in surrounding villages always watched the weather, not so much for rain, but for that fateful shift in wind direction, which if missed, or ignored, meant the ruination of the week's washing!

After the cement works and repair yards went, the waterfront a became magnet for fledgling yacht clubs and a number of house barges. One of those barges, now hulked, remained and was being used as a wharf. Here in more recent times a yard, the Ferry Boatyard, maintained barges. It had rebuilt a barge, and a miniature spritsail barge, the *Blackthorn*, and a yacht were built from steel on the foreshore too. The mate knew of this and, sensing that the skipper was about to embark on some tale of his youth in these waters, pulled him away towards the inn door. Upon entering they were met with the mixed aromas of good food, for it had essentially become more a restaurant than a pub. They settled down with a beer and chose their victuals. The mate was, of course, right about her premonition of another tale!

The skipper, choosing his moment, said, 'Did you see the old barge alongside the wharf? It's owned by the yard's owners you know. They've put a round bow on her. Last year it was the stern that had been altered, giving her a transom. Surely you remember we saw her round the East Swale at anchor off Harty Ferry. She was a swim head lighter originally. A neat little job she is too. I looked closely at her from the dinghy recently; she's as pretty as a picture!

'The wharf,' the skipper having started had no intention of being allowed to falter, 'the one that the barge is berthed at, is itself an old spritsail barge hull. She's the old *Dorothea*; she was one of the many yacht barges and house barges that had made this little bight their home. When I was a lad at school, near here, a few barges still rested in this quiet haven, seeing out their last days as people's floating homes, close into the shore, with two inns across from their front doors. None of the modern housing existed then, just the little row along the front.

'A marine artist, John Chancellor, lived on a barge here too, his barge was the *Viper*.

Above: Upnor as it is today. Left to right: a wharf built upon a graveyard of barge hulks and now used as a boatyard, modern waterfront housing stretching back into the wooded background, an ancient riverside public house and finally the spritsail barge *Whippet* alongside a wharf built from the hulked spritsail barge *Dorothea*. Further to the right are the wharves of a long-dismantled cement works and barge yard.

'The wharf with the crane on it, where the boats are all lifted out, was extended out into the river many years ago. A number of old barge hulks were floated and sunk in position alongside, and the wharf swallowed them up under tons of landfill.

'One was the *Emma*. Some parts of the barge hulls could be seen for years afterwards. It's all been modernised now, re-piled and concrete faced.

'You remember some years ago when we came here, there was a barge beneath the wall, where the floating pontoon now sits? We came back a year later and only the bottom of the barge remained and that too has all gone now. They don't last for ever, unless rebuilt, used, maintained and rebuilt again as time moves on!

'There's another wharf up in Curels Bight, in Bridge Reach, just before the old entrance to the Strood Dock – the old canal entrance. The starboard side and bow of a barge has recently come into view as the wharf has crumbled – I bet it and the others, 'cos there'll be others buried with her too, could tell a tale. You know – I can almost hear the old hulks in the wharf yonder chattering away, can't you?'

The mate had been looking at the skipper, intently listening to the yarn, yet thinking, 'I've heard some or all of this before.'

The skipper paused, briefly, and this gave the mate her opportunity to stop him. She said, 'Here, drink up your beer' – for he had dawdled over his beer – 'I've finished my cider, so please fetch some more before the supper arrives.' She then continued, 'Tomorrow you can explore Hoo while I laze around and read – after the shopping and laundry has been done of course!'

Here, drink up ... I've finished my cider ...

As their food arrived the mate said, 'There are a lot of hulks and that old concrete ship to keep you occupied over the next two days; but that, as I said, is for tomorrow – oh look the food has arrived.' They then remained relatively quiet, while the food, eagerly awaited, was enjoyed.

The skipper, the boat's cook too, although enjoying the fare, said, 'You know it'll be great to get some fresh stores in Hoo village tomorrow. It's all very well eating ashore, but real fresh food simply cooked can't be beaten – don't you agree? – like a brace of succulent lamb chops, cooked pink, with fresh new potatoes.'

The mate said nothing, thinking 'Here he goes again', but knowing in her inner self that he was right!

Later, lazily rowing back to their boat, the skipper rested briefly on the oars, letting the last of the ebb do the work, for he had seen that the night although star-filled above them was partially blotted to the south by the mass of light emanating from the maze of housing now firmly ensconced on Saint Mary's Island. It was some years now since the old naval dockyard had been closed down and been redeveloped, with a marina too based in the western basin.

Across the placid water, they felt the eeriness that existed under the shadows of the wooded slopes that came down to a pebble beach that ran from Upnor to Hoo. From the unseen beach came quietly, but clearly, voices, and also the gentle but clearly audible scrunch of pebbles under foot. Those noises ... had they been the sweet nothings of courting couples? The solitude of the beach here had, for a long time, been to their advantage. The skipper saying nothing to the mate let the dinghy quietly drift by – leaving them in peace.

The next morning the mate and the skipper awoke to a flat calm. With breakfast cleared away, they dropped the buoy and motored slowly towards Hoo and its marina. The buoy barely nodded as they left it behind sitting on a placid surface to await another visitor. The mate, idly looking about, looked across to the passing beach and said, 'Look at that pillbox over there. It's fallen further down the beach since last year – I'm sure.'

The skipper responded saying that indeed it seemed to have done so, adding also that he knew that a book had recently been written about those concrete fortifications, built during the early 1940s. He then said, 'I used to play in that one, when a lad – I don't suppose it was a wise thing to do; it lay a little back from the top of the beach then.'

They headed across the mud-flats that formed a wedge along the shore here as the river channel curved southwards, motoring down inside rows of yachts resting on their moorings. It was on these very mud-flats, the skipper, when a child, had come on a barge. The moorings were clear of this area then – allowing sailing space. The tide was nearly made and there was plenty of water for the passage. They were bound no further than the little tidal marina that sat behind its perimeter of old concrete lighters and a sill, to stay for a quiet couple of days. It was a place they both enjoyed.

After calling the marina for berthing instructions the mate remarked, 'See that yacht coming in behind us? They left a buoy close to us earlier, they motored out into the deep water channel and have come in following the marked channel all the way – while we cut across the flats, saving your precious diesel.'

'And time!' quipped the skipper. 'For although we've pottered down, we arrived first … they're probably charging their batteries.'

After berthing the skipper and the mate wended their way up to the busy little village of Hoo, where a good selection of stores were situated, and re-stored their larder.

The village, situated on rising ground above the waterfront, is reached along a sleepy lane, beyond arable fields sweeping east and west. The ground to the southeast, towards the river, fell away to low-lying fields of arable crops fringed by a sea wall, and inland the rolling fields rose to meet the backbone of this isthmus of the Kentish Downs. Approaching the village a sense of stepping back in time greeted the newcomer and the more frequent visitor too. Passing the back of the parish church with its rambling graveyard, the lane was fringed by an old hedge where a stream ran away to fall into the river at East Hoo Creek, at the back of a distant power station. The road seemed to narrow as it passed over a bridge and on past the first of the older village dwellings. At a junction two public houses lay across the road ready to welcome the thirsty and road weary sailor … The day was sunny and warm with little or no breeze and the walk although not extensive had been steadily uphill …

Down on the waterfront, an extensive mobile home development had evolved over the years. It stretched across from the lane towards the edge of the high tree-covered ground to the west. The site sat on an old brickworks. To the south it looked over the modern marina with its permanently floating yachts, locked in for about seven hours twice a day, and the older western section built at the end of the Second World War. Concrete lighters originally built for the carriage of fuels and fresh water had been sunk to form the outer perimeter, maintaining their usefulness years beyond that originally envisaged. The western area had now become a home for houseboats.

West of the marina, along a beach, some recent development had taken place and an old ship sat along the fringe of what was a brickfields wharf. Further west, the remains of an old West Country schooner, the *Rhoda Mary*, sat at right angles to the gently sloping shingle and broken brick beach, sitting in seaweed-covered glutinous mud. Beyond the wreck were the remains of an ancient fortification dating back some five hundred years. These had suffered from the ravages of time and the ever-encroaching tides, ripping out the soft red bricks, from which it had been built, causing chunks to fall away. The scattered debris had the look of a pile of LEGO – some joined in larger blocks.

Trees, along the edge of the thickly wooded hill, dangled over the water's edge along that stretch of the River Medway and made it one of the prettiest on the East Coast. Another, the skipper and mate had always maintained, to anyone that would listen, was situated just a little further up stream under the old dockyard church opposite

Above: The marina as it is today … an eclectic conglomeration of vessels; some have been converted into floating homes, others have the look of stalled projects.

Left: Spritsail barges at Hoo Marina in 1952. The author's childhood home, the *May Flower*, is in the foreground and astern of her is the *Henry*. Beyond were, probably, the *Alice May*, *Venta* and *Winifred*, all of which were based at Hoo during that time. (Courtesy of Gwendoline D. Ardley)

Chatham Ness. The skipper and his mate had often gone to that latter place, mooring to some buoys out in the river. The church sat high up on the hill above the river and was surrounded with trees; below it sat an old public house by what was known as The Admirals' Stairs. The scene was a beautiful sight indeed, an enclave, amongst the morass of the modern town. Little or nothing remained to show that this waterfront had once been a busy and prosperous maritime port.

East of the marina, behind a wharf now no longer used by commercial vessels, was an industrial estate. A footpath ran through this to exit by the entrance to a little yacht club with its moorings arranged round wooden staging, and beyond this was a yard. The yard contained a varied collection of vessels and some old spritsail barges, some in permanent decay, some being worked on and one or two, depending upon the time of year, fully rigged. One of these had a living connection to the skipper's childhood, for one of its spars had come from his old sailing home.

An old wharf lay buried hereabouts; it used to be known as Buttercock Dock. The foreshore had grown out over the mud-flats as the years had passed, and with it, the natural coastline had gone for ever – or had it? The sea had a habit of reclaiming its own, at some time or other, and it was the skipper's view that man had often forgotten this point: the future was bleak for many low-lying areas in the skipper's sailing grounds due to ever-rising temperatures around the globe, and with this, sea levels were on the rise too.

One vessel in the yard bore closer scrutiny. It rested in a line of vessels sunk to form a jetty. She was one of two concrete ships built at Faversham towards the end of the First World War. Concrete, or ferro-cement, had been used because there was at the time a shortage of steel. The two vessels had been built as motor schooners with three masts, rigged with gaff sails and no topsails. They sported a bowsprit and had two foresails. They could load some 600 tons, but were essentially unsuccessful. One, the *Molliette*, became, for a while, a yacht club headquarters at West Mersea, before being used by the RAF as a bombing target out on the Mersea Flats during the Second World War. Her remains were still out there, marked by a beacon which the skipper and mate had often passed by. The other, the *Violette*, became a fuel lighter here on the River Medway. It had ultimately been abandoned at Hoo. Here, in this little backwater, it had sat forlorn and all but forgotten – by most casual observers. But would it be her last berth?

The skipper said to his mate, 'You know, I believe that that old ferro-cement ship should be saved. It is essentially a maritime treasure, not beautiful like the *Cutty Sark*, of course, but still, it is part of our heritage, as much as an old building is, surely.'

'The *Violette* was one of many vessels that came a cropper against Southend pier,' the skipper added, 'I don't remember exactly when though.'

'A little coaster did that a few years ago – you were still at sea then,' the mate interjected. This had the result intended: the skipper was stopped in his tracks!

The second day in the marina was a bit dismal; a spell of wind and rain came rattling up from the west. The mate and the skipper had rigged their boom awning the previous evening as a precaution. It gave them some protection from the heavens and allowed the cabin to remain open – giving space to move about with access to the cockpit. It could be a trial on a relatively small boat during inclement weather. A good book is an essential necessity during those times. The rains did not last long and by dawn on their second full day, it had broken, leaving bright sunshine and scattered high clouds. The day had a good look to it; they were not disappointed, for it was later confirmed to them in the local weather forecast.

The skipper during the morning had, while the mate stayed put to do a spot of cleaning through their boat and other odd jobs, embarked on a walk round the hulks to the east of Hoo.

The *Violette* is a relic from a bygone age, when the country not only needed man power but ships too. An innovative solution during the First World War was to build ships with concrete. This view shows the slight hollow lines in her bow. She was not pretty, but nonetheless sits waiting for rescue and reclamation ...

Later returning back to their little clinker yacht, with washing fluttering from a line tied off between the forestay and a shroud, the skipper hailed his mate and said, 'I've had such a morning!'

The mate said, 'I bet you have. Let me pass the lunch out into the cockpit. There, set it out on the table for me', and coming back out into the cockpit, she continued, 'Now then, we can settle down over our bread and cheese while you give me an account of your sights.' Looking across at the skipper she poured a tin of beer into two glasses.

The skipper, settling down on a cushion with his bread and cheese, his glass to hand, began, 'It was not all sad. The *Marjorie* has always looked resplendent, I couldn't keep my eyes off her topmast though – it's a lovely piece of wood. It was a different spar on our barge you know.

'The *Ena* looked a bit forlorn. She is in need of some work. You remember she was featured on a television makeover programme a few years back. Not sure what's happening with her

'There is a big steel barge in a lighter. She's the *Niagara*. Her hull rebuild appeared to be complete and odd bits of gear have been assembled on her decks. She had her windlass in place. Her mast case is strangely the same shape as the one that was fitted to our family's barge.'

The skipper was aware that the mate had been trying to get a word in and stopped a moment to respond and reflecting a moment longer, as if trying to dredge something from the back of his mind, he then continued, 'Do you remember the *Felix*? she was owned by a lady many years back and was featured in a magazine or news article, can't remember which. The barge seems to have a broken back and her hull looks twisted. It seemed to me that she is finished. Decks are littered with all sorts of gear. Though you know with a barge, never say die – but she will!

'I walked round the sea wall past the offices of Lapthorn's, the coastal trading company. The chap that started that business began by buying up a few old barges. The family lived aboard one, she was the *Alice May,* and they later put her back to work too! Mr Lapthorn was the chap's name; he carried anything that would go into a barge, just about anywhere. Mum and Dad knew the old man well during the first two decades of their own barge-owning era. The company worked some barges in sail until quite late on – engines were fitted though, but most were motorised from the start. We see their modern workhorses from time to time out on the estuary, don't we – those little squat black-hulled freighters.

'I remember being towed by one of their fleet during the early 1960s, on our barge when I was a child, at least a couple of times, after being becalmed somewhere down river.

'The Lapthorn family later kept the *Spinaway C* for their use. She used to race in the early '60s. They cruised on her abroad too – quite a lot.'

'A couple of their modern coasters were laid up on the mud near the hull of the *Dannebrog.* You know the one, she sits just off the sea wall; she has had a chequered time since being re-rigged in the late 1970s. She was barely sailed either, a waste of effort really. She sank in St Katharine Docks many years ago and after she was re-floated, she came to Hoo for restoration. As you know she's been here some fifteen years or more now. She is falling to pieces now. It's her last berth, that's for sure!'

The skipper needed a pause to refresh himself, if not for a breath!

He continued, 'I walked out over the chunk of marsh from where I did that sketch of the *Esther* a couple of years back, when we both had a walk round the sea wall. The marsh gave off those heady scents of brine and the, almost, sweetness of the abundant plantlife in flower, the purple pink headed flowers of the Thrift were out in bloom too. Sorry you missed it! Anyway, the *Esther* has deteriorated enormously since the last time I saw her.

The *Esther's* gnarled and rotting stern quarters, sketched during the skipper's visit to Hoo.

'Leaving her behind I sauntered across to the edge of the marsh and looked over the other hulks in the graveyard. The *Spinaway C* and the *Ethel Ada* have all but gone to pieces: only the fore end of one and the transom of the other remain intact.'

Looking out over the two hulks, the skipper saw that the broken hulls of these once lovely spritsail barges lay scattered where timbers had rotted and been washed about by the daily inundation of the tides. Frames gnarled and splintered had remnants of plank fastenings from which dangled fronds of the black bubble seaweed. Within the open hulls a plethora of an obvious sign of human habitation showed; rusting tanks, pipes and cookers etc. protruded amongst the debris from the mud.'

The skipper went on, 'So I climbed down and paddled across the mud.' He stopped because comment from the mate was a certainty: the skipper was not supposed to go mud larking. Nothing was actually said so the skipper grinned at the mate, before going on, 'I climbed aboard the bow of one of the barge remains and went across to the big steel *Adriatic*. She is rusting slowly away, but completely intact shape-wise – she still displays her pleasing shear and deck cambers.

'The *Remercie* – we saw her from the distance last year coming through West Hoo Creek – now rests alongside the *Adriatic*. She has gone from a floating vessel to a hulk that is rapidly breaking up in a very short space of time indeed. She was in Faversham only a year or two back, awaiting a re-build.

'Her stern has dropped away, but you know, it's sadder still because all her winches, windlass and steering gear have been left aboard – it's such a waste!

'My friend, the old bargeman, would be saddened by the sight of that old girl: he was skipper of her, when a motor barge, during the '60s. She came into Maldon for some repairs when I was there sometime in 1964 on our sailing home. For a while we had to be moved off of the barge yard blocks to make way for her, because she needed some urgent repairs.'

The medley of barges that lay in the barge graveyard along the marsh edge, to the east of Hoo. These are, from the front to the background, *Adriatic*, a steel barge, *Ethel Ada* of Ipswich, *Spinaway C*, *Alan* and the *Esther* beyond. They have since been joined by the *Felix* and the *Scotsman*.

It had gone well on into the afternoon by the time the skipper had got to this point, so the mate suggested that the skipper should finish the tale later, saying, 'I think I've taken in all I can at the moment – I need a rest even if you don't!' Glancing into the cabin and looking at the clock, which glinted back at her from the varnished bulkhead, he saw she was absolutely right: it was indeed siesta time!

Later that evening at the little clubhouse, they enjoyed a couple of drinks to wash down their splendid supper. The skipper had prepared a delightful dish of pork cooked in cider. It was one of his sailing specialities and it held a particular place in the heart of his mate, especially: it had been produced in a far away anchorage up a Suffolk river, some twenty-five years earlier, at a time that she had discovered that she was expecting!

The original club at Hoo had been known as the marina barge club, hence the spritsail barge in the fly of the present club's burgee. The club had been set up by a firm which bought up old spritsail barges for conversion into floating homes and yachts. No spritsail barges resided here anymore, but the club fly remained as a poignant reminder.

Later, comfortably sitting inside the club, near the veranda, with the evening sun reflecting its glorious majesty down the long length of the river reach beyond the sea of moored houseboats, the skipper sat back and contemplated the day. The mate was in a similar mood; she wanted to hear more of the skipper's story. A cooling breeze gently wafted through the open doors and it ruffled the long hanging edges of the pulled-back curtains, occasionally puffing them out as if a spinnaker, which then collapsed again at the lack of a holding breeze.

The mate, choosing her moment, after seeing her skipper take a long pull of the Kentish ale he was enjoying, wanted the rest of the earlier yarn. 'Come on then, I'm ready for the rest of your tale you started this afternoon.'

The skipper took another quick pull on his tankard, then, after he had licked his lips in appreciation of a decent drop of real ale, continued as requested. 'I looked at the old *Alan*. She hasn't really started to break up properly yet, although her stem has split and some her planks are breaking away. The old boy at our greengrocer's sailed on her in the early 1950s; he sailed on the *Sirdar* too, for that matter.'

'Then I walked round to the old farm wharf, Abbots Court Dock. Not a lot left though, much less than the old wharf in Benfleet Creek; it's almost completely obliterated. It seemed strange, especially as I remember vividly visiting a barge, the *Ernest Piper*, with my mother – we had tea! We also berthed there ourselves on a visit some forty-five years ago for some weeks over one summer!'

'Wasn't it there that your mother did a mass of sail stitching?' said the mate, hastily getting a word in.

'Oh, err … yes' was the short reply.

'Along the way, I looked over a fleet of hulks that were sat next to the sea wall years ago. They had something to do with stemming the tide after the 1953 floods as far as I know. Little left of them now though, a few timbers here and there, some recognisable stem and stern posts and a section of a barges side holding up a pile of sea-wall stones!'

'That was it really,' the skipper said, picking up his ale glass and indicating that as it was now empty he would be having another.

The following morning they left for the tranquillity of Stangate. Having cleared the marina some two hours before high water, they set the main and jib and with a decent northwesterly breeze passed through into Middle Creek and followed the buoyed channel to the River Medway, crossing this to enter South Yantlet Creek, below Darnet Ness. It was easy sailing, allowing time to look around and enjoy the sights. Using those inner channels avoided the wash from the myriad power craft that had proliferated on this river over the last decade. The skipper had nothing against motor boats, but some of the present crop of craft produced a wash that caused violent boat motions that at times did not feel natural. In any case it was always an interesting passage.

Leaving Yantlet Creek, to the north of a wreck, an old dockyard dry dock caisson, they sailed into the entrance to Otterham Creek. The skipper said, 'We'll not go far in – one day we'll go right up and, perhaps, stay the night. It's possible now to get a berth up the creek against a pontoon. So I've heard.'

The skipper pointed to the sea wall and said, 'the old London & Rochester barge *Sirdar* was abandoned over there for a while around 1970, until she decided to go for a voyage on her own!' then looking at his mate, he added quickly, 'Sorry, I've told you that story before.'

Back outside the creek they looked across at a row of small navigation buoys, and in the distance some moored yachts, to the south-west. The mate, looking at their chart said, 'Rainham Wharf is over there, its off Bartlett Creek. Didn't you tell me a story about an old trading barge going in there and a lad who visited your barge?'

The skipper nodded as he replied, 'It was the old *Cambria*. She sat there a few days waiting to be unloaded.' Then, pointing, (he was going to change the subject: something had come to mind) he said, 'You know there is enough water to anchor under that little hill on that spit of marsh over there, at the head of the creek, especially on a neap tide. I was going to do it a couple of years ago, when you left me for a day or so to go back home, I didn't 'cos I caught the edge of the spit on the Yantlet side and sat in the ooze for several hours!'

After a moments silence to reflect upon his mistake the skipper said, 'Later I sailed back up to Upnor instead ...' leaving the comment hanging in the air.

The mate, looking away into the distance, smiled to herself: the skipper was embarrassed!

The tide was approaching slack water so reluctantly they put the helm about and reached up Half Acre Creek, not heading for the main river, but into the back entrance of Sharfleet Creek. Leaving a beacon well to port they headed, it seemed, into a morass of marsh with a number of masts on unseen hulls indicating that navigable water lay beyond. Soon though the eye had been able to discern the way ahead!

After they had threaded their way through Sharfleet, where the rich ozone flavours drifted off the marshes across their boat, filling their nostrils with the heady scents, they came out into Stangate Creek. Here they set course southwards, towards the foot of the creek, where they planned to anchor. On the way up, the skipper dropped the mainsail and at a comfortable ground speed they slowly pottered up over the early ebb, along the western edge. The skipper felt in no hurry.

The mate mumbled about getting anchored. She looked at the sky: it had darkened appreciably.

'I hope it isn't going to rain ...' the mate murmured in the quietness of their slow passage along the edge of the mud. There wasn't any rain: the clouds drifted away inland, though a covering of cloud, with sunny breaks, did return towards the evening to give a glorious sunset – but that was later.

Along this western side of the creek it was not unusual to see numerous snow-white egrets. These had colonised the area in huge numbers, it being to their liking, and food, an essential of course, had been found in abundance too. The island of marsh, which was the remnants of flooded sheep-grazing land, was probably free of the marauding fox, that modern blight of the town and country, thus preserving good numbers of the birds hereabouts, of many differing species.

At the bottom end of Stangate Creek the marsh island still had a bulwark of ragstone cladding protecting it from erosion, which was all to the well for the small

Sunset at the end of the day, with the tail end of a threatening evening sky clearing away. It left the skipper and mate in the solitude of a Stangate Creek, virtually alone, in one of their favourite places, anchored along the edge of Greenborough Marshes.

boat sailor. The end, a chin shape, had a strange name; it is known as Slaughterhouse Point. It was probable that a slaughterhouse had indeed been sited ashore here when sheep were grazed on the now-flooded land. The end of all of this had come about nearly one hundred years ago after a bout of flooding and sea-wall damage had rendered the land untenable and it had been abandoned to nature.

Rounding the point, the skipper indicated to the mate where he intended to drop their anchor. So, passing over the helm, he ambled forward to haul the chain from the locker, where it had lain since leaving Pyefleet some days earlier. Unlashing the anchor as the mate started to round up, the skipper watched as the boat came up towards the wind and slowed, then he let the anchor splash overboard. He paid out the chain, and then snubbed the boat, ensuring that it had dug in.

After dropping and tidying up the jib, the skipper thought, 'I'm ready for my tea ...' Then, as if his thoughts had tumbled below into the cabin, the mate's call coincided with the comely sound of a whistling kettle.

'Tomorrow,' said the mate, 'let's go up into Lower Halstow for lunch. I know we've been there recently, but the tides are just right.' With those thoughts they settled back onto some cushions, with their respective books to hand, to have their tea.

Some time later they looked across the cockpit at each other. They smiled ... that knowing smile: here was one of their favourite places.

8

Once Again, a Bob Fluttered in a Forgotten Corner

Far beyond the big river where modern ships come and go, a system of creeks, where yachts can be seen in large numbers on a summer's weekend, leads up to a sluggish stretch of water; a dock moulders at its head.

The dock is surrounded on one side by a rough country park, whose contolling force is Mother Nature. To the other, an ancient rambling church built on a low hillock, seemingly floating; a mere fraction higher than the spring tide level that regularly changes the surrounding inter-tidal world into massive shallow lagoon stretching as far as an eye can see. At the top of the dock sits a low bridge surmounted by rambling sea wall with a sluice, shutting out the tide from the low habited hinterland beyond. The dock bottom has silted up from deposits left, year by year, by sluggish tides and layers of decaying sea grasses.

The once bustling quaysides have collapsed in many places, tumbled wharf infill material blending in with the upper tidal levels, sloping downwards into a smelly, weed-infested, mud bottom, through which a gutway trickles, draining water from a stream which issues from the sluice after each tide. The stream has its source beyond the village, amongst the green gently rolling hills that fringe the skyline. The green hills are varied in hue, depending upon the seasons, with pink and white of heavily scented blossom mixing with the wooded edges of the narrow country lanes. The orchards are set strangely below road level, the ground having been denuded of brick earth by labourers, sweating day in and day out, to match the demand from a brickworks that sat by the dock. Along one length of the dock some semblance of order has somehow survived and a semi-serviceable quay remains. The bottom of the dock, though, is littered with the detritus of villagers' unwanted possessions: prams, bicycles, supermarket trolleys, children's scooters, chunks of clinkered brick, broken bottles and a melee of indiscernible objects that poke, dangerously, through the mud and weed. Its disposition is seriously inhospitable.

Life had come to this inexorable state, slowly, from the moment the brickworks began to turn out fewer and fewer bricks. Time began to sit still, its past and heyday all but forgotten. At a first casual glance only an unusual quantity of broken bottle glass, old Victorian pottery ware and small pieces of brick, all with edges rounded by the wave action from countless tides, scattered on a beach close to the dock entrance gives clues to an industrial past. Other signs lie away from the dock, buried under wild banks of hawthorn, bramble, cow parsley and thick knots of tall grasses waving in the breeze. To either side of the dock entrance lies the rotting remains of a few sailing barges – once numerous, these humble, but picturesque vessels were the Victorian floating lorry, carrying cargoes from far and wide, their bones are the only reminder.

Some folks living by this waterside connection to the sea remember the time before, and lament in the way older people do what has been, what has been lost,

Looking into Lower Halstow Dock in recent times. Remnants of crumbled wharves can be seen in the foreground.

and the glory and grandeur of a bustling working environment. The old brown-sailed (though some say they were red- or even black-sailed) spritsail barges have long been a memory. They came in with holds full of muck from London and went away again, and again, full of bricks, millions of them; these went into building that sprawling metropolis far up the big river, out beyond our smaller tributary. The bustle of unloading and loading barges, dust from furnace coal, the mess of mud, clay, dirt and detritus of other brick making needs had all gone and with them; the belching chimneys and smells went too.

All is now a memory. The air is now clean, smelling of sea salt, seaweed and that almost indescribable waft from the decaying remains of millions of sea creatures left after the tide recedes, mixed with the sweeter scents of bramble, grasses and the myriad of wild plants growing abundantly upon this old industrial landscape.

On the tide a few small boats and yachts come and go. The few visitors head for a quick pub lunch. The sailors, being very wary of the gnarled old timbers holding up part of the dockside, fear to take the ground and leave as soon as the tide started to ebb away. A few brave souls keep their boats here. They risk damage from remnants of wharf timbers, or bits of old barge rudder which lay half buried at the edges in the ever-increasing levels of silt. They visit regularly to clear away an old bicycle or some other item dumped by the unscrupulous. These boats are held clear of the wharfside by ancient floats or logs and are old, battered and weathered, receiving only rudimentary attention: they are nearing the end of their lives, although still useful. The picture, if framed, would show a sad, dilapidated, sleeping tableau.

The wilderness that covered the old brickworks, the country park, is riddled with pathways where walkers enjoy the rejuvenated environment. The scent of wild flowers, the buzzing of a myriad of different bees and many other winged insects can be seen as they walked from clump to clump, and the space above their heads is clouded with

Spritsail barges in Lower Halstow Dock during the early 1930s. The *Suffolk* and two stumpies, one loaded down, sit amongst their reflections. Bricks sit piled up ready for London. (Courtesy of Pauline Stevens; from the Kitney Collection)

a myriad of winged life. Butterflies abound and they flutter lazily from flowerhead to flowerhead. Birds not seen when smoke and dirt pervaded the environment have returned here, in ever-increasing numbers, feeding on the abundance of seed and winged life. The land is riddled with burrows housing numerous rabbits which looked up, as walkers come near, hopping under a briar patch, coming out after they've gone by, looking up, as if to say, 'Now move on.' They continue grazing: this all belongs to nature.

In the winter, after a heavy frost, the brambles and hawthorn are coated with a layer of white crystal icing; the ground has a crusty top and scrunches under foot announcing the presence of early walkers exercising their dogs. On the mud-flats beyond the dock, brent geese, with the resonant sound of their almost constant growling 'Aark,' feed in large numbers upon the eel grass. Soon they will be heading for fresh feeding grounds on farmland to the east which fringes this wild place, the succulent weed not lasting long. Mixed in are shelduck, mallards and widgeon all foraging in the tidal pools and little run-off streams from the mud-flats. Sit quietly and the watcher is rewarded with the sight of curlews, gulls, oystercatchers, sand pipers, red shank, turnstones, dunlin and, if you look carefully, some bar-tailed godwits with their slightly turned up bills, all foraging in this tidal and inter-tidal domain. In amongst all these are hundreds of knot, which, when agitated, or for no other reason, fly up in ever-increasing numbers, swooping, weaving and swerving in sharp turns, above the mud-flats, as if waltzing to some unheard tune.

In summer, on a hot day, children come down to skim stones across the placid surface of the water. People are to be found sitting, contemplating – thoughts about a host of troubles, concerns, happy moments – or just resting, cleansing the mind and watching nature at work. Artists can be found, too, perched on canvas stools, sitting on a chunk of clinkered brick, or seated at the edge of the sloping Kentish ragstone wall, sketching and painting the world about them. A lady of the village is one regular, often seen with a pad and pencil quickly catching a moment, or laden with all that is needed to paint on the spot. The lady, now much older, had once lived on a barge berthed nearby and had once, too, stayed in the old dock during a summer some forty-odd years past.

Amongst the brambles near the ragstone wall, the remains of a few timbers are found; these are from old spritsail barges that were hauled ashore and broken up for fire ood, good for nothing else after a hard life, to be burnt in the kilns to bake the bricks of which they themselves carried countless cargoes. The remaining timbers, gradually returning to the elements from which they came, give life and a home to insects, beetles and fungi of every description.

Jutting out from the wall the shattered hull of a barge lies with its stern to the beach. She arrived here many years ago, tired and worn out, was stripped of her sails masts and rigging. Strangely, her leeboards were left on; she sits as if ready to go. Gradually she fell to pieces, her decks sagging, beams giving way until finally dropping, ultimately her hull sides collapsed. Her leeboards can still be seen, standing grimly upright, until they too eventually succumb to the caress of the tide. Her stem still stands, as too does her sternpost with parts of her transom boards attached – a sad, forlorn sight. Nearby, in amongst the seaweed that fringes the base of the stone-clad sea wall, the bones of another hull pokes out. If those old ladies could talk, the conversations would contain vivid, or perhaps some lurid, tales of people and places long gone, voyages through storm and gentle wafting breezes, hulls heavy with creaking cargoes, memories perhaps of the reek of a hold full of Londoners' rubbish – for after several days drifting down the London River with only fickle winds to help, it would be 'high' indeed. Yes, if only!

Out on the flats an old wreck sits with the noticeable remains of stem and stern posts pointing upwards. It has a mound towards one end which was the mast deck, where a fine mast and sails were supported, garnering the breezes, allowing the effortless carriage of cargoes across the waters which now daily cover her. She came here, some say, nearly seventy years ago; she was anchored up and left with her bilge bungs out. She would pick up on the tide, flood and settle. This went on for quite some time; eventually she failed to lift. Gradually her hull fell to pieces. Her bottom timbers, which would be preserved in the mud and would take aeons to break down, knew this only too well. For if they could talk you might hear, 'Ha, you thought I'd be gone in a trice! Well beware you sailors of the here and now, I'm still alive and waiting, so mind your keels!'

The churchyard contains the bones of a few old sailormen. However, most would have gone to the weathered, grime and smoke-stained brick chapel at the edge of the village, they being not a 'high church' lot. But the farmers and gentle folk lie here peacefully, the bustle of past times gone, with only the breeze and quiet sloshing of gentle waves to pervade their environment – except of course, the weekly hymns sung by the small congregation that wends its way into the old building, year after year.

At Christmas, the happy sound of carols sung with gusto, though often out of tune, can be heard drifting and mingling with the sounds of seabirds calling out as the rising tide creeps inexorably across the flats. In the winter too, if one is lucky, a moon, an orb the colour of polished brass, sends a dazzling shaft of light across the still water, broken at times by ripples set in motion by a seabird alighting upon its surface. The brightness, too, often lights up the shoreline with ghostly images which appeared to move eerily about. The night visitor feels the solitude of this place keenly and will either linger to enjoy it, or hurry back towards the bright lights of the village.

Towards the end of the brick-making era, the old men of the company had kept one last barge sailing. She was raced each year in the annual sailing barge matches, held on the London River and her smaller sister. The challenge was for silver cups and they were manned by old skippers and mates. Year by year, fewer and fewer of her sisters had remained as trading barges, for it was only these that were allowed to race with each other. For those coveted cups were special, being presented by a Victorian entrepreneur who had come up with the idea of a race, to further the advances in the hull design of the spritsail barge, without impairing its cargo carrying ability. When they won, a victorious crew gained a month's wages for their labours!

During those last few years the grand old burghers that controlled these summer jamborees were forced, due to the dying numbers of trading craft, to admit yacht barges owned for pleasure or sailing homes. This caused consternation amongst some of the 'sailormen' – as a barge crew were called. Some were homes skippered by their owners, with a few experienced sailing crewmen. A wife or woman was not allowed to take part in the sailing of the barge. Others were sailed by old skippers for the owners with professional crews.

One year a barge entered into a London River match had a young family aboard, it being their home. They had split the tops'l during a hard thrash up-river to a place eerily called Gravesend, where all the barges were congregating for the early start next day. After dropping the sail to the deck and spreading it out on the hatch top, the skipper's wife set to and let in a new length of cloth. By the time the sail was hoisted, the next day, all of the other barges in her class were away down river. The barge, consequently, started late, but eventually finished well clear of the fleet's tail end.

The barge that split its tops'l came into the dock and spent part of the following summer moored up near the top end. The children who lived aboard her were often seen exploring the fringes of the brickworks, sea walls and creek beds when not working about her decks, helping to do what needed to be done to keep an old barge in trim. At the end of the summer she sailed away, 'Where to?' you may ask, it would

Visitors to the old dock during the 1950s included the motor yacht barge *Percy*, in the foreground, and the yacht barge *Venta*, the outer vessel. Eastwoods *Westmoreland* sits between these. The *Percy* finished her days alongside the *Henry & Jabez* at Conyer, and is mentioned in Chapter 11; the *Venta* at Cuxton marina, under landfill. (Courtesy of Pauline Stevens)

One visitor to Lower Halstow was the *May Flower*; she came into the dock in 1963. The church is framed beneath her airing topsail. (Courtesy of Gwendoline D. Ardley)

be good to think that the old wharf knew: old timbers communicate in some strange way!

The last brickworks sailing barge had gone, given away to a barge sailing club whose express intention was to keep barges sailing. The brickworks then sent all their bricks away by lorry. Mud and blue clay were collected from diggings in the marshes to the east of the dock using a steel motorised barge which had a grab crane in its middle. She used a small section of the dock only. The old barge wharves were sighing, even then, for busier times, for now no barges came in on the tide, settled for a chat and rested together after all the workers had traipsed wearily off to their homes for a supper. The men after their suppers would wander down to the pub for a glass of brown ale and a game of dominoes or cribbage and bemoan the dock's idleness.

The wharves knew that their days were numbered. No one came down and did any work on them. Bits had started to fall off, and disused leeboards were wedged behind rickety posts to stop the sides crumbling. An old rudder appeared and was leaned against the wharf. A sailing barge, which had been used as a lighter with a cut down rig of small mainsail and foresail used to be filled regularly with mud and clay from the outlying marshes, lay abandoned and unloved, hulked at the creek entrance. Her hull hogged and took up the shape of the beach, the tide entering and leaving at each rise and ebb. Sometimes, on high spring tides, the old girl would lift; sigh with the weight of water running into her, through tired seams, then settle. After many years, her hull, by now ramshackled, from parts being stripped off and general vandalism, was burnt. The beach still gives up her fastenings, they remembering when with the timbers lovingly crafted they held her elegant hull in shape: with her brown sail and brickworks' name emblazoned upon the mains'l, she was a once familiar sight. Some say that the old rudder, still propped against the wharf, half buried in silt, came from this old barge. There was now no one to ask: only the old timbers could say.

In time, too, the steel motor barge had gone away and the brickworks were closed down. It was then that the dock was abandoned to its lingering death.

The only sailing barge that came on odd occasions was one of the barge club barges. Old hands always tried to visit these old docks of days gone by, whenever they could, and if able to lie alongside all the better. This now was no longer possible because the poor old wharves had continued to slowly crumble, year by year. The once familiar spritsail barge had become a memory; the only sighting perhaps, if one was lucky enough to see one through a spyglass, was in the anchorage away on the eastern horizon …

Then, many years later, on a bright spring day, a team of men appeared and started to repair a length of wharf up near the sea wall. Fine new posts, shuttering and concrete edgings made the wharf better than in its heyday.

'What's going on?' thought the old dock.

Into this bustle of activity came a sailing barge, an old lady, rigged with empty spars, but a sailing barge none the less. People came down from the village behind the sea wall, to witness this event, a sight thought no longer possible by the old boys and girls who remained from the original community – most having come from far beyond

The old barge, before her gear was completely removed. In the foreground is Church Wharf, where a barge could still sit as late as around 1970. Now this is no more than a beach made up of debris from the collapsed quay.

these parts, with little interest of history and what was here before. This was a sight to behold. The old wharf timbers chattered away, remembering ... For once again, they could feel the weight of a hull leaning against their posts, her chine itching at them, as the barge moved to an evening's breeze.

'What's going on?' the wharf timbers had continued to exclaim.

During that summer, the barge was used as a committee boat for a sailing club raft race; she motored out bedecked with bunting, code flags going back to Nelson's time fluttering gamely from her lofty spars. Next workmen came and set up a pattern of blocks in the dock bottom; onto these the barge was floated near the top of a series of spring tides. Here she sat, slowly being stripped of her gear.

Her decks disappeared beneath a huge shed built over the hull. From this, week after week, emanated the smells of resinous wood, wafting sweet and peppery on the breeze. The resonant sounds of hammering, the scream of electric saws and planers being used to shape the many new timbers greeted passers by. Listening carefully, the softer more natural swish of a hand plane or spoke shave, perhaps putting a finishing touch to a beam, a chamfer on a deck carling, or just to take the edge off a plank; these offset the harsher noises of modern tools. All this had brought about a remarkable rebirth within the hull of this old lady. Indeed, she had become a floating shipyard!

The barge was being worked on, being given new life; but what of the old dock? It continued to moulder, whilst men from the council came and went, promised to do something and, as is the way of the political world, did nothing. One day only the newly repaired wharf for the old barge would remain and the rest of it would be gone as others, around a myriad of the areas creeks and rivers, had before them. The outer dock seemed to know this and continued to sigh, sag and fall, the timbers forever chattering to one another, until rotted and crumbled they returned back to earth and mud ...

'... resinous wood, wafting sweet and peppery ...'

The mast and sprit: the last remnant of a once proud, stately racing lady, the *Veronica*. The spars were fetched from Greenhithe, then the headquarters of the Everard fleet, by the *Edith May* when based at Maldon in 1964.

Lorries, piled high with new timber, arrived at regular intervals. The wood, with its familiar sawmill smells, as if alive with its perfume, fresh and sweet, disappeared under the shed. One lorry driver recognised an old lady sketching on the sea wall. Calling across, his voice a soft Kent burr, he said, 'Are you the Mrs — from a barge that used to be moored round the wall?' for he had delivered timber, over a quarter of a century earlier, to another little wharf close by, round the sea wall.

'Yes I am,' the lady replied in a measured tone, and she blushed, a little, being unsure of how to handle this enquiry.

'Well I'm blowed,' the driver quipped, and then he continued, 'I was the boy in them days, it was oak then too – I seem to remember!'

The lady, with a rueful look said, 'We stayed here too, some forty or more years ago – on the barge.'

'Did yer indeed … Err do you miss it?' asked the driver as he busied himself and his mate with unloading the timber.

The lady with a wry grimace let out a long, 'No …!' following it up with a straightforward, 'No, not now.' She was sure of that. Staying awhile to watch the activity, she continued drawing in her sketchbook. An onlooker would have observed moments of thought as the lady had cast her mind back to days spent working on a different tired old barge all those years ago.

Ashore, close to the barge, two long steel poles sat on trestles. They had gradually been buried beneath mounds of brambles; gathered too was a plethora of graffiti. Many a visitor to the wharf knew not the purpose of what appeared at first hand to be a load of scrap. Some knew – they were of course her mast and sprit. They stuck out over a drop, and a swing had been set up on one end of a spar, used by local children

In 1963 off Garrison Point two stately ladies, the *Sirdar* and *Sara*, race into the River Medway. The old dock's last barge, the *Westmoreland,* is seen on the far left-hand side. The *Westmoreland* was then operated by Eastwood and carried the company logo in her sails. She was kept purely for racing from around 1957. The *Dreadnought* can be seen past *Sara's* mizzen. Beyond the *Sirdar* is, probably, the *Memory*. She was first home in the staysail class ahead of the *Westmoreland* – it was the last trading barge match. (From an original print by Leslie G. Arnold, courtesy of Keith and Marian Patten)

as a harmless past time. One day a fine fresh coat of paint would adorn these spars, but in the meantime they remained resting and useful. It should be mentioned that those lengths of steel tube had a famous past; they came out of a grand old racing barge owned on the London River, the *Veronica*. Her sisters, the *Dreadnought* and *Sara*, were broken up by their owners: a sad and egoistic decree, similar to the King's ending for his beloved *Britannia*, at the end of the 1930s, a selfish and needless act of maritime destruction. But that was life then.

Time went on: another year passed by. The barge had more and more work done to her hull. Planking, frames, decks, rails were renewed with a plethora of other, smaller parts – but ones equally as important to the whole. The old dock, however, continued to crumble and fall away. Most of the walls were now more beach than dock wharves; dinghies lay pulled up, tethered until needed by their owners. Often children jumped and played in these. One, long neglected, lay with her bottom stove in.

One day, late in the morning, into this little dock another visitor sailed: a wooden clinker sloop, towing a pretty little similar-looking dinghy, with two people aboard. She had appeared in the distance earlier on the tide, tacking back and forth, from shallow to shallow, working closer up to the dock. The breeze was steady, firm but not strong, allowing fingertip control and immediate response. Eventually the skipper, sensing that the boat was feeling its way with little or no bottom clearance, went forward and was heard to call out, 'Shoot up, this is as far as we can get now.'

At the helm, the mate, all concentration and with a look of enjoyment, put the tiller over and as the yacht came up into the wind, went forward to drop the mains'l.

The skipper was seen to let the jib run down the forestay, before letting the anchor splash overboard. While paying out some cable to bring the yacht up with a gentle snub as the tide swung the boat, he called to the mate, 'You make the coffee while I tidy up the sails.' It would be an hour before sufficient water allowed further progress – time enough to muse about the surroundings.

Away to her starboard side the remains of an old fisherman's hard that still showed above the mud-flats rose in hummocks of shell and seaweed. Beyond the hard, the ragged remnants of the old barge marked by its beacon, poked above the water. 'I remember these from my childhood' thought the skipper, 'and that was some forty years before this time.'

Later, the yacht came in under power, moored up next to the old rudder, the skipper not being concerned about its presence as the tide still had two hours to run. The two crewmembers then disappeared over the wall, to return some time later accompanied by a lady. Knowing onlookers would have recognised her as the one seen regularly sketching around these parts. She sat and watched as the jib was hoisted, then as the boat was pulled round by the jib she sailed away into the distance, with a zephyr of an afternoon's breeze to help her along.

Before leaving, the skipper looked over the barge being repaired. He said a word or two to a worker, recounting a smidgen of his own barge life. 'The owner will be back later' the worker said, but the little yacht could not wait: the tide was on the ebb. He glanced too at the remains of the old gnarled rudder, knowing that old boats and their bits had souls and feelings, he thought silently to himself, 'I know what you are, I can only dream of where you came from and what life you've had: I was a sailorman too, a barge boy, on a barge which visited here over forty years ago.'

It would be nice to think that the rudder appreciated those sentiments and was glad that no harm had come to the charming little yacht, for it too had once been attached to a vessel and still remembered the feel, the flow and pressure of the passing waters, in its efforts to turn a barge and go where bid. 'Oh, they were happy days!' the rudder sighed gently as the water continued to creep up it.

The wharf sighing at the rudder was heard to murmur, 'It's alright for you, but we have been here all our lives', after more murmurings, 'We've only the tales told by a friendly old barge to know what's beyond!'

The rudder sighed too and murmured quietly, but in a positive manner, as the wash from the departing yacht lapped at its rotting baulks, 'Well, at least our recent visitor comes here from time to time!'

Time went by, so slowly it seemed; men continued hard at work on the barge, sawing, hammering, sanding and painting. For some day soon, the wharf had overheard, the covers would come off. Then at last, as masts, rigging and sails were put back in place, a gracious lady would be reborn. The old wharf timbers would know what they had witnessed, through the many seasons of the rebuild, and sigh with happiness – of memories long past, for sure, and too for the pleasures to come. Men, women and children from the village might or might not come down to the old dock to watch from the sea wall as those final happenings occurred, marvelling at the picture she made. The old dock might be both jealous and pleased, but only it knew that, as it wondered about the future, a silent witness – perhaps the only witness?

But what of the old dock? What would happen to her, would the men from the local council eventually take off their covers too? Wonder by all means – but do not stray into excitement – for few people really cared enough, it seemed, about the fast disappearing riverside heritage that surrounded them here.

One day, the eerie sound of a curlew was heard to cry out. As if to echo it, another responded, and a cacophony from a myriad of other waders rose above the breeze as it rustled the trees in the lonely churchyard. A spring tide was on the flood; soon

In a forgotten corner, Lower Halstow Dock, the lovely old barge *Edith May* lays afloat. She was nearing the end of her long reconstruction during the spring of 2008 and was expected to be sailing for the 2009 season.

the mud-flats that spread far beyond would be covered, and the sea would creep inexorably up the old dock and around the grand old lady, lifting her buoyant hull, shipshape again and ready for the open waters that lay beyond.

Earlier, as the barge had sat on the blocks, looking resplendent, smelling of Stockholm tar and tanning, decks tidied and ready for sea, a bystander was heard to say, 'A hundred years old, yer say – she doesn't look it.'

That night her rigging thrummed gently and tremors travelled down her lofty spars, where they were dissipated into the rejuvenated hull. It too, no doubt, felt the lean from the pressure of the breeze that pressed against her newly raised sails and rigging: once again in this forgotten corner, high up, above a topmast truck, a barge bob fluttered. It tugged and snapped audibly: it sang its own tune, as if to say, to anyone who might be around to listen, 'Tomorrow, we're off sailing …'

9

A Faversham Idyll –
Betwixt Land and Sea

It was high summer; the sky was wide and blue with some fluffy clouds that, on occasions, fortunately shielded the sun. The air felt warm and muggy. That morning, the skipper and his mate had left the picturesque waterside town of West Mersea for a passage into the East Swale. Now they lay at anchor under the rolling green mound that constitutes the Isle of Harty, contemplating a few lazy days' wandering around in these waters.

They departed at first light, taking the ebb to the Wallet Spitway and then crossed into the Swin before the ebb had run its full course. By the time the young flood had set in they were passing the Whitaker Beacon, a lonely sentinel many miles out marking the eastern point of Foulness Sands. With the flood under the keel, they ate up the Swin, it had seemed, and headed east of south when clear of the Barrow sands, sailing obliquely across the tide to pass the Middle Sand Beacon, a shoal on the approach to the East Swale.

From time to time, the mate or the skipper looked astern both to check that their little lugsail dinghy was still firmly attached, and of course purely for navigational reasons! The dinghy was seen, with its mast lashed down on the thwarts, to be tripping along obediently behind them. On a recent occasion, upon looking behind, the dinghy was seen trailing some distance astern.

'I should really fit a second towing painter,' said the skipper to nobody in particular: the painter had parted!

Leaving the Barrow sands behind them the skipper looked back, before the distance was too great, at a colony of seals that they had passed earlier, basking on the sand bank, lapping up the warmth of the sun before getting down to the serious business of chasing food. He remarked to the mate, 'There was a number of seals on those sands last month when the "boy" (their son) crewed with me up this way. It's great to see them.'

The moderate northwesterly breeze that had kept them tramping along at a decent rate had held and the passage across the shipping channels was glorious, running with their big genoa out to windward. The Red Sands towers passed by well to starboard and soon the Middle Sand beacon hove in sight and it was in turn left behind them. They had made even better progress, in the slacker west-going stream, over the shallower Four Fathoms Channel.

Here, with the greater part of the passage completed, they relaxed from the greater level of vigilance needed and tension caused by crossing the shipping lanes where ships at times appear from numerous directions – the feeder channels towards the Medway and Thames river outer marker buoys.

'Tea! It's time for tea …' said the skipper, grinning, as he stepped below to put the kettle on.

The mate, helming, closely passes the Middle Sand Beacon, out in the middle of nowhere, before crossing the Four Fathom Channel bound for the Columbine and the East Swale.

'In the locker there's the remains of a fruit cake ...'

'Enough for me,' he thought, 'you shan't want any.'

Drinking their tea, the skipper and mate had ruminated about the Four Fathoms Channel. It was only such at high water during spring tides, and was an old route from the Cant, an area of flats to the north of the Isle of Sheppey that was once fertile land, to a broad shoal area off the North Kent coast, inside the numerous shoals and sand banks that abound – this part is known as the Overland Passage! The channel runs almost east-west.

Draining the last of her tea the mate said, 'Look, we've not been into Whitstable for a few years,' pausing to let the message sink in, 'so, let's go there tomorrow if the weather is good – the fish and chips are always worth the effort, aren't they ...'

Looking longingly across the wide stretch of protected water to the south, she continued, 'I know the aim is for a couple of days up in Faversham, but we've plenty of time for both.'

So it was agreed.

The Columbine Spit buoy was left trailing in their wash as they came round on a reach, into the East Swale, with the freshening breeze nicely on their beam.

Upon anchoring the skipper smiled at his mate, for they had had a good sail, and said, 'Today's passage was excellent; one to relish, don't you think?'

'It wasn't the classic we had running into the Medway a few years back, but definitely a a little pearl to remember!'

After supper that evening, and after lighting and hanging up their anchor light, they rowed ashore for a little walk. Both had agreed that some refreshment at the hostelry on the hillside overlooking the ancient anchorage would be nice. The scents of the surrounding fields and scrub seemed powerful to their senses, especially after a

The Isle of Harty under a moody sky, seen from the south of Shell Ness while sailing into the East Swale.

few days away from a rural landscape, for they had had a stay up in the old port of Maldon and at West Mersea, before arriving here.

The public house where they had their refreshment had changed a great deal over the years. It had been modernised and extended, but from the water it still looked pretty, nestled comfortably into the hillside. Inside, it was all a bit rustic; beer could still be had from the tap, it still had flagstone floors and water could be obtained from a tap in the yard. The mate had always appreciated a good cider and had for a long time judged an inn of any description by that benchmark. She was not disappointed! Ruminating on the past few days, sitting outside, with the sun approaching the distant horizon, they watched as its golden orb changed slowly to orange, then to red. The water below them glinted with those changes, it was iconic. Watching they had both felt content with life.

The mate said, 'Let's get back to the boat: it could be a starry night tonight and you know how I enjoy those.' So as the sun had sunk below the yonder horizon, they, with dual accord drunk up and wandered back down the hill to the hard where they had left the dinghy. The skipper had to slip off his shoes to retrieve the little anchor that tethered their dinghy to terra firma. The water felt tepid to the skipper as he had waded out: the tide as it had climbed the sloping mud had garnered warmth left by the day's hot sun.

On the row out to the boat, the mate saw that a sliver of a moon had appeared with the setting of the sun. As the oars dipped and lifted from the water, their splashes lit up shards of electric blue phosphorescence that danced away: they contained many unseen minute sea creatures that caught and held, briefly, the light. They both watched entranced. 'Oops, we're here,' the skipper said as he suddenly realised that they had, with their lack of attention to rowing and to their direction, nearly run into their own boat!

The stars did, as expected, appear and to celebrate they had a nightcap of flavoured coffee before turning in. The skipper indulged himself with a little cheese and a biscuit or two as well. It had been a long day. The mate said, 'We've had some marvellous sights of the night sky whilst here at Harty. Remoteness does have its advantages ...'

'Err ... yes, I agree,' said the skipper, as the mate headed below. Following her, his thoughts moved to the morrow. Before that his eyes took in the cosiness of their cabin: the flickering glow of the cabin oil lamps cast comforting orange reflections around the varnish work. Then returning to the thought he'd had, said, 'Tomorrow the forecast has promised a lighter northwesterly. It would be ideal sailing, but I bet we get a sea breeze in the afternoon too.'

It was a quiet night; there wasn't even a gentle lapping from under the clinker plank edges. That noise, so familiar to clinker yacht owners, was at times strangely soporific, friendly even, and its busier beat would awake the sleeping crew, telling them that a change in the wind strength had occurred.

Waking to a bright day, the skipper cleared away the riding light, then he gazed at the green bulk of the Isle of Harty. Its shades coloured the smooth water between the marsh edge and his position. He felt awe for the remote beauty of this anchorage, in the quiet of the first of the day. For many years it had been a safe haven, but the Columbine Spit and Horse sands had had their share of vessels' bones. These days it was used by some fishing craft, a few spritsail barges waiting for the tide to reach Faversham and a large number of yachts.

The skipper noticed immediately that a friendly, light northwesterly breeze was evident: it was flicking at the burgee. At the time it seemingly struggled to do its duty. The skipper, however, was undaunted: the breeze would fill in, so he called to the mate, 'Look, why don't we have some bacon sandwiches underway: it's just gone high water and the breeze may not hold out – burgee seems a bit listless.' They were in the wind shadow behind Harty though!

They soon weighed anchor and sailed serenely away on the first of the ebb. Soon they had left the ferry anchorage behind them. Passing the entrance to Faversham Creek, they passed a spritsail barge anchored along the shore.

The skipper looked at the barge with a practiced eye. Then, to no one in particular, for the mate was now below grilling bacon for breakfast, said 'It's the *Mirosa*. She must have dropped out this morning. The Iron Wharf tug plucks her up and down the creek: she's engineless.'

'Ah, bacon ...' murmured the skipper. The aroma, when the bacon rind had begun to sizzle and crackle, was rising from the stove, wafting from the cabin below to circulate around. It made the skipper salivate: he longed for that anticipated enjoyment!

With the ebb helping them along they ate up the short distance to the Pollard Spit buoy then, passing inside of it, set a course across Whitstable Bay. The skipper made an allowance for the outgoing tide, which was more or less on their beam. The harbour beyond was about two-and-a-half miles away.

Away to the east Herne Bay and further on The Reculvers could be picked out. Herne bay is a seaside town. The Reculvers are two navigation towers erected by Trinity House at Reculver on the site of Roman marks. Reculver was once the exit of the Inland Passage inside the Foreland. The Inland Passage was the River Wantsum and came via Sandwich, on the Stour. Sandwich itself was once a coastal town too.

The Wantsum separated the Isle of Thanet from the body of Kent, but it had long since silted up. The Inland Passage had gone round the Swale and through the Yantlet, before coming out into the Thames, all within protected waters.

'What wonderful sailing that passage would make today,' thought the skipper, 'and the Wantsum would have been a glorious playground for sailors and a feeding ground for a multitude of wildlife species too.'

Reculver was fortified by the Romans and formed part of the bastion against the Saxon hordes that eventually flooded these shores. An ancient church dating back to early British Christian times sat within the walls of the old fort – no doubt built from Roman rubble!

The fort fell into disrepair and its northern wall crumbled with the cliff into the sea around 1780. Up until around 1900, when coastal protection was erected, the coast eroded by nearly one metre each year. Off the coast lay the Pan Sands, which are scattered with cement boulders – a natural phenomenon. From these sands fishermen for centuries have dragged up fragments of pottery and other ancient artefacts. It is thought that the sands were once a low-lying island. These sands, amongst others, sit on the extensive Kentish Flats and have no more than three to four metres of water covering them at low tide.

Along the shore to the west of the yacht club hard, clear of other moored vessels, they dropped anchor in about two metres of water. They had disposed of the sails coming in, because the skipper wanted to ensure that the anchor was pulled hard to ensure a good hold on the bottom. The boat would be aground for less than four hours, which would give them a tidy amount of time to head for Faversham later in the day.

Clearing up and locking the hatches they rowed ashore leaving the dinghy by the yacht club, pulled up on the beach. The club was open because racing was in progress: it was their cadet week. The skipper mentioned that they had left their dinghy on the beach. A club member said, 'That's alright mate. Bar will be open later, there's food too today, come in before you leave.' The skipper and his mate always had an excellent welcome from the Whitstable Yacht Club sitting atop the beach, and they said that they would return later.

Whitstable High Street, a quaint and pretty street with a plethora of charming old buildings.

Clapboard houses line a passage, Beach Passage, and spill out over the beach. A house at the eastern end, The Nore, was once the home of the author Arthur S. Bennett.

The skipper and the mate had to get some fresh bread and other odds and ends. But first they made for a little museum on the high street that ran beneath the protective shingle – it was always a pleasure too. Along this beach sat a large barge and yacht building concern until it had closed in the early 1980s. A spritsail barge had not been repaired at the yard for fifty years or so. The last, the *Major*, a motor barge, had been on the ways for repairs around 1961. She was owned by a partner of the yard. Sadly she was lost the following year after initially giving help to another motor barge. Her remains lay buried in the Gunfleet Sands, a remote island of sand that is awash at high water, lying off the Essex coast.

The museum was a quaint, but enjoyable, informative and interesting place to visit. Whitstable has had a long and varied history. The present docks were built by the burghers of Canterbury, during the early 1800s; they also built the railway line from Canterbury. Before the proper harbour came into being, cargoes such as coal had to be unloaded on the beach from sailing colliers. Barges continued to unload on the beach until about 1939. Oyster fishing, or farming, was the mainstay of the town now, although other forms of fishing took place too. The docks still had some commercial trade from small coastal traders. During the summer spritsail barges were often seen, their lofty topmasts towering above the dockside sheds, a reminder of a past age.

Before their saunter round the museum they went into one of the delightful pantries for coffee: their bacon sandwich eaten earlier, while coming out of the East Swale, had seemed an age ago. Over their coffee they quickly decided to buy some local fish for that evening's supper, but that would be obtained later from the fish market located on the harbour quay before heading back to their boat. For lunch – without a doubt and this had no competitor – they were going to have fish and chips. The town was

The skipper and mate's yacht *Whimbrel* at anchor in the shallows off Whitstable beach. A barge and yacht yard used to operate along this beach. The harbour wall can be seen beyond with a spritsail barge in the dock. During recent summers a spritsail barge has operated from this old but still busy fishing port, adding to its charm.

famous for its fresh fried fish! This they always ate sitting on the beach, gazing out over the water. They did all those things, finally calling into the club for a restorative glass of local Faversham ale.

The skipper drained his glass of ale, and seeing that their clinker sloop had picked up on the incoming tide, they departed. Getting back aboard and stowing away the fresh stores, they soon got underway and crept across the shallows towards deeper water and the East Swale. The breeze had come in now from a north to northeasterly direction; this made for an easy departure under sail and would give them a spanking sail up to Faversham.

Soon the buoy on the end of Pollard Spit had come abeam. The flood, now more urgent, gurgled round it. Trailing past the buoy were little wavelets that swirled and hurried westwards. The flood tide and the breeze picked up the little yacht as she hurried on: the skipper had eased the sheets to run before the wind, whereupon he sat back and relished the easy sailing.

The mate appeared to be in a reverie of her own, staring out across the water. That was suddenly broken: for she had pointed across at a line of white cottages that sat on the end of Shell Ness, speaking as she did so, 'That must have been a lonely place in previous centuries.' They were the home for coastguard families.

The day had turned into a glorious summer day with a deep blue sky marred only with some odd fluffy bits of high-level cloud. The water captured the sky and as they turned up the East Swale, along the Harty shore, the greens from the hills could be seen mixed in, resulting in a splendid tableau.

Sailing along the edge of the sands near the Sand End buoy, the skipper pointed out, in the distance to the north, two barge hulks that sat in a line coming out from the

Rows of smacks and fishing vessels line Faversham Creek near its junction with the Swale. The skipper and mate's yacht is heading in, under sail. The boatyard at the entrance to Oare Creek and the old inn, the Shipwright's Arms, can be seen ahead.

shore. He reminded the mate that he had recently promised to point them out when sailing round the Swale. The mate looked at him quizzically, so the skipper said, 'You remember, I said that they were part of a boom defence system here during World War Two, and have since sat in peace, rotting slowly away.' Looking thoughtful, he then added, 'I'll go for a look one of these days.'

Sweeping past the buoy marking Faversham creek and leaving it and the mud spit to starboard, the skipper realised that they were fairly humming along and he checked the time. He saw that the mud-flats under the marsh edges of the creek were still above the rising tide. 'Have to watch the bends,' the skipper said to the mate, who was at the helm.

The mate said, 'Here, you take over. I've been hard at it from Whitstable ...' Close to the beach, or mud as it were, the mate preferred to watch the passing sights rather than have to worry about mere pilotage details!

Soon after entering the creek, the hot sweet scents of the land wafted over them, for the land behind the sea wall had had all day to heat up and was now being brushed by that incoming sea breeze. Moving onwards, the marsh edges closed in as the creek narrowed. Here the heady saline aroma of marsh plants reached out to them too: they had been freshly washed by tides which at that time were at a height to partially flood their fronds. The saline scents mingled with those from the farmland beyond, creating a rich mixture. Many of the marsh plants displayed their summer colours in all their glory. Sailing along, with the decks above the level of the marsh, the skipper and mate were able appreciate and enjoy the awe-inspiring sight of nature at its best, with pleasure. There was more to come.

Passing an ancient rambling old inn they also passed a pretty smack yacht moored along the bank. 'A smart little vessel,' the skipper remarked to the mate, expecting no answer. The inn, which dated back many centuries, sat at a junction to another old creek that led up to the village of Oare. By the inn was a yacht club that sat on the site of an old barge yard. Years before its clubhouse had been one of the yard buildings, a boat shop in fact. The area had become a centre for smacks and other similar craft and, sailing past, it had all been very picturesque. Often a smack could be seen arriving or about to depart – this was always a delight. On the day of the Swale Barge & Smack Race, traditional sails abounded and the spectacular sight, once seen, was never forgotten.

Leaving all that behind them they shaped up closer to the wind to reach round the start of a horseshoe bend where mud-flats, to the west of the creek, ran out ever so gently, waiting for the tickle of a keel, to grab and delay, or indeed to keep the unknowing or too casual sailor for longer. Not so many years back both of the creeks had a considerable level of commercial trade. The Oare died first, many years ago, then Faversham, where the last cargo had come in about a decade ago. Now Faversham creek was used by a few spritsail barges, fitted out for chartering, a small ketch and a number of yachts that berthed in the ooze.

Rounding the corner the mate started the engine at a slight nod from the skipper. He smiled, because he'd wanted to get round under sail. By luffing up and using the tide under them he had worked their way round Skiff Reach. With a shrug the mate switched the engine off – the skipper had not said a word. Approaching Nagden Reach, the skipper said, 'Here, you take over. I'll take the mains'l down and we'll run up under the jib.'

'What funny names these reaches have!' commented the mate, 'Bit like the names given to the sand banks and swatches out in the estuary.' Then with more of a quizzical look added, 'I doubt if anyone really knows the whole story of any of them.'

The creek edge to the west of the creek along that section was fringed by a strip of marsh that grew into a wide swathe of grazing marsh. Across the flat carpet of marsh, a flock of sheep were busy keeping the grass short, meandering along the low-earth sea wall beyond. Their low-pitched bleats could be heard coming clearly across the expanse.

... a flock of sheep busy keeping the grass short ...

Shelduck, little egrets and various waders were often seen, for the marsh were riddled with gullies and tidal pools providing rich feeding. If helming, it was a distraction to the primary task of controlling the boat's heading, and the skipper often had to carry out a sharp correction of the tiller to ensure an approaching bend was negotiated in a proper manner, or that the mud did not claim them!

From June the marshes were a sea of colour, first from thrift with their pink to white flowerheads, then later sea lavender and finally the yellow flowers of the sea purslane, which lasted well into September. When the spring tides flooded into flat tablecloth of marsh plants, the myriad of flowerheads rising above the still mirror surface added to the tableau. It was a sight to behold. It was something the mate, a 'townie', had begun to enjoy many years ago upon being introduced to sailing up mud and saline marshland creeks. As they sailed onwards, the landscape was becoming more land than water: it was enchanting.

A couple of cottages were passed on the eastern bank as they skirted round some mud-flats that extended out at that point. Here, beyond the wall, out of their line of sight, the roaring whine of a combine harvester could be heard, spewing not only grain but the smell and dust of the harvested cereals. On the gentle breeze husks and chaff wafted across them; some fluttered down onto the decks. It left the air gritty. 'You'll need you hay fever tablets,' the mate said to the skipper. Then, as if to order, he sneezed involuntarily, again and again. The mate, both a caring wife and good boat mate, fetched and dispensed the medication! From then on, the sea wall gradually closed in on both sides all the way up the rest of the creek and on into the ancient port where it was largely bordered on both sides by wharves in use, redundant wharves and wharves now crowded with closely packed modern waterside housing.

After clearing round an S-bend they were now on a dead run in on a fairly straight stretch towards their destination, the Iron Wharf. Thinking ahead, of their berthing, the skipper hauled out the fenders for the mate to tie off on the guardrails either side. Mooring lines were then prepared. The tide still had nearly two hours to run so the skipper said, 'As we come past the sewage works outfall, you dowse the jib and we'll potter up under power. I'll go past, nose into the bank and let the stern swing, then crab over to a berth.' The mate nodded her approval: when early on the tide they had carried out this exercise during many visits here.

They berthed sweetly alongside a motor yacht. Along the quay was the usual collection of loafers and boat owners standing gazing, at the sight of the pretty cream-painted clinker yacht towing a similar dinghy, some in awe, the skipper liked to think, others waiting, perhaps, for an expected maritime cock-up – they didn't see one!

The mate had then gone ashore to check on the berth. They had not known a casual visit to cause the yard a problem and the skipper doubted that their present visit would have been any different. The skipper had worked out that they would be afloat for some three to four hours at least before the keel started to sink into a soft sloppy bottom. 'Plenty of time to move if needed', the skipper said to himself.

The mate returned with tokens for the washing machines and news that they were all right. She then departed ashore to stuff a washer. The skipper meanwhile had put a kettle on; the tea was ready for the mate's return. She had left the washing machine churning round, giving intermittent flashes of the colours of their clothing as it ran its course. After tea, the skipper set his dinghy up for a sail along the creek. His intention, apart from having an enjoyable sail, was to nose along the quays to look at all the changes and to appreciate the vessels which, he knew, lay up towards the town.

The skipper left the mate sitting propped up in the cockpit with her book, at ease with the world, comfortable and happy: Faversham was another of her favourite places. What better place to sit back let the world go by, enjoy a good book and perhaps snooze! The skipper would join her later. He sailed contentedly away, almost

The old shipyard of James Pollock & Sons can be seen across the murky waters of Faversham Creek. The spritsail barges are the shapely *Remercie* and beyond the *Beatrice Maud*. The hulk of the *Remercie* is referred to in a previous chapter about Hoo. The site of the shipyard is now a mass of waterside apartments and silted up moorings.

on a run, the wind behind his back, sitting to one side with one foot casually at rest on the varnished gunwale. In his position he was able to look at all that was going on along the southern, more interesting shore.

The north shore had been cleared of industrial concerns. Along it had sat the yard of James Pollock & Sons. The yard had been in operation for over a century and was run by the Pollock family from 1916 to its closure in 1969. It was originally developed at the request of the First Sea Lord, Lord Fisher. Like at many shipyards around our coasts, as vessels got bigger sideways launching became the custom – these were exciting events as a wash wave was produced! The old shipyard had turned out two concrete motor schooners at the end of the First World War and had, up to its closure, built over a thousand ships of up to 1,000 tons. After its demise another firm operated for a short time on the site, before it too had to close. The land has since been covered with a mass of modern housing and apartments fronting the creek. Moorings have been arranged for the use of householders, but the developers and town council have forgotten, or do not appreciate, that once regular use of the wharves and water way stopped, silt will build up and up and so it has! Cord grass, that demon of the estuary and creek, has grabbed a firm hold and the mud has risen rapidly where only a few short years ago a viable waterway and wharf front was in use. The skipper giggled, but also sighed with more than a little sadness at the folly.

Along the southern side to Gillett's Quay, just past Standard Quay where barges were usually berthed, the creek was still relatively clear. Many of the barges were away on summer charter work. At Gillett's some smacks and traditional craft were moored. The skipper noted all the changes to enable him to give the mate a run-down later! After eventually reaching the head of the navigation, up by Town Quay, upon which stood one of the older buildings in Faversham, the skipper turned for a casual beat back against the late-afternoon breeze. The tide had started to ebb so was a help as he beat with long and short tacks homewards, from time to time raising a nonchalant hand to idle observers – their voices carrying all that they said easily across the water to the skipper's ears!

Returning to the boat, the skipper found that washing was strung out on lines from various shrouds. All looked the peak of domesticity and definitely not very nautical! Over the years their boat had become renowned amongst their sailing friends for the profusion of washing that appeared in the rigging in a variety of anchorages and marinas. The mate asked once, 'What do you do then, when cruising for several weeks – wear nothing?' With a harrumph and some other noises, they admitted to washing on the boat ... the Dutch, in particular, were always to be seen with bits and bobs drying in the fresh air. An observer, if he so wished, could giggle at the often interesting and colourful collections! It was part and parcel of their type of sailing, it was a need. In any case, in the skipper's mind, was there a better place to do it, than alongside, at Faversham, with three nights and two whole days to gently meander through?

Over dinner, which they enjoyed out in the cockpit, they talked about the day and what the skipper had seen up the creek. The breeze had fallen light and with the sun still relatively high in the sky, it was warm. Dinner, some scallops cooked in wine and some herbs on a bed of rice with salad, had been delightful. After clearing away they headed for the shore and a walk – the skipper was very much intent on a glass of ale or two: they were safely tucked up in port, as if at home.

Waking the next day after a warm and sultry night, it was obvious that it was going to be warm. Looking outside the skipper felt that it was very hot, even at that early hour – before people were properly out and about. The forecast, still listened to, spoke of high pressure, very little wind and no cloud cover. This had been on the way for a few days now. Breakfast was enjoyed out in the open, as their stores were in need of

Looking towards Standard Quay, in Faversham, during the 1980s. In the foreground is the last of the once huge fleet of Eastwood brick manufacturers' spritsail barges. She is the *Westmoreland*. At the time she was undergoing a rebuild, following a stranding at Hoo when owned by the Thames Sailing Barge Trust. Her bow was broken off after getting atop a concrete lighter. The rebuild has since stalled and the poor old barge sits forlorn and, possibly, without hope.

some rejuvenation – they were down to toast and coffee. The skipper always carried a jar or two of their favourite homemade marmalades aboard the boat and this was an occasion to sit back and enjoy it, especially on hot buttered toast!

That morning a herd of cows sauntered along the top of the sea wall and came down to graze the tender grasses below, on the flat marsh beside the creek edge. Some stopped to stare across the creek, with their huge, dark brown, glassy eyes which had seemed to rest fixedly upon the mate and the skipper, before they continued their journey. 'Been up to the dairy and been milked', said the skipper, 'I heard them go by some two hours ago.' This was one of the facets that made a stay at Faversham so idyllic: it was betwixt land and water.

Over breakfast the mate mapped out the day and finished up by saying, 'We have got to get a few fresh stores, but we can stock up properly tomorrow and pick up some fresh meat before leaving the following morning – "at around high water" you said. So let's have a morning in town then walk out to the gunpowder mill after coffee – perhaps pick up some food for a picnic.' It was heartily agreed.

They left the boat locked up, but not forlorn: she sat still, afloat, as if aground, looking as pretty as a picture while the ebb gurgled past her stem. They walked away, through the Iron Wharf boatyard, nodding to the staff they saw. The yard was essentially a do-it-yourself place and displayed a patchwork of activity. In some cases the obvious signs of productive work could be seen, while from others total inactivity saw yachts and boats, which had once been loved and prided when afloat, sat forgotten in odd corners – some partially covered in a creeping growth. The wharf was also home to two spritsail barges, the *Mirosa* and the *Orinoco*. The latter has been rebuilt over a number of years and is now sailing again.

At the edge of the yard towards the town was another boatyard. This one was a repair and building concern. They had built the little GRP-simulated clinker dinghy that the skipper and mate towed along obediently behind them wherever they went. The yard had a continuous throughput of traditional craft: some came in for pretty minor repairs and others were in for larger jobs or for complete rebuilds. The yard and moorings adjacent were on the site of the old Anglo American Oil Company wharf. It was a fascinating place to walk through; the public footpath passed the top of the slipway in front of the shed. The skipper often looked in to say hello. The proprietor always welcomed them. It was doubtful if he actually remembered them – it didn't matter!

The path then became enclosed and wound past an old granary, known as Chambers, now converted to flats and offices; they passed through a length of rough footpath, the site of Goldfinch's barge yard. Here, for a number of years, had sat the old *Westmoreland*, the last survivor of the Eastwoods brickmakers' fleet. She was brought here in the 1970s following a stranding at Hoo, when her bow had been sheared off. She was then partially rebuilt, but she had since sat forlornly, becoming increasingly dilapidated and her fate may well have been sealed, for she had not floated for an age. To the landward side of this area the land had been cleared ready to build houses on ground marginally above the level of the ever-rising tides. 'Madness!' thought the skipper when he had first heard of this – and still thought it!

Leaving the enclosed footpath they passed out onto Standard Quay and Gillett's, where spritsail barges and smack types were berthed. All but two barges were away. The path turned into a lane that led away to the road that, in turn, led to the town. A gorgeous public house sat close to the water here, where good food and ale has been dispensed since time immemorial ... Some years ago, a drama group had put on a series of plays in the pub garden: they were very good. When a man had the need to use the 'Gents' it was possible to watch rehearsals at leisure: an open window provided a box seat!

Market Square, Faversham. It is always a buzz of activity and life.

Walking casually up the street, leading up to the town, the mate always marvelled at all the old buildings – they were stupendous. Many of the homes along that street had been continuously lived in for nigh on five hundred years. Some were Tudor, timber-framed, and others built of ragstone and flint. Reaching the town square, they saw that it was market day. In the middle of the square was an ancient town burgher's building, beautifully maintained and still in use.

Reaching the town square, the mate said to the skipper, 'Let's have a coffee. You order at that place', indicating with a flourish of her hand, 'and I'll fetch a newspaper!'

'Bun?' asked the skipper.

'Oh, yes please,' the mate called from over her shoulder, as she headed for the newsagent ...

Later over a beer ashore, sitting outside a pub near Standard Quay and enjoying the gorgeous evening, now cooler than the heat and heaviness of earlier, the mate and the skipper reminisced about their day. 'The Heritage Centre was interesting,' she said, 'well worth the visit and there was so much information about the town. I know we've been here many times, but ... there's always something new.'

'I thought the water-driven gunpowder mill was interesting, and I enjoyed the picnic up by Stonebridge Pond too. They were both originally part of the gunpowder manufacturing industry.'

'Did you see that there had been some canals built to transport materials? Fascinating, I thought.'

The skipper chipped in, 'I read somewhere that there had been a huge explosion a century or so ago, at one of the Faversham works, which caused absolute devastation', pausing to enjoy a sup his local ale, 'It was a good job that it was one of the works out of town. That's why the factories were rebuilt out alongside the Swale.'

The Pent, looking back to the disused lock gate and sluice. It is a shame: the crumbling wharves were in use until twenty years ago.

'Over one hundred people killed ...' He stopped: the mate had been telling the tale and the skipper let her finish.

'The industry here was given a helping hand by a flood of refugees from France. They were the Huguenots. They had better skills at milling the powder and their expertise was a boon for the trade. The Huguenots were experts at so much and their influence can be seen throughout the channel and North Sea counties.' The mate paused, and then added, 'Remember our visit to Ipswich – remember all the fine merchants' houses? Many of those date from that influx too.'

The skipper merely nodded. Then they both listened as the dulcet sounds of music struck up from inside the pub. The strains crept their way outside – 'Probably the local shanty man' they thought, as their feet tapped to the rhythm!

The mate, looking thoughtful, said, 'It is such a shame that the local authorities in Faversham have let the sluice at the Pent Swing Bridge fall into disrepair, but typical though: "if it doesn't affect landlubbers, then it doesn't need fixing," you keep telling me. The creek has silted up badly and rapidly too, these last few years – even I've noticed!'

The skipper chipped in, 'It's the same too in our creek, in any creek in fact that was dammed off, or not allowed to flow, especially since the floods of 1953 and the building of new sea walls afterwards. Dozens of creeks have slowly died. The sea will have its revenge – mark my words – I for one would rejoice!'

'Come on,' said the skipper, 'it's time we wended our way back – I feel the call of a nightcap or two. It'll be lovely and cool in the cockpit – there is a nice piece of cheese to nibble too.' So with the hum and bonhomie that continued to ooze out of the open doors of the pub, enticing the like-minded inside, they silently slipped away ...

'You know, just walking up this street is enough to warrant a visit to this fabulous place,' said the mate, the following morning, while they were walking towards the

The evocative spire of Faversham's abbey church, framed by the buildings of Shepherd and Neame's old brewery. A fine church and a fine ale.

town to have a late breakfast. It was hot, very hot – it was really a day to be out on the water, not mooching round the land.

'Just look at all these old frontages,' she continued as they walked along, pointing out a bow window here and there, indicating the building's use as a shop in the past. Looking down a side road towards the church with its intricately built spire, they both marvelled at the patience of the stonemasons long ago.

On this fine morning, after again leaving the boat afloat on the mirrored surface of the creek, they were heading for the market square for a late breakfast treat of croissants and coffee. Afterwards their plan was to walk round the sea wall to the Shipwright's Arms for a bite of lunch. The ham sandwiches there were known to be divine. This fact was later borne out: they were not disappointed.

It was exceedingly hot by the time they left the Shipwrights' cool interior. Both had had several soft beverages to quench their thirst, the skipper saying with a chuckle that it was far too hot for a beer – even for him! The walk home along the path to the head of Oare Creek was interesting, but by the time they had reached the hot streets it had begun to be a little tiresome. The tar-based surface of the roads and pavements had softened and in places and was almost running.

After stopping in the town for a few stores, it was a tired and wearied crew that returned to the creek. The tide with its slightly cooler feel was just creeping up the rill again; shortly they would feel its effect. With an accord, they both collapsed on their bunks. It was siesta time – but how sticky it had been!

It was hot and humid. The skipper dreamed of a pirate from these parts: he had read something or other about him earlier that day. An Englishman, a John Ward, had turned into pirate after a short career in the navy around 1600. He set up in Tunis and took the name Issouf Reis. Reis did not care who he enslaved, Englishmen, Christian or otherwise, it mattered not so long as they could man an oar on his ships: it was a case of 'Join me or work until you drop.' The skipper awoke with a start – dripping in perspiration!

The early evening came none too soon, it had been an amazingly hot day and the lower sun came as quite a relief as they walked ashore. Over dinner in a hostelry along the street towards the town square they talked about leaving in the morning. It would be around nine, not too early, and the forecast had mentioned a southerly breeze. They then settled down to enjoy their evening and to discuss the day's sights.

The mate said, 'I did love those cottages – Brents I think they were called. The whole of that side of the creek is so pretty and it can't have changed a lot since the homes were lived in by fishermen and watermen. But, it's such a shame about the silting up and the mass of reeds. Those moorings, too, were mostly useless!'

'It was so picturesque down past what you said used to be an island and that ancient public house. Then there were all those new waterfront buildings, houses and flats, all with moorings … silted up and sad, along where there used to be the shipyard, "Pollock's" you said to me.'

'It was fun looking for the footpath because there have been so many changes, and wasn't it strange walking over and along the old creek bed opposite the stretch we're moored in?'

The skipper then said that he had heard that a plan had been openly discussed within a forum for Faversham Creek about reopening the original course of the creek. The plan was for perhaps a marina with a sill. Water would be used to help flush the creek. Nothing had come of it though.

The mate continued, 'It was a lovely walk to the confluence of the two creeks, but it was getting too hot by then. After lunch I really wasn't looking around me – you know what I'm like in the heat!' She looked at the skipper gravely.

The skipper took over at this point. 'I enjoyed looking at all the smacks and numerous yachts moored up Oare Creek. That old spritsail barge, the *Gwynronald*, at the boatyard some way up the creek sits on the site of an old powder wharf. I wonder if she'll ever be put back into sail again.' After his rhetorical question, the skipper paused then added, 'Doubtful, I think – the present fleet of charter barges are struggling with upkeep costs.'

'That old smack that we saw awhile back, at the head of the creek, had been broken up – a chain saw job by the look of it. Then leaving the creek we eventually passed the site of an ancient old abbey on the slopes or rise between Oare and Faversham. It was probably almost an island six hundred years ago.'

Later, walking back to their little floating home, the mate said, 'This has been a lovely break in our sailing, but I'll be glad to get out and feel the boat move, in its own sweet way, alive to the tide and the breeze,' then ruffling the skipper's hair, she said, 'The solitude of the South Deep awaits our evening tomorrow.'

'Yes it has been good,' said the skipper, remembering that the previous year they had taken the train into Canterbury. But this little interlude had allowed them to really see and appreciate this old harbour, for its history and its present strivings to keep going.'

Waking the next morning, a little later than they should have done, and going on deck the skipper called below, 'Come on Mr Mate – a lovely southerly is gently lifting and fluttering the burgee up at the mast head, the boat's afloat – let's get underway.'

'What about some fresh meat?' said the mate.

Responding quickly, for he felt the urge to feel the boat's movement under him again, he said, 'Oh, we've stores enough for our supper. Let's just go!'

The mate nodded her approval: it would be cooler out on the water.

Looking back towards Iron Wharf across the site of Foreman's Hard (now covered in salt marsh) with Chambers' old granary building in the distance. This is the view when arriving or leaving by water.

They were soon ready. Their big genoa pulled nicely and as the bow came clear the skipper slipped the last line astern and they were underway. At first the boat moved slowly and silently against the flood with barely a rustle under the stem head. They crept clear of the moorings. Then, coming abreast of the lower end of the Iron Wharf they gradually, almost imperceptibly, picked up speed. Leaving this wonderful place behind was always hard and it was as if the boat too had those feelings of regret.

They looked back down the sun-drenched shaft of water; this spread out from their little yacht's stern and receded into the distance as if to a spears point. They cast a last lingering look astern, together. Both released a couple of deep, audible, contented sighs, but the skipper, who was at the helm, had to concentrate on navigating. The mate though, had continued her reverie – to look back fondly until the receding spire of the abbey church and the lofty spars of the resident spritsail barges merged into the general panorama.

The skipper heard a quiet, almost reverential, 'That was nice … so nice '

'Yes', he answered, contentedly, in his own mind, not wanting to disturb his mate.

10

Two Cautionary Tales

The skipper and his mate had sailed for a considerable number of years in their little clinker yacht and, before that, on their first little yacht. The skipper, too, had spent many an hour pottering in a dinghy. The skipper had been brought up on the water, on a spritsail barge, so all in all had gained a fair amount of experience. Most of their sailing was pretty straightforward and they both thought that they had, in general, learnt from their mistakes as time had passed. There were a number of incidents, though, that had taken place over the years that they both remembered only too well, some, they would have rather forgotten …

In a time before their present yacht, they had a dark blue painted *Yachting World* People's Boat. This boat sprang from a competition sponsored by a sailing magazine of the period and was built in 1954 of marine plywood. She was a pretty little yacht with pine spars. Two of her sails, one called a 'bob-a-link spinnaker' (a bit like a modern cruising chute) and a fine genoa, were of Egyptian cotton – they set like a dream.

The cabin space was without standing room and cramped by modern standards. It had a two-berth main cabin, which doubled as the saloon and galley (a two-burner camping stove!), and a forecabin which had a berth and a chemical toilet. At the time of the tale, the forecabin had a Moses basket secured to the single berth, for their young son. In this boat they cruised quite extensively around the East Coast and its fascinating collection of rivers and creeks …

The skipper and his mate met up with a sailing buddy and his crew aboard their *Peter Duck* ketch. They had met in Queenborough and agreed to a few days cruising in company around the River Medway. Both boats had just returned from higher up the East Coast. The weather was threatening to break, with a mixed forecast, but at the time it was still sublime. The two yachts departed from Queenborough to make a pleasant passage to Upnor, managing to moor to adjacent buoys off the shingle beach, under the wooded slopes, just below the yacht club. The evening, after aperitifs aboard the larger yacht, was spent ashore, supping at one of the local hostelries where food could be obtained and youngsters were allowed in the eating area. It was all rather pleasant.

Over their supper it was decided to take the tide down to Sharfleet the next day to soak up the aura of the summer marshes and wildlife. The variety of wildlife was not as abundant then as has become, but was worth seeing all the same. Another attraction, which still has merit, is that during the week it was clear of weekenders and its remoteness and solitude could be more greatly appreciated.

The forecast the previous evening had spoken of some wind from the southeast. The strength was considered at the marginal stage, but agreement was made to listen again in the morning and look at what happened. In those days, the local radio forecasts now given out regularly during the day had not become the useful tool they now are – let alone all the other modern contrivances that are available to be fitted aboard yachts, spewing out details that confuse some or put other crews off getting underway! The skipper and his mate were to become ardent supporters of local radio forecasts: they were very much honed to the particular areas detailed. In those days, the skipper and mate relied upon the standard shipping forecast – with the Thames area running all the way to Belgium! – and, of course, basic observation.

The morning came with sunshine, but scudding clouds were buzzing in from seawards. In the wooded slopes above the moorings, the trees were as if alive, actively swaying about. A number of yachts had come in, either under power or with only their jibs set. It did not look good. During the night both the skipper and the mate had been aware of the increasing wind, being woken by the bump of the dinghy coming alongside and the general slop that built up with the wind over tide.

The mate said to the skipper, 'I wonder what they're planning over there', pointing to their friends' boat. The skipper and mate did not even have a VHF (marine band) radio then, although their friend did. Mobile phones – of a size that were smaller than a military field telephone – had not entered the market either. It was a different age.

The skipper said to his mate, 'Let's see how the morning progresses. We don't have to leave for a while yet.'

Later in the morning the skipper and mate heard a hail from the larger yacht, 'Fancy a coffee?'

The skipper, cupping his hands to throw his voice, called out, 'That would be great. Look, we'll be over in a jiffy.'

With that the mate put the babe in the baby carrier and put him on her front, his favourite position! The skipper meanwhile had hauled their dinghy up alongside. Although breezy the river's surface was quiet as the tide was still on the flood. On the ebb it would be very different!

The row over to the other yacht was short and simple. Coming alongside, the topsides seemed to loom above the mate and a warm friendly hand reached down to help her aboard. The men aboard this yacht, both at the time confirmed bachelors, had a watching brief over mother and baby while the skipper was away at sea. The mate had been on this proper little yacht a number of times and had spent a pleasant few days onboard a couple of years earlier – for an initiation into the wiles and ways of cruiser sailing … into which she had been confirmed.

Over coffee in the spacious cockpit of the *Peter Duck*, sheltered from the wind, it felt warm and sublime. Deep inland it was a glorious summer day. As they sat nattering they watched a gaff-rigged yacht coming in past Gillingham. As the yacht approached it was

Coffee? We'll be over in a jiffy ...

The *Peter Duck* ketch that belonged to their good friend, seen sailing in company with the skipper and the mate down the River Medway in quieter times. In the illustration, too, is the *Cabby*, when owned by Crescent Shipping (London & Rochester Trading Co. Ltd.) and before she was rigged with a bowsprit.

obvious that it had a very deep reef-tied down indeed. The boat was later seen to be flying a Dutch ensign and had probably just completed her voyage over, so it was dismissed.

Prior to departing their friends' boat, the two skippers decided that at about half ebb they would both get underway. The crews acquiesced, but the skipper's mate had given him a searching look, for they had the baby aboard.

Back aboard their own little yacht again, the mate said, 'Are you sure that we should be doing this?'

Don't worry – what can go wrong on a sail down to Sharfleet?'

Later they set off with a few turns in their mainsail. It did not seem to be too bad. The boat was balanced. The baby was in his basket, snug and warm, secured between the two main cabin berths, where eye contact could be made from the cockpit. This in itself was often not necessary because the baby always fell asleep whenever they got underway!

Rounding Folly Point, the skipper heard a rumble from the foredeck. He said something indiscernible and went forward to investigate. The anchor had gone overboard and some cable had run out, fortunately not all the way …

Calling for the mate to luff up, the skipper hauled away on the cable for what seemed an absolute age. Eventually their fisherman anchor was swinging from the bow roller. Pulling it aboard, he lashed it in place and was to continue the practice ever after. It was that day's second lesson!

Their friends' boat had luffed up briefly to make sure that all was well aboard their smaller companion. The skipper waved and both boats carried on – they were not alone as others were out enjoying the sailing too. Turning into Long Reach it was apparent that a few tacks would be needed. The larger boat started to pull away and they pulled another reef into their mainsail to reduce speed. Going down towards Oakham Ness all had continued to go well, but soon after rounding it, it soon became obvious that the skipper needed to roll the mains'l up some more.

Well over towards the Stoke Ooze mud-flats, the entrance to Stangate Creek was in sight. 'Not so very far', the skipper and the mate both mouthed to one another. The baby remained asleep, even though they'd been sluicing along with the wind almost on the beam, the boat bouncing over short, wind over tide, waves. In Kethole Reach they crashed through a number of fairly hefty seas; the spray was thrown across the boat, showering the crew with sparkling droplets.

The skipper had to start tacking again after clearing Sharp Ness and here he made a mistake. It could have been nasty. Trying to squeeze the last few metres out of a tack he had pinched and when he had eventually put the helm over, their little yacht with its shallow draught had stalled. By the time they had enough speed for another attempt, the hard low tide clay beach to the east of Sharp Ness grabbed them. There they bumped sharply on a seemingly rock-hard bottom.

The skipper thought, 'What have I done?' Then, handing the helm to the mate with hurried instructions to sheer the boat off and as soon as the jib hauled aback, filled, to bear away from the shore, he quickly went forward. Whipping some chain out from locker below, he hurled the anchor out towards deeper water. It bit. The boat swung, and with the wind slant off the shore the boat was away on the new tack. The skipper hauled in the anchor as fast as he could, glancing aft as he did so, where he could see that the mate was doing a sterling job.

After tidying the anchor and cable, a much-chastened skipper crept aft and apologised to his mate for his foolishness and foolhardiness. It could have been so much worse. The skipper then asked, 'How's the baby?' but after looking below he saw the angelic smile still in place; the thumb was in and the little man was fast asleep! A pale-looking mate grimaced and said, 'Here, you take over again – it'll settle you down!'

The skipper, now keeping well clear of the shallows, continued to tack towards Stangate Creek. The tide had turned, the skipper noticed, because the wind-over-tide waves quickly seemed to have diminished to mere trifles. On a board over towards

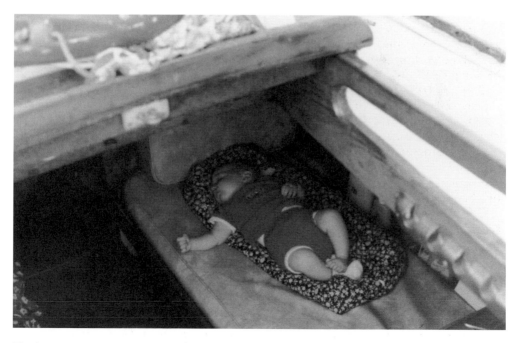

The boat was once again at rest: after a feed the 'babe' still slept on, but no longer in his Moses basket. The muted breathing seemed to say, 'Oh ... this ... is a ... grand ... life ...'

the old refinery side of the river the skipper said, 'Look, we can bear away now, we'll clear the spit and fetch into Stangate.'

The mated nodded. The skipper noticed that some colour had returned to her cheeks: she knew that all was now well. The skipper thought, 'But not forgotten, I'll probably have some explaining to do in a while ...'

Soon they had cleared the spit at the entrance and continued on a glorious sail up the creek, before dropping the mainsail to run under jib into Sharfleet Creek. Sailing round the western side of a clay spit they rounded up well to the south under the marshes to drop anchor. The spit in those days still had islands of marsh that at high tide seemingly sat out in the middle of the fairway. Now, though, the islands had eroded to the point where it often caught the unwary, especially at the approach to half tide.

During that afternoon, the skipper of the larger yacht rowed his crew, an older gentleman, with short-cropped greying hair, over for afternoon tea and cake. While passing the time, as people do aboard a yacht on a sunny afternoon, the two crews agreed to meet aboard the *Peter Duck* for dinner. Their friend said, 'Look, we've both got steak and kidney puddings. Bring yours over, ready cooked, and I'll do all the rest. I've got something to start with and some cheese to dawdle over afterwards.'

Later, at around six, they rowed the baby and the pudding over to their friends' yacht to spend a convivial evening together. The baby had his share too, but the two gentlemen (they said) hadn't noticed the little suckling bundle buried amongst his blanket and mother's jersey under the gently flickering orange glow of the cabin lamps.

During the evening the skipper and the mate had talked to their friends about their passage, the skipper said, 'I've learnt several things today: firstly, that we should heed the forecasts; secondly, I should have lashed the anchor down; thirdly, It was foolhardy to pinch close into the shore, with a hard bottom too; and I hadn't noticed that the tide had turned against us.'

'That's four', quipped the mate as she snuggled the babe.

Smiling she added, 'We'll jolly well not forget them – I hope!'

And so they didn't – on the whole!

... (they said) they hadn't noticed the suckling bundle ...

Another incident of some note took place a couple of years later soon after they had taken delivery of their newly built 24ft clinker sloop, the boat that they now sail.

The skipper and the mate had enjoyed a few weeks' cruising around the East Coast rivers. They had been up to the Orwell and came home in lazy stages, poking their boat up into various little holes. The Walton Backwaters and rivers Blackwater and Colne had kept them entranced, as usual. Although time was not of the essence, they had felt it was time to get back to their home, but were under no pressure to do so.

There had been a run of misty mornings with light breezes, but each recent day had brightened quickly leaving it warm and sunny. 'Very pleasant in fact', the mate said to the skipper, referring to being able to read outside, in the cockpit, in such pleasant conditions. That was after the skipper had returned from a sail in his sailing tender. He'd gone through the marshes and poked around Shepherds Creek looking at barge hulks, after their arrival in the little port.

Their last night on the River Medway was spent in the ancient watering hole of Queenborough. They had supper ashore, getting back to the boat about mid-evening. The sky above was clear, but down on the water the air felt damp; it had the fuzziness of a creeping mist that was almost unseen in the darkness. Lights too had rimes; angelic haloes caused by the mist. It did not bode well for the next day.

The following morning the skipper poked his head out, fairly early, to find a deep foggy malaise hanging over the boat. It blotted out the surrounding Swale. The shore could not be seen. The forecast, listened to with severe intentness, spoke of mist patches and bright sunshine, with a light breeze from the south or southwest. Looking at one another, they both shrugged. High tide in the late afternoon meant that they had plenty of scope for leaving and arriving in time to reach their little creek and the boat's berth.

By the time breakfast had been produced, eaten and cleared away it seemed that the fog had lifted somewhat, because some old pier ruins near the entrance to their stretch of water had come into view. Soon the mate made out a cardinal buoy which sat at the entrance, marking a spit on the western side of the channel, out in the main river.

'Great!' said the skipper, 'We'll give it a bit longer and get underway.'

Looking astern to the south the skipper could clearly see a wharf, its cranes and a coaster alongside. This was at least half a mile away. Visibility was creeping up to the mile mark. It was time for the mate and skipper to discuss the finer points of the approaching passage.

There was no wind as such, so, with the trusty diesel beneath the cockpit floor, always ready on those occasions, running sweetly, they dropped the mooring off and soon left it astern. The plan was to cross the main river, leave the old fort well to port, but inside the channel buoy, then follow round a two- to three-metre contour of the grain sands, locate another buoy in the Nore Swatch and head north for Southend Pier. It was a passage that they knew well – in normal conditions. They had good visual contact all around them and the wharves at Sheerness loomed out of the swirling mist too. However, on the passage across the Medway entrance, the mist dropped down again, enveloping the boat in a clinging shroud.

The skipper grimaced and said, 'This is not good, Mr Mate', borrowing a phrase he had picked when at sea on big ships years ago.

Maintaining their course until in the shallows the skipper turned eastwards, slowly running along the shallows. Gauging his distance, they stopped and ran the anchor overboard to await developments. After a very short while it seemed that the sun appeared to be nosing through the cotton wool canopy above their heads. They stayed put.

Eventually, the mist began to lift, imperceptibly at first, but soon Sheerness sprang into view. This was it: the sun had, at last, won its battle. Outside the river, looking down the channel, the skipper saw the outer Grain Sands buoy. This was the moment of decision. 'Let's get underway,' he said to the mate.

So, with lightness in their spirits, they weighed anchor and headed out of the river. All seemed to be going well. Crossing the Grain Sands they had visual contact with the swatch buoy that they were interested in; from there it was an easy and relatively short hop across the shipping channel to the pier. Well, it was this that had been the skipper's concern.

The main Thames channel had undergone a period of quietness for a number of years, although slowly trade was building again. But that worrying width, which was effectively quite narrow, still had to be crossed. Under power, though, the skipper and the mate knew that it could be traversed quickly.

Then it happened. Shortly after passing their point of departure on the southern shore along the Nore Swatch, the mist came swirling down upon them. In a short space of time they were blanketed in a thick oily fog, a proper 'pea soup'.

Considering the position that they were in and the fact that a ship had not been spotted before the fog enveloped them again, the skipper made the decision to continue. 'Was it the right decision?' was a question that had troubled the skipper and in retrospect, afterwards, he knew that he'd have made a different decision if faced with it again: fog has been the enemy of the seafarer for eons. The age of power-driven vessels has in many respects made the situation facing fog-bound vessels more dangerous: a ship travels at speed, all seeing, it believes, with its array of electronic wizardry. Oh so different in the gentler age of sail! The humble yacht, without electronic instruments, generally relies on twists of aluminium encased in a plastic tube set up on its mast. It's a trusting world.

Shortly after that, the mate said, 'Listen! That was a fog horn – from the port side, I think.' Then another piecing blast reached them.

Listening too, the skipper closed down the engine to an idle and turned into the still out-going tide, slowly stemming the last of the ebb. 'Yes,' he said, 'that was a single long blast, two minute intervals; a ship is coming down towards us.'

'We'll stay put, stem the tide. He'll have seen us on his radar.' The skipper had wanted to add, 'I hope', but did not do so, for he had seen the look of concern on his mate's face. She trusted him!

They had both continued to listen carefully. Then a much closer long resonant blast rent the air, seemingly from above their heads. 'That's not far away', said the skipper, with more than a little quiver in his voice. He hoped too that the mate had not caught his intonation: he could almost feel the great ship. He was worried. After a minute – but it had seemed an age at the time – the skipper sensed that the ship had passed by. The next bellow from the siren came from their starboard side, with that they had continued on a course for the pier, passing the propeller wash wake of the ship moments later. They both shuddered, involuntarily.

Then, as if by magic, they burst out of the clinging wet fog into clean bright air. The sun streamed down on a sunlit panorama; the pier was dead ahead, to the north, and about half a mile away. 'Bloody Hell!' said the skipper, for he knew that they had had a close shave. He shivered as briefly he thought of the worst …

The mate said with a sudden brightness, for she had been silently scared witless earlier, 'Just look at it on this side its …' Looking back, towards the way they had come, it seemed as if the fog was being rolled up and dragged skywards. It had literally melted away before their very eyes.

Later, moored up and waiting for the tide to get into their creek, the skipper said to the mate, 'Unless caught out, on a passage over, we will never again cross the River Thames in a fog.'

'That was close, too bloody close!' He added after a pause.

The outcome of that short passage, for the mate and the skipper, and their son too, could have been dire. A severe lesson had been learnt. That autumn they bought a VHF communications radio for the boat.

11

'Nothing Round the Swale, You Say?'

The departure from their moorings had been idyllic. It was a typical summer day during late August; the air was warm, even though a light northerly had been blowing across the estuary. Thunder had been forecast to come up from the south overnight and clear away by the following morning; but as it happened, the sun shone from an almost cloudless sky. The London River had taken on shades of blue and greens, dappling and reflecting patterns of light close to the boat as she curtsied over the wash waves created by passing shipping and motor yachts buzzing by on their way to Queenborough or some other honey pot up the River Medway.

Their progress over the last of the flood had been slow at first; but time was on their side, for they were, that day, bound for the East Swale for a cruise round the Isle of Sheppey. Once the ebb had set in, they progressed at an easy and sedate pace, giving them a relaxing sail.

As the austere and eerie masts of the *Richard Montgomery* hove alongside, the skipper recounted, again, to the mate how the ship had been ordered to anchor where she now sat to await its turn to go up river and unload. Unfortunately it was too close to the Grain Sands. She had swung and grounded, breaking her back before tugs could pull her clear. The bulk of her cargo of ammunition still sat inside her rusting hull, although some had, at the time, been unloaded before her cracked hull disappeared beneath the murky estuary waters.

'Look,' said the skipper, pointing away on their starboard side, 'you can see the twist in the hull. One of the masts is at a different angle to the others: her hull is broken.'

'When I was a boy sailing out of here on the barge, I remember the funnel was still in place and when the tide was out you could still see the top of the wheelhouse. She's sunk further down into the sands now though.'

'We [my siblings and I, he explained] use to think it great fun to look upon her as we passed by.' The skipper explained that they didn't then know that she was full of ammunition, enough to wipe Sheerness off the map and badly damage Southend–on–Sea on their own side of the estuary too!

The skipper was making reference to his childhood afloat and a book he had written and had published, *The May Flower: A Barging Childhood*.
'What's going to happen to her?' the mate asked, looking at the skipper with her quizzical expression – any old answer would not do.

The skipper filled in what he knew, 'The authorities say she is safe to be left alone.' Continuing after a moment's pause, 'The problem is that due to shifting sands, her hull is getting ever closer to the deep water channel, so I assume something will have to be done eventually.'

Leaving the masts of the wreck and the apparent shadow of her hull with its cargo lurking ominously beneath the surface behind them, they made a passage across the

A colourful sight, the ship made slowly
and effortlessly into the East Swale. The
Columbine Spit buoy is in sight, under
the boom, with a moody sky brewing
ominously over her towards the south.

Cant, an area of shallows fronting the ever-crumbling, soft, clay, northern coast line of
Sheppey. This area was littered with wreckage, vessels, aircraft and old wartime boom
defences. But on the top of the tide little of this was of any danger to their clinker
sloop, provided they stayed outside a line of beacons.

The skipper mentioned the cruising chute to the mate ... the mate, her face
puckering, had said, reluctantly, 'You play, I'll steer!' That sail was not her favourite,
though after it had landed on the foredeck with a light thud she resigned herself to it.
Busying himself on the foredeck, the skipper soon got the sail out of its bag, grinning
as it was set. It was soon pulling well, giving an extra bit of speed over the ground.
They continued in this lazy fashion for nearly two hours, with the wind more or less
on the beam, when the mate looking away through the starboard shrouds picked up
the Columbine Spit buoy.

Shortly after coming round on almost a run towards their marker, the skipper said
to his mate, 'Look, it's lovely and quiet. We're making nicely over the last of this ebb;
I'll take the camera away in the dinghy and get a photograph. The sun shining from
behind "your favourite sail" would make a great picture! It'll catch those colours in a
way not thought possible. Look at those clouds too, over the hills, south of Faversham,
they'll add a bit of drama to the back drop of the shot.'

With that the skipper pulled the dinghy alongside and lay off astern, easily keeping
pace with their progress. While taking the picture and concentrating on framing the
boat and the reflected colours in the water, he noticed a white sail away in the distance
ahead of him. A thought suddenly struck hard. 'Why is that boat running towards
us?'

'Look out,' he had called to his mate, rowing rapidly back to their boat. Leaping
aboard and handing the mate the dinghy painter to tie off astern, he panted, 'the wind

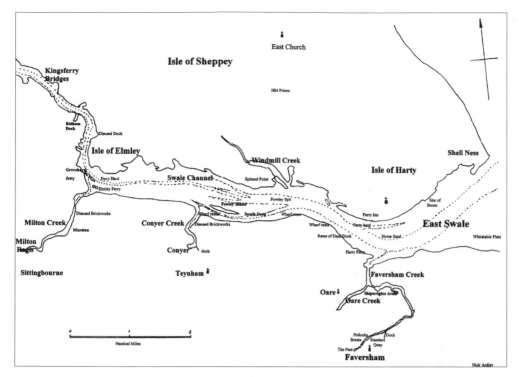

Chartlet of the East Swale on the north Kent coast.

is about to shoot round to the southwest. I've got to get the chute down. Look at those clouds now – they look threatening.'

With that the skipper shot forward. No sooner had the lightweight sail been rapidly dumped down onto the deck, than the wind, with no warning patch of fitful light airs beforehand, came at them from the southwest! Around them, the water that had only moments earlier been placid and almost oily-looking, had changed to a quite a typical slop, with the crests of little waves almost at breaking point.

The skipper soon had the jib up and they then proceeded to tack into the East Swale. A yacht, the one seen in the distance, came surging down towards them, her wings spread, enjoying a grand sail. The skipper recognised them as fellow sailing club members, and waved, although her burgee set from her crosstree had been hidden until they were close. At that point the other boat's crew waved cheerfully too! A call drifted across the water, 'We thought it was you – but didn't recognise the sail!' The two boats were clearing each other fast, so with a nonchalant wave in response, the skipper concentrated on tacking the boat.

The wind came in quite fresh, so, with only the last of the ebb to fight against, they made swift progress, tack by tack up the channel, with the hump of the horse sands standing well above the water. Reaching the cardinal buoy off the entrance to Faversham Creek, they made a final tack to reach along the southern shore of the East Swale, looking for a spot to anchor, or find a mooring that was vacant further in.

'Look,' said the mate pointing through the port shrouds, 'there's a buoy vacant inside of that red yacht, can you see it?'

The skipper nodded and, after their usual conversation on who would do what, they had picked the buoy up. Sitting over a late-afternoon repast of tea and cake, the skipper congratulated his mate on her excellent sailing onto the buoy for him to pick up the mooring: passing the buoy they had dropped the mains'l, to fetch back on an almost slack tide, the mate bringing the little yacht round onto the buoy for the skipper to easily haul aboard the trailing line.

Shortly after tying up to the buoy, the wind swung and dropped to a gentle southerly, then on round to the southeast, eventually falling further until no apparent wind could be felt at all. The burgee hung limp at the masthead. As things stood, there would not be a sail in the dinghy for the skipper that evening. Both settled down with reading material and with the movements out on the water they passed a pleasant hour or two before supper.

Gazing across the marshes towards the shore to the south, the mate wondered to herself about the stumps of wood sticking above a grass-covered indent in the sea wall; also she had noticed what looked like a solitary post sticking up above the flat marshland, further to the east. Other than this the shore looked featureless and empty.

Looking at the skipper she said, 'I'm certain you've told me before, but what was that indent in the sea wall where those posts are?' pointing towards the southern shore.

The skipper looking up from his book had explained that it was the remains of an old dock. Spritsail barges shipped in the commodities needed for ammunition manufacturing and took away the finished products. A huge factory had existed on the site. On the other side of the sea wall remnants of the buildings could still be seen. The whole area was now a nature reserve.

The mate, not getting all of her question answered, had prodded the skipper, 'Come on,' she said, 'what's it called then?'

'It's called Dan's Dock. There is another similar dock on the western side of Elmley Island', he'd hurriedly said, feeling a little scolded for rambling on!

He went on, as was his way, 'You remember, surely, on our visit to Faversham, a while back, when we walked out to the old gunpowder mill that was powered by the very stream that feeds the creek.'

'We learnt a little about the gunpowder industry that took place in these parts.'

They had learnt too about a huge explosion and the immense damage caused to a factory out here. A tragic loss of life of the townsfolk had resulted too. After that the authorities forced factories to move out to more remote places, where they were better served by water transport. It was fortunate that that particular explosion had occurred out of town.

The mate said, 'Oh yes, I remember now, the town works – the old workings – is right in the middle of a modern housing estate now.'

Then her gaze drifted eastwards, and continuing quickly before the skipper could set off on one of his rambles (which he was prone to do), said, 'So what is that post over there then?'

'Well,' said the skipper, 'it's not a post as such, it is actually the stem of a spritsail barge, long abandoned. The bottom of her hull sits embedded in the marsh. She is the *Pride* and she was a local barge from Faversham.'

'Look through the binoculars at the top of the post; you'll see the remains of her lower stayfall tackle block. Don't you remember a couple of years ago we walked along the sea wall to look over the dock when we had gone ashore for some of the water that issues freely from the natural spring at the top of the hard?' The skipper paused a moment to remember something and said, 'I did a sketch.' Then he briefly disappeared below and came back with his sketch pad, flicking the pages over to find his drawing of the *Pride's* stem as he'd done so.

The skipper, after he had shown the mate the sketch, continued, 'There is a whole line of other barges, a buried fleet, that rest with their decks awash with the top of the marsh, abandoned since around about the First World War. The rigging irons

The upright stem of the *Pride* stands proudly above the present level of the marshes, surrounded by a sea of sea pusalane, thrift and cord grass. It stands as if a sentinel, saying, 'Look, I may be no longer be of any use, but I'm still here!'

A veritable fleet of spritsail barges rests here. Rows of rigging irons and other recognisable features poke out. The knowledgeable eye will run back to stem heads and rudder tops. The old hulls rest, as if tucked up, sleeping under the coverlets of their marshland beds.

can be seen on one and on others the stem heads and stern posts poke up above the sea lavender and grasses. The grasses are almost a land variety: the marshes have reached such a height that they are not flooded very frequently.' Then adding as an afterthought – a pet subject – 'Although with the more rapid rise in sea levels I'm sure that balance is bound to change.'

'You remember, I said that it was similar to walking round a churchyard, to walk on the almost ghostly shadowy shape of those hulls. They are, after all, to me, something that was alive long ago. They're not yet invisible, not completely interred, but are at rest. It had a feeling of trespass. It is a sad and lonely sight, both eerie and evocative. They have been here about eighty years now.'

With that the mate gazed awhile through the glasses, then wondering aloud, 'Isn't it amazing how marsh can build up like that over there, yet in other places, is washed away, at will, by waves and tides.'

The skipper, pointing across to the other side of the creek, indicated to the mate the scattered remains of a few other barges, now well buried in the mud, but still a hazard to craft. He concluded, 'There are two more on that shore down near Sand End.' The skipper had, some time ago, told the mate about the anti-submarine boom that had been constructed across the East Swale during the Second World War. The two hulks near Sand End had been part of that boom. He added, 'Remember too, there's one further up the Swale, under Elmley Hill. It sits when the tide is around her hull as if deeply laden, eerily coated in fronds of weed.'

The mate chipped in, 'Yes, I do remember', but wanting to continue, quickly added, 'do you remember when we visited the little church on the hill many years ago?'

The skipper, looking at the church nestling amongst some trees, let out a slow 'Yes', for he thought he knew what was coming next.

The mate continued her story nonetheless, 'The church had been broken into, well not exactly, because in those days it wasn't locked. Wasn't an ancient chest stolen from inside? I remember being told about it. I wonder if it ever turned up. I seem to remember that it had been originally retrieved from a wreck of a ship that got caught on the horse sands hundreds of years ago.'

'Maybe we should make a return visit one of these days and find out,' said the skipper lightheartedly.

'You know,' the mate started, 'the Swale …' she paused again, 'What better place to sit back, a book in hand and watch the world go by. It's such an open panorama, a fluid canvas on an ever-changing picture – yet it is timeless too: the backdrop doesn't appear to change.'

Later that evening after a fine supper of braised pork chops cooked with onions, tomatoes and lots of cider, (a wonderful ingredient that conveniently imparted good flavour) and with the clearing up out of the way, they sat back in the cockpit to enjoy the warmth of the balmy evening. The sky had cleared away leaving it cloudless; there wasn't going to be a moon, so they were expecting a starry night. The threat of thunder had evaporated, thankfully, as the clouds had receded back beyond the hills of the North Downs to the south.

'You know,' said the skipper, leaning back, sighing and looking around, 'the place looks so empty, but yet, beneath that empty veneer lies so much.' He looked at his mate, 'We'll see more tomorrow.'

'In Roman times too, and until not such a long time ago, this waterway was the main artery through to the London River and further on up the coast. Ships could sail inside the Isle of Grain to come out, opposite Leigh-on-Sea and to the west of the then treacherous Nore Sands, at the Yantlet.'

Over a coffee, laced with their favourite nightcap, they enjoyed the sounds of the night. Flourishing colonies of various sea birds had made this area home for the summer; others were there all the year round and the skipper and his mate always felt it was a privilege to be afloat, to be able to enjoy nature at such close quarters, especially in such an anchorage as this.

'Listen!' they had both chorused together. 'The birds are agitated.' Curlews, oystercatchers, redshank and others were calling out frantically.

'Must be a fox', said the skipper quietly, for the stillness of the night gave a feeling of intimacy and anything else would have seemed out of place.

'It's gone quiet now: Mr Fox has his supper tonight!'

There were an enormous number of stars in the sky. A slight haze was present, but not enough to affect clarity. Down on this stretch of water, the skipper and mate had found that the light pollution here was the lowest to be found around the River Medway and Swale. The mate suggested another coffee before they turned in. For the morrow a lazy day had been planned. A gentle potter up into the South Deep was all they desired.

During the night the skipper, realising that there was a bit of a disturbance in the main cabin, and that his mate had obviously abandoned her side of the bunk, got out too and went aft, through the boat, to investigate. He found his mate, her coat on, looking up at the sky. It was an incredible sight, so brightly lit by a plethora of intense pinpricks of coloured light. It seemed that there were blues, near whites, yellows and some oranges. The latter were probably some of our world's sister planets.

Giving him a hug and then telling him to get his coat on, the mate whispered softly, 'Let's have a hot toddy and enjoy this: it's a night in a thousand. We don't have to be up early in the morning.'

Waking the next day – late – they had breakfast outside on the cockpit table. On the boat it was generally the skipper that did the cooking, although they did share this duty, but breakfasts were usually prepared by the mate. The skipper enjoyed a coffee while he watched the world go by as his pleasant – he knew – repast was produced below.

Boats were on the move. People on passing craft always looked their way, calling over a comment or two, if close, complimenting them on the appearance of their old boat. The skipper always having to say, 'Well she's not that old ...' Incredulous expressions often follow with a typical, 'Oh, only 1984 is she!' or with an eyebrow raised, 'Oh, she's younger than mine then,' from an owner of a glass-reinforced plastic (or as it is commonly termed, GRP) sloop obviously manufactured sometime in the early '70s. Their incredulity being met with a grin from the skipper – the only possible, or sensible even, response!

'The thing is', the skipper had often told anybody that was interested, 'with a wooden boat, an owner who keeps on top of the paintwork and does things as they need doing, reaps the harvest of their efforts.'

The skipper and his mate had found that painting the hull of their wooden sloop only needed, in general, a four-year cycle; but they, or just the skipper, promptly dealt with any scrapes and such as and when they occurred. This philosophy was extended to the bright work too, where overcoating took place every two to three years, none of which was an onerous task.

Over breakfast they decided to get under way as soon as the clearing up was done. The tide was still on the flood and, what with the fickle southerly, they would need it if the engine was to remain 'locked up' beneath the cockpit floor: the skipper only used fuel when he had to!

The skipper hauled up their big genoa; then, as the mate gave the boat a sheer, he dropped the mooring overboard. They were away. The mate luffed up, for the skipper to heave the mains'l aloft, then she had the boat round to head westwards up the Swale.

The remains of a disused explosives jetty that sits near to Dans Dock, to the east of Stinket Ness. It was used for transportation of gun cotton.

Passing some moorings and the ragged remains of an old wharf, the skipper remarked, as he was wont to do, 'See that ragged pile over there?' pointing to the shore. 'That's the remains of an old barge wharf from which gun cotton was shipped out. See how it is well separated from the powder works we've already passed. The remains of an old barge lay hereabouts too; no sign of her now though.'

The moorings of the old wharf were owned by a local farmer. Here, there was anything up to four yachts during the season, and nearly all had an interest in them. One was an old-fashioned gaff-rigged yacht. It had a straight stem, typical of a punt, with a long bowsprit reaching out for the unwary. Another was a fairly modern yacht, but almost uniquely it was constructed of Cupronickel. It had never been painted, not needing any protective coatings; it had an all-over green patina, slightly dull but not too much so. There was too an old gentleman's day yacht, fitted with a cabin. It sat low in the water, was narrow gutted with a counter stern and almost a clipper bow. She was a beauty, if not functional for cruising. The skipper had seen her sailing a few seasons before and appreciated her for that alone. 'She was built for those lazy days of sailing, when a gentleman had a yacht and a man to help work her, at the end of the Victorian age', said the skipper.

'Away past the green conical buoy over there', the skipper said, pointing northwards, 'is the silted up remains of a creek: Windmill Creek, it is called. It is no more a creek as such, but a dead end, full of cord grass-covered mud banks and marshes. An old boy we used to know came here regularly during the 1950s and 60s, shooting for duck.'

'It's a classic place where the sea walls could be breached to let nature reclaim the marshy land beyond; it might clear out the old creek too.'

'The whole place is a history book; I wonder how many sailing past have any clue about what's happened here before them. Look across there,' the skipper pointed to the southern shore abreast of a spit buoy, 'there are the remnants of another wharf, once a hive of industry, in that patch of weed.'

'The only visible activity this end of the Swale is farming and the odd fisherman.'

Lazily sailing slowly up with the tide, with a long spit running eastwards from the remains of Fowley Island on their starboard side, they decided that once anchored in the South Deep, between the Island and the sea-walled shore. They would take the dinghy up to Conyer for a visit to the local hostelry for a light lunch, it being such a day for a 'Swallows and Amazons' summer adventure.

The food had been consistently good at the waterside pub for many a year and going up in the dinghy would re-enact a trip made years earlier in another dinghy when they'd had a different yacht, a Yachting World People's Boat of 1954 vintage. It was an early plywood yacht, the design sponsored by the yacht's namesake magazine when they still dealt with the 'man in the street', as it were. And, too, the reader will know this from an earlier tale, when the skipper had ignored all the warnings weatherwise!

Shortly after anchoring and ensuring all was snug aboard, they set off in the dinghy. The breeze was of sufficient strength to push them along nicely. The direction would mean a few tacks up the creek, but the tide helped greatly. The passage back, the skipper had jovially said to the mate, 'Would be easy.' The mate had given him one of her looks: she had heard that story before!

Looking at his mate he remembered what he saw reflected in her look: written in that look was the time that they had had to tack their boat out of the Walton Channel, a stretch of water behind Walton-on-the-Naze, up in North Essex, part of an archipelago of islands, mud creeks and cosy anchorages nestled in a sunken valley there about. They had had to do the very same the previous day on the way in. He'd then said to the mate, 'Tomorrow the tide will be on the ebb and the southerly wind would give an easy run out with it.' The skipper had said this tongue in cheek: for at the time he couldn't have known!

They had a couple of hours up the Conyer Creek, time enough for lunch and for the skipper to have a nose around at the remaining old spritsail barges still residing in the dock. The *Mermaid*, which had been in the dock since the early 1950s, had recently been broken up and now nothing remained of her at all. At the time, two others were still up inside the old dock cut. A dock built to ship out cement (the works being now long gone except for one building at the junction of the lane near the head of the dock) had become the home for a number of yacht barges, which in the space of a few years became virtually static floating homes. A row of modern clapboard houses now sat on the cement works site, most with an enchanting view across the low marshes beyond the creek.

The skipper and his mate looked over the hull of a barge called the *Persevere*. She was built close by across the marshes at Murston, a hamlet on the eastern bank of Milton Creek. She was being broken up; her decks and all her beams had been removed and her hull was open, like an empty tin of sardines. The skipper grimaced at the sight.

Later that same summer, on a return visit, they found that the hull had gone. From a garden up at the head of the dock there emanated the sweet, resinous scents of pine. A pile of wood, the twisted, broken and sawn remains of her hull planking, showing clear colours of yellow and orange, sat heaped up. Close by sat what was obviously her sternpost and knee, all of it ready to be loaded onto a lorry. 'The very vehicles that took away the jobs of the humble spritsail barges will soon be removing the last of this one,' muttered the skipper to his mate.

'The *Gold Belt* remains as the last of a veritable fleet of ex-sailormen used as yachts and floating homes, based in this dock,' said the skipper. With more than a tinge of finality in his voice, he added, 'though I don't believe the *Gold Belt* will last much longer. It's truly the end of an era.'

Only the *Gold Belt* now sits in the old cement works dock, the last of the old spritsail barges that made Conyer their home. Her days are numbered: although still 'lives on' she does not seem to have lifted for a while. 'Is this her last berth?' the skipper muttered; another, the *Persevere*, had been broken up recently.

'It had to happen. Just like your old home too.' The mate said with a reassuring voice, knowing that the skipper tended to become melancholic and saddened when witnessing these events.

However, back to their present visit: there was more to see. Further up the creek, from the dock, a yacht marina sat on the site of an old barge yard at what was Mercer's Wharf. Opposite the marina, some remains of old barges, used for homes during their last years, lay in a morass of dredged spoil. A few years previously the skipper had investigated the spoil and seen the remains of the side of a barge. It was the section that would have been between the fore and main holds. Her rigging ironwork poked above the dried silt. A section of her inwale was seen too. The skipper had gazed adoringly, and in awe, at a beaded finish to the bottom edge, as good as the day it had been crafted.

The tide waits for no man. King Canute, so it is said, found this out centuries ago when he had endeavoured to command the rising tide to stop, on the banks of the River Crouch, below a place which sits well above the tide on a hill and is purported to be his namesake, Canewdon in Essex. So, reluctantly, they returned to where they had left their dinghy, at a small yacht harbour downstream of the pub. The mate said, as they passed through, 'These houses were built on the site of a boatyard that built those bespoke yachts in steel, weren't they?'

After donning his life jacket, the skipper finally responded, 'Yes, but before that, this was a barge yard too. The creek had three barge yards at one time! The other was downstream.'

Alas, all that had all gone now and it all had become a part of the fascinating and live history of the little creekside hamlet. Along the bank, some small-scale building

'At the head of the creek, across from Mercer's old barge yard, now the marina, two spritsail barges lay buried in the detritus of creek dredging. One, the *Henry and Jabez*, her outer sides gone, showed some of her rotting frames and parts of her inner lining, the other, the *Percy*, was completely obliterated. It left me cold', the skipper said.

of traditional craft in GRP, with a wood finish, still took place at a yard over looking the yacht berths.

The marina site had a group of waterfront, clapboarded houses, some virtually hanging over the creek; they looked idyllic in many respects. 'They'd make a good place for us to be based', said the skipper as they readied themselves for the return trip.

'Only trouble is, is that there are no facilities locally – Faversham or Sittingbourne for those!' the mate added to ensure common sense prevailed …

Further down the creek were the remnants of brick workings. It all lay half buried in a maze of scrub. Hundreds of rabbits inhabited this place; the grass in many places had been nibbled to a carpet texture. Walking through during an evening stroll from the creek, some years back, the skipper, his mate and their young son had stood watching as dozens of rabbits, not being aware of their presence, came out to graze. The sight of the younger ones acting in a similar fashion to that of human young was a sight to behold.

Beyond the scrub was a line of poplar trees; these ran along the line of the fields which lay below the path due to the removal of brick earth used in the manufacture of millions of bricks. Most fields in this part of Kent had this feature! The skipper noticed the tops of the poplars swaying, their lofty fronds swishing, like the skirts of a female dancer waltzing, in the breeze.

On their way out of the creek they looked at the remains of two spritsail barges abandoned many years ago. They sat along the sea wall fringing the old brick workings, just above an old wharf. Beside the wharf another still sat, now virtually gone. The stumps of her stem and sternposts are the only recognisable features – to knowing persons. She too would soon be forgotten. The phrase from the Christian funeral rites came to the skipper's mind, 'Ashes to ashes, dust to dust ...' is true for all things organic, and ultimately, all things have a finite life span.

Leaving the creek behind, the mate said, 'Do you remember that early morning sail up this muddy creek, when we saw the kingfisher?'

'Of course I do,' was the softly spoken reply, for it was one of those wondrous and never-to-be-forgotten moments she had enjoyed on the water.

They decided after supper that evening that the next day they would have to stop off, at Queenborough, the waterside town at the entrance to the West Swale: some fresh provisions were needed.

That evening as the sun approached the horizon, the skipper had a short, yet idyllic, sail in their little lug sail-rigged tender. The colours reflecting across the water had been fabulous. Their sailing home was gradually silhouetted against a spectrum of colour, a hazy rainbow; it floated on the creek's mirrored surface. The skipper appreciated all of this before he slid gently back alongside the mother ship and the eager hand of the mate reaching out for the painter to make the dinghy fast.

The night had been exceptionally still; the only noises heard were the grumble of the anchor cable dragging across the shells on the turn of the tide in the early hours, the skipper popping on deck to savour the tranquillity. The following morning had dawned bright, with a gentle southerly breeze that wafted warmly the scents of the land across the water.

After breakfast they took the flood tide, which had about two hours to run, over the shoals at the head of the South Deep. The wind was by then a decent southerly and made for good sailing. The skipper, knowing the flatness of the bottom, had kept the boat on a course to gradually work over to the main channel.

The mate, looking around as the skipper enjoyed the good sailing breeze, said, 'Do you remember a previous occasion when we had left near the bottom of the ebb? We

It was late afternoon. The skipper and the mate felt their way, their boat's keel scraping the shells now and then, westwards along the narrow channel, barely deep enough to float them.

sailed eastwards to the Fowley Spit buoy, before turning west about, to sail up the main channel. The banks were uncovered all around – it was late I think.'

'My body always tingles when we go through at the bottom of the tide – almost scraping the shells beneath us.'

She shivered. A natural enough reaction!

'We had worked up the shallow swatch and enjoyed the sight of a small colony of seals, basking in the late afternoon sunshine, soaking up the warmth while waiting for the turn of the tide and a fresh meal.' She grinned, 'Remember the cormorants?' They'd seen a long row of them, their wings outstretched, drying in the breeze as they digested their last catch. 'Their heads turned to and fro, warily, as we passed by.'

'There was that the old wagon wheel sitting up on the southern bank too!'

From where it had originally come, the skipper and mate had debated at length, over and over again! Over many years they had repeatedly completed the same passage and each time it had lost none of its fascination. For in many ways it was a wilderness, a wilderness that could be appreciated at close hand. Recently, though, the wheel seemed to have disappeared.

'I was enchanted and it is something I'll always appreciate.' The mate beamed as she looked across at the skipper.

The mate, a whimsical look on her face, had not expected an answer to her questions and could have been in the world of her current book, so the skipper let her be, to enjoy, to savour, to relish and to remember, in peace.

A while later when they had reached the main channel, near Elmley Ferry, the skipper had pointed at the hulk of a Second World War wooden mine sweeper. She sat lolled to one side, up on the mud-flats, the tide reaching into her insides through the many missing planks. 'She's really started ...'

The skipper stopped, his ear had heard the fast approach of a noisy, powerful boat. Casting his eye astern, he saw the raised razor-sharp bow obscuring a sloping deck that seemed to continue up to a flying bridge containing a laughing group, curving, it seemed, towards them.

'Hold tight', the skipper had said, needlessly, for the mate had already clasped a grab rail tightly.

At the last moment, it seemed, the monstrosity leaned away from their stern and showed her buttocks as she careered by. The wash hit them moments later, throwing the little clinker yacht every which way. Articles that never normally moved were thrown awry.

The dinghy, picked up by the fast-moving wash wave, surfed as if free of its tethering painter. 'Spectacular' you might think, but its fun and games were stopped abruptly as it made heavy contact with the yacht's transom and rudder, slewing round and bouncing about in the confused water.

'Bloody Hell!' the skipper shouted as he was thrown bodily across the cockpit into the opposite guard rails. He grabbed, instinctively against a pain, at the tiller that was freely slamming to and fro: the boat had careered off course. He shook his fist, in extreme passion, the more so: there was little hope that it would have been seen on the power craft that had rapidly receded to a blob with its white propeller-induced flume spouting out from behind, like a lolling schoolboy's tongue!

'Hullabaloos!' shouted the mate, shaking her fist too at the dot, now disappearing round a low hilly point ahead.

'Arthur Ransome was quite right all those years ago when he canonised the word for those types of people in his book, *Coot Club*.'

'Hullabaloos, Hullabaloos,' she shouted again!

In the confused, broken water left by the wash waves, the skipper and mate sorted out the sails and got their boat back on course.

The skipper shook his head, smiled (at the mate) and … said nothing.

Then he continued, 'Oh yes, where was I?' then, of course, he remembered …

Pointing to the old wreckage with the sloshing remnants of wash waves lapping the sides of the deteriorating hull of the old minesweeper, the skipper picked up from where he had left off prior to their close call with the water-borne missile.

'She's really started to deteriorate much more rapidly these past few years. Look at that bit over there, I'm sure it has collapsed since we passed this way last.'

'You know, there are the bottoms of others up on the beach at the top of the ferry hard. They were broken up for scrap metal and firewood – precious commodities in those austere days at the end of that dreadful conflict. Now those remains sit as reminders of an age long gone. A conflict to stop all conflicts – it was said! They're probably unique too.'

'Difficult to believe that now, isn't it?'

'Still that one rests in tranquillity, greeting the tide twice a day, year after year, outliving the men who built and manned her. Like those brave men too, in time, she will eventually return to the earth, leaving little trace.'

'It could be fifty, or even a hundred years yet!'

Passing between two sets of sturdy posts that sat at the foot of the hard, on both sides of the low-water channel, each sporting a sign warning of a gas pipeline, they continued westwards. The skipper pointed out, again, across the water, but it had been to the north. 'Look, see the ghostly shadows over there under the marshes. It's that barge I mentioned the other day.'

He'd stopped his own speech, abruptly, for he concentrated for a short while on looking through the binoculars. The mate knew that more was to come so waited patiently – keeping an eye on their path westwards.

'You can see her stem and breast hook. I'm sure I can make out the rusting remnants of her lower stayfall block. You can see her mast case and at her stern. The rudder looks like it still has some of her steering gear attached. In the waste of flat water, between those recognisable parts, lies her broken and rotting hull.'

'She was abandoned years ago, some say still rigged and ready to go; eventually she sank and there she has sat ever since, sleeping and gently merging into the environment.'

The hulk is the *Webster* of Rochester, built at Lambeth in 1863, so her remains were of an incredible age. The skipper obtained the information from the Society of Sailing Barge Research, an honourable society that studies the numerous trading sailing barges of Britain. Details such as where the barges were built, their owners, crews, types of cargoes carried and the known sites where they now rested were matters that the society records.

The mate changed the subject: she'd enough of barges. 'There's a tradition that King James II (VII of Scotland, too, of course) was picked up at this ferry point and taken down river to await a ship to carry him into exile. He'd upset Parliament by becoming too close to the Holy See in Rome. It was too soon after Cromwell's parliamentary revolution.'

'He was captured though and taken to Faversham and the rest is history!'

'Is that so?' said the skipper, and adding, 'Many a tale could be told about these desolate shores, that I'm certain!'

The skipper pointed to their port side, having switched attention back to a more recent history. 'Look,' he said, 'that creek leads up to Milton Regis; it has a long history of attachment to the water. Barge and ship builders co-existed up here with brick makers and cement works. A huge quantity of London's rubbish came here too!'

'Just like they are still dumping in our part of Essex now', said the mate with a more than a little irony.

The burgee of *Twitch*, the skipper's dinghy, flutters in the breeze on the way up Milton Creek. The creek has an industrial past of cement, bricks, rubbish and paper; it came and went by spritsail barge. It has been said that then you could cross the creek from barge to barge. Now it has all gone. Only crumbling wharves and rotting ribs of a few craft remain, all peeping out from amongst a sea of salt marsh and mud.

The skipper continued after a moment to concentrate on a course change and to adjust the sheets, 'Now it is all dead and silted. Hulls of vessels lie sleeping deep in the marshes, some completely smothered, and others rotting away gradually. Wharves are abandoned and crumbling.'

'There used to be a yard at the top of the creek, it had been saved from developers years ago and used as a museum. It was a working place too, the old crafts were kept alive, but it had to close. I did hear that it was to reopen – the barges have now gone though. The desperate need to destroy more of our maritime heritage cannot, it seems, be assuaged.'

'The powers that govern have decided to put a low road bridge across the creek, effectively chopping the top end off, so that barges, or any vessel larger than a dinghy, will not be able to navigate the waterway. Might as well fill it in and build over it', said the skipper finally, with a huge chunk of spite embedded in his voice.

'There's a yacht club still using the creek too. It is based at an old barge wharf.' The skipper had paused as he spotted something he hadn't seen before.

'Look!' The skipper pointed across the water into the entrance to Milton Creek, 'there are some new withies marking the gut way. We'll have to investigate another time ...'

Again, having to concentrate on his steering, the skipper turned almost downwind; the mate eased the sheets some more as he did so. Passing a jetty where a freighter was being unloaded, the skipper remarked, 'That jetty used to be a coal jetty. The coal was needed by the paper mills.' The freighter's cargo of a greyish powdery matter was being dropped onto a conveyor by grab cranes. This disappeared ashore to be added to the huge pile that made up a substantial man-made hill to the south.

'That stuff goes into some, if not all, of the plasterboard made in this country,' he added, 'and there's still a specialist china paper works too.'

'Well at least the water is clean,' said the mate, remembering her first passage round these waters as a young wife hailing from a town in Warwickshire, when effluent from the famous paper making mills had been disgorged at random into the Swale, rotting vegetation along the banks, murdering crustaceans and invertebrates, and creating a discoloured stinking flow of total deadness.

Now all was sweetness: the smell of mud, weed, sea life and brine predominated; it had returned in a few short years to normal. Nature had successfully reinstated itself.

Leaving the jetty behind them with the rotted bones of an old Baltic Trader poking out of the mud bank close by, they continued to run northwards down the reach. They passed by the remnants of another crumbling jetty and dock on the northern side of Elmley Island. This had been abandoned a long time ago. A hulk of a vessel sat mouldering in the silt amongst the seaweed covered terrain. The skipper was unsure what it had been, the vessel that is: the docks were used by the cement works that once sat here. Little remains of this industrial complex now, except for the odd noticeable man-made section of masonry not covered by grass.

Leaving the old dock astern, they were approaching the still active and vibrant Ridham docks and the bridge beyond. The mate had called up the bridge keeper to be told that they would have a wait of nearly an hour before they could transit. This was only a little less by the time they had arrived.

The docks at Ridham were built originally to service the local paper industry. Wood pulp had been shipped in from Newfoundland. Now rolls of newsprint and wood came in from Scandinavia. Ballast too, dredged from the outer Thames, arrived daily in deeply laden dredgers, loaded to the gunnels, spewing settled water as they surged

Part of the Swale's industrial past, the remains of an old cement works wharf on the western side of Elmley Island.

up on the tide, churning the river bed, thus ensuring, strangely, its sustainability as a ship channel. Those ships, though, left a severe and vicious wash that could throw a mug of tea off of a yacht's table, if taken unawares.

Eventually, after sailing up and down the Swale, in view of the bridge, for some forty minutes, they transited the bridge, or bridges. There were now two: a new high-level bridge took the road high above the water, thus allowing traffic to go over and under. The lifting bridge had been retained: the railway still needed to cross, but river traffic was still held up more often now than a few years ago – how so? Sod's law, of course!

'Ah, if this were Holland', thought the skipper aloud, 'tunnels would have been constructed and all the riverside paraphernalia would have been cleared away.'

The mate, thinking of the recent past said, 'Remember, years ago, when you told me to haul the dip bucket up in the rigging, so that we could let the bridge keeper know we wanted transit. I thought you were mad!'

'It was only when you put the pilot book under my nose and I read about what we had to do to get through the bridge that I believed you!'

'It was a strange custom, but before the age of the radio, it made sense', pausing to look across the water back up at the bridge keeper to give a wave of thanks, a link with humanity, she continued, 'It seems that the radio, as functional and sensible as it is, has taken away some of the more endearing aspects of life on the water.'

Humming to himself and deep in thought the skipper suddenly said, 'Do you remember seeing the spritsail barge, *Mirosa*, sail through the bridge?'

It had been a moderate westerly, or more or less, that day and they had had a good passage round the Swale, beating up from the South Deep. 'We had passed through and had anchored up to have a quiet lunch. The barge had come round from the Medway; she fetched up under the edge of the western mud bank, mains'l brailed up

The stately lady, the *Mirosa*, sailed serenely towards an obstacle, without a care in the world. The skipper had looked behind: a ship was approaching the obstacle too.

A sight rarely seen today, here it is framed by the obstacle of King's Ferry Bridge. The *Mirosa* had followed a ship through. The ship can be seen beyond the right-hand-side buttress of the bridge.

to the sprit, her tops'l left sheeted out and her foresail lay on the deck. A short while later a ship had come through the bridge from Ridham Docks. Then we watched as the *Mirosa* had quickly got underway. Up went her topsail and foresail – it had been held aback by the bowline as the anchor was brought up short. Then as the anchor broke out, she paid off and swept round on a gybe, the mains'l being run out as she came round.'

'It was a fantastic sight, do you remember? She had tracked across the water, perilously close to the eastern bank – it seemed – before swinging back in line with the bridge and then she'd shot sweetly through.'

'For me it was another one of the most magical moments that I've witnessed on the water.'

'Yes, I remember', said the mate. For her too it had been a sight never to be forgotten: it was something from the distant past – almost.

The skipper said, 'My father brought his barge here too, Mother says that she can't remember going through, but another of the crew assures me that they did.' Like those in the days of sail trading, neither of those barges had an engine.

Reaching a long spit and a sharp turn, they had to haul their sheets onto a close reach to sail past another commercial jetty. Here coasters unloaded scrap steel, which was used in a steel works nearby.

The skipper laughed because he had suddenly remembered the glue works. Bones used to be shipped here in huge quantities to feed a glue factory. The stench on some occasions was very severe indeed. The mate was introduced to this place some time before that era ended. The factory used to be to the south of the little creek that ran round the back of the town. It looked as if a housing development was being built there, the skipper had seen recently.

'Do you remember the glue factory smells?' he asked the mate, grimacing as he did so.

'Yes! It's something never forgotten, an abiding memory. The place is so much pleasanter for its demise.'

Cutting through the lines of some moored yachts along the northern bank of the jetty reach, Loden Hope, before rounding another bend to sail northwards, they were soon off the little bustling waterside town of 'Queensborough'. It had been named this long before, when it was an important town, some six centuries ago; it had a castle belonging to Queen Phillipa. The town still commemorated her, with a public house near the site of the castle, now just a low grass mound. Nowadays it was simply 'Queenborough'. It was a haven for yachting and had a varied collection of inshore fishing craft too.

After picking up a buoy opposite the hard, the skipper and mate went ashore. They stopped at one of the hostelries for a sandwich and a shandy, for it had been a long time since breakfast and it made an enjoyable late lunch. Later they walked up through the town, a fascinating collection of ancient buildings with a few newer in-fills, the result of wartime bomb damage years ago, to a baker's and butcher's, purchasing their needs for the next couple of days.

Having earlier decided upon a quiet little backwater for the evening, they were departing the Swale and leaving this singular place behind, but they were not going far: the backwater lay just out of sight, over the low marshes to the west. Looking carefully through binoculars, on a busy weekend, one could see yachts lining the creek beyond; some, under sail, were more easily seen. But for the sea walls in these parts, it was likely that a direct passage through, at the narrowest point of separation, would be possible – perhaps one day it will be so.

Settling down that evening after supper had been cleared away – a pair of succulent lamb chops each and some fresh fruit after – the mate commented on the beauty of the place. They had anchored quietly, near the bottom of the tide, in Funton Creek. It was a little creek, running initially east and west from the eastern foot of Stangate Creek, where the bird-life on the ebb went crazy, chasing each other off what had been deemed their patch, in a frenzy of food hunting. Shell banks, packed with mussels, reared up on the southern side like camel humps, seemingly in the middle of the creek. Shells lay, too, at the foot of a clay hump of an island, known as Chetney Hill, thickly covering the shallow lower slopes. It was idyllic.

A while later the mate, looking up from her novel, a reflective expression on her bronzed face, had turned to the skipper and said, 'At first glance the Swale appears to be such an empty bleak place. There is little tangible to actually look at but, in that emptiness, lies more, far more than that casual look can tell.'

'You've brought it alive for me these past few days; they were enchanting.'

The skipper, as he looked across at the mate, smiled, and said, 'Yes, you're so right.' Then as his gaze wandered about him, looking intently at what looked to be such a natural environment, a thought occurred to him: 'This place, so natural looking in every respect, is in fact ... well umm ...' a look from the mate had stopped him from speaking. That, whatever it was, was for another time!

The mate, seeing that the skipper had taken her unspoken, imploring look on board, said, 'Let's just sit back and savour it ...'

12

Cooped Up!

It was late in the day when they bustled, with rustling skirts, into the little harbour of Queenborough.

Earlier, when they had set off from their upriver mooring, the breeze had only been a light northerly and with it a bright sun, tinged yellow, had shone down from an almost clear sky. Towards the east, though, a haze blurred the horizon. During the passage down towards the river's juncture with its mightier sister, the Thames, the wind had threatened it seemed at times to become more of an easterly. The skipper, from time to time, watched this with the odd sort of grimace he was known to exhibit: he was thinking that perhaps the weather was on the turn. Nothing untoward had been heard on the radio though. Quietly, to himself, he had had some misgivings.

Nearing the end of their passage and sailing gamely down the long reach that fringed the marsh edges, opposite the wharves that had once been the old British Petroleum refinery, they had to come harder on the wind, when it should have been nicely on their beam. With the fetch across a longer stretch of open water, the river had become increasingly boisterous too. It had been grand sailing, though, and the boat had frolicked with joy, it seemed, in the purposeful heavier puffs. Those puffs had caressed the sails, heeling the sturdy hull as it threw up spumes of spray which glistened brightly in the sunlight, before the droplets fell away to melt back into the ever-changing facets of the river's surface.

By the time they had been able to bear away for their destination, the West Swale, the wind which had also been increasing in strength throughout their passage down from Chatham, pressed the boat across the tide and short waves into flatter, protected waters. Here she had picked up her skirts and literally skipped into the ancient harbour of Queenborough. The skipper dowsed and loosely stowed the sails as the mate rounded up towards a vacant mooring buoy, this time under power, whereupon the skipper slipped a line through the ring. It made a delightful end to a pleasant afternoon's sail.

Previously they had lain for a couple of nights off Chatham, tied fore and aft to a row of vacant buoys under the shadows of the ancient, disused dockyard church. The picturesque church, built of the light buff Kentish ragstone, nestled amongst a stand of tall deciduous trees on a bluff above a valley where once had run an old creek. It was a pretty little anchorage, but, in general, little appreciated. Under the trees and church stood a public house, with a Georgian frontage, and below it a flight of steps, set in the wall. The steps had once allowed the navy's admirals and captains access to the river from the western and older end of the old dockyard.

An interesting foray into Rochester had been enjoyed the previous day too. During that evening they savoured the sounds of music lifting from beyond the squat tower of the solid workman-like cathedral of this quintessential city made famous in the (some would say dour) books written by Dickens during the Victorian era. The strains of

The delightful old town of Queenborough on a pleasant day, seen from across the water from the skipper's yacht fastened to a buoy on the mooring trot.

an outside evening concert had been heard, coming it appeared, from the grounds of the ancient castle. The castle keep, built in the immediate aftermath of the Norman Conquest, visually still dominated the city, rising above the surrounding buildings, as did the strident chords of Tchaikovsky's 1812 Overture as it built up into its final crescendo. The music was carried to them over the water quite clearly, and the sky was lit by colourful streams of rockets bursting in a cacophony of resonant explosions in time with the music. They both savoured the atmosphere in delightful harmony. The skipper considering that even Pickwick, too, and his young friends, would have concurred …

On a separate occasion, at this time of the year, but years later, the same year as their spring sail in fact, the skipper and mate had spent another evening under the shadows of the old church surrounded by its richly leaved trees. Coming into the Limehouse Reach earlier on that day for a sail round to Strood, before dropping back to pick up a buoy, the skipper was astounded to see that the paraphernalia of the wharves along the river frontage on the Rochester banks had all been cleared.

No ships would be berthing there anymore. Gone were all the warehouses, piles of baled paper, stacks of timber and piles of glass for recycling – all had been obliterated. The old wharves, many of which had been re-piled or were in the process of being piled, had been gentrified; elegant handrails fringed the edges. Tall cranes were still at work. It all looked very nice … but this was a thriving hive of industrial import and export activity. It had given the river vitality. It was all gone.

The freshly opened panorama was a delight though. The view from the river was, probably, something that could not have been witnessed for centuries. The old cathedral and castle keep were no longer obscured, no longer hidden away – from a distance – and were imposing indeed. As imposing as when built, some ten centuries before this time, to remind the peasants who was master and not to forget it. The skipper and the mate were enthralled!

The skipper said, 'That cathedral would have looked more or less like that in medieval times, surrounded by a little hub of low buildings. The original cathedral was built around the year 604, I understand. It was and still is one of the senior bishoprics.'

'The original abbey church was rebuilt around 1080, then further developed between the twelfth and fourteenth centuries. It's only modern man that seems to want to preserve these old buildings in aspic, rather than fully develop their usefulness.'

Chatham: the old dockyard church sits amongst the trees and a waterside public house sits above a flight of steps. What famous seafarers have alighted here?

A view of Rochester not seen for a couple of hundred years, if not more, and soon no longer to be enjoyed: waterside housing will blot the powerful panorama. The skipper and mate saw the castle and cathedral tower above the landscape, reminding people of their (once powerful) presence.

Along the lower Chatham road, a road that has glimpses of the water down alleyways, sits the Hospital of Sir John Hawkins, an old alms house and still in use today.

Moving their eyes leftwards from the castle a long line of trees, in full leaf, greens of varying hues were seen. 'Oh, what a revelation', the skipper said. The mate chimed her appreciation.

In amongst those trees could be seen the rustic red browns of ancient brick buildings. One of those was topped with a white pillar tower above which was mounted a weather vane, clearly visible to the eye. The skipper peered through his binoculars and could see that the vane was an old-style sailing ship. The building can be seen too from the old high street in Rochester: it was the Old Town Hall.

Another of the buildings stuck out. The skipper could see that it was built of ragstone. It had a slate roof. 'Ah!' he'd said, 'that's the old synagogue along the old Chatham road.' Along that old Chatham road also sat the Hospital of Sir John Hawkins, an old almshouse for the needy of the parish. Its design was Dutch-influenced and its gables could be seen amongst some trees.

The views they had thought were exceedingly beautiful. 'It would be nice to think that this is going to be left open,' said the skipper, but without any conviction what so ever.

Along the water edge towards Chatham itself, cranes, tall slender talons, were busy engaged in driving piles and concrete was being poured. It seemed as if it were a conveyer system: one end – towards Rochester – was completed. Men were first fitting the railing frills and beyond, towards the workings, fresh concrete was being scrubbed. No ships will come here. It shouted – 'Keep Away!'

The skipper looked across at his mate almost in tears, for he had seen the green lung ripped out of the area when his old home of Whitewall Creek, on the Frindsbury shore, had been filled in and turned into a giant industrial park. He said, 'You can see why I spoke earlier with no conviction.' He paused. 'They're doing it again – in the name of progress. Why can't a little bit be left green? An open space for the populace – a park would be grand indeed. What a legacy it would be!'

Huge earthmovers were scraping and levelling mounds of imported earth. The ground had been cleared of the detritus of industry and sanitised. It was ready for the builders.

The land beyond the smart new piling with its concrete topping and garden fence frills was being readied for building. 'My!' the skipper exclaimed, 'They're going to fill the area with waterfront flats.' For, passing the completed sections closely, and looking, they had seen that inlets for private moorings, perhaps, had been built too.

'My!' said the skipper as it dawned on him, 'The next time we come this way there'll be blocks of hideous concrete flats, a LEGOLAND, characterless and devoid of any charm.'

'The buildings will sprout up like spring flowers, slowly at first, then with more rapidity, imposing themselves on the environment – saying, "I'm the king of the castle now!"'

The mate said, wistfully, 'Well, we will have to treasure the views we've seen: for as you say, they'll soon be gone ...'

But I digress ... The passage to Queenborough was the penultimate leg before their departure, across the River Thames, to their home moorings up Smallgains Creek at the eastern end of Canvey Island. They'd had a lengthy period touring the waters between the River Deben and the north Kent coast: an annual affair, but one always enjoyed. In fact it had been more than merely enjoyable, but the crew of the yacht knew that their holiday was over and a slightly downcast atmosphere pervaded the boat.

Queenborough, which nestles just inside the West Swale, off the River Medway, makes an excellent bolthole when the wind is heavy from the east or the west. This was just as well: the forecast that evening was, as the skipper had thought about earlier in the day, a little worrying – which added a something extra to their end-of-term feeling. Strong winds were expected from the east. That would not be good.

It had not, though, completely dampened the spirits of the mate and skipper as they departed ashore with their young son for an end-of-cruise supper. One of the hostelries then had a decent restaurant attached, and it was an enjoyable experience. It had since been dumbed down into a 'fight-for-all-you-can-get carvery', which they had, for sometime, not felt the urge to patronise. Now, too, good food could be had at other places.

After a convivial evening they returned to their boat. All had noted that the wind had not moderated, as was the usual natural pattern: usually the wind died away as the evening drew into the night. Later that night the wind went past the humming stage and was heard whistling through the rigging, thumping the halyards (although tied back, as was the skipper's custom) against the mast in a steady heavy tattoo. The skipper went out to release the halyards and frap them back, further from the mast; it helped a little. Sleep for the rest of the night came in fitful patches. At some unearthly hour, on the turn of the tide, the boat for a while rolled and scrunched her clinker planks in a noisy symphony that made sleep nigh on impossible.

The mate murmured some comments about sitting it out the next day. The skipper just muttered and said, 'Let's see what the morning brings, shall we ...?' He was apt to make this or similar responses to his mate's enquiries on these matters – they had rarely worked!

The early forecasts, starting with the BBC Radio 4 shipping bulletin (because they were awake), through to the forecasts from both BBC Radio Kent and Essex had been nothing but bad news. The wind, as if to echo those, whistled and howled above their heads. A glum and thoughtful-looking skipper at some stage put the kettle on. The boat's youngest crewmember continued to sleep the sleep of one who had apparently been deprived of such activity for quite some time, and eventually stayed seemingly comatose until mid-morning!

Waiting for the kettle to begin its cheery whistle, the skipper poked his tousled head out through the hatch. He was met with a blast of wind coming from the east, which caused more disarray to his unkempt locks. It was, at least, off the shore and the boat, although jumping about and tugging at her mooring, was sitting comfortably enough. The mud-flats between the sea wall and the channel were well exposed. 'It'll be different when the tide's on the flood and there's a fetch across from the seawall', the skipper mumbled to some enquiry that had seeped past him and into

... caused more disarray to his unkempt locks ...

his consciousness. He had been studying the main river beyond the moorings: it was a mass of white water churned up by wind over tide waves. Spume and spray flew before it ... it was nasty indeed!

Looking aloft the skipper saw that the burgee was sheeted out with barely a quiver along its length cracking and snapping audibly, its outer pointed end, though hardly seeming to move. Far beyond the top of their masthead, ugly grey clouds flew across the sky at an incredible speed. Their bellies had the look of rain and, as if to reinforce that view, large droplets began to bounce across the cabin top and others stung the skipper's face. The skipper shivered. Reluctantly he braved the ever-increasing raindrops that were driven nearly horizontal by the force of the wind, stinging his face, bare legs and arms. He pulled the cockpit cover over and buttoned it up before going below again. As he had slid the hatch back over his head he grabbed a towel to dry himself. 'I won't need a wash now', he thought, not speaking aloud: he could even then hear the mate's retort – usually an exclamation of his name in full!

The kettle was by now singing for attention. The mate buried her head beneath the covers, hoping for more sleep. 'Coffee!' called the skipper, giving his mate a gentle prod. 'I don't think we're going far today.' He did not expect an answer – for both questions hadn't needed one! Eventually the crew were all wide awake, and some semblance of order was created. The main cabin was gradually returned to its use as a living room, instead of its nightly duty as a bedroom! A late breakfast ensued which seemed to run on and on ...

Some time later the skipper, glancing up from his book at a cabin window, caught a ray of brightness, so, stiff from sitting over several mugs of coffee and a natural need to move, he eased himself out past the table and centre plate box and looked outside again. The clouds had indeed broken up somewhat and some sunshine streamed down. Looking northwards, the shafts of sunlight cut like pencilled lines from behind the cloud banks and lit up the river beyond in a moving patchwork of alternate wild whiteness and dark foreboding. It looked frightful. The skipper shuddered involuntarily. It was, however, warm enough to sit outside in the protected cockpit and watch the world go by.

The harbour boat did not appear, that morning, to collect overnight mooring fees. It was full of wind-bound yachts from several of our North Sea neighbours and many local cruisers too. The authorities were missing a killing. 'Tough!' thought the skipper.

Upon the coming of the brightness that morning the skipper doubled up the mooring lines onto the buoy to which they were attached. The moorings here were generally considered to be good and well found ... the additional line was a seamanlike precaution ... 'We'd at least stay attached to the buoy', thought the skipper, not expanding upon this point for fear of worrying the mate – though she would have silently known.

While out on deck, the skipper saw a number of yachts coming in from the river. He had watched as several plugged away against the wind to reach the outer mark of the stretch of water, before being able to turn, and then broad onto the wind; they had seemingly sailed, without a scrap of cloth up, at speed into the anchorage. Those boats thought the skipper had probably initially sat it out in Stangate Creek and had considered this a preferable place to hole up in. The efforts of weary foredeck crews, on plunging platforms, to pick up a vacant buoy had been perversely fun to watch, but, 'Hell!' said the skipper, 'There but for the grace of God go I.' Happily, they had all succeeded! There were no more boat movements that day at all. Fortunately, too, during the rest of that day, the sun had continued to shine down on the wind-bound yachts, which at least allowed people to sit out on cushions to read or just watch ...

With the enforced confinement the skipper had carried out a range of small jobs about the deck, ably assisted by the boat's smallest hand. He controlled the toolbox. Well, that was until the enforced captivity, the boredom and frustration of it had forced from the youngest member of the crew a cry, 'I don't want to do this.' Poor thing: he hadn't an understanding of the situation and could only grasp that his needs were of importance. A change of tack and other activities were presented by the mate – that was one of her specialities.

The forecasts during that day had talked of some moderation, but not a return to any form of settled weather. Options were discussed and discarded. Both agreed: they were not going to go anywhere! The boy was promised a run ashore on the morrow, provided that the wind moderated sufficiently to make a safe passage ashore in their dinghy.

The larder was raided for their usual standby meat pie for supper that night, pasta having been given the thumbs down! The skipper and his mate had a novel way of cooking these pies; they used the best, made by an old established manufacturer. The lid of the shallow tin was pierced and placed in a saucepan to simmer for about forty minutes – the level of water needed to be watched, though. A second smaller tin, placed on top of the larger one. Once gauged ready (by experience) and after removing the lid, the pie in its 'dish' was carefully grilled to puff up the pastry. Eaten with fresh new potatoes and carrots dressed with butter and salt and pepper … it had made a delicious repast!

As night came on, so quickly it seemed, streams of ragged clouds were seen tearing across the face of a crescent moon. Above them, too, a myriad of bright stars twinkled, intermittently, beyond the light looms of the town and the port complexes of Sheerness and Thames Port away to the north on the Isle of Grain. It was a magical sight. In its way, and as is often the case in these sorts of conditions, the sight had majesty, a beauty. It was a powerful reminder that it is nature and not man that rules this fragile world of ours.

Later, sitting in the cockpit over a nightcap and some supper of cheese and crackers, the mate said, 'You know, we could go into Sheerness tomorrow.'

'Don't you remember there are some interesting parts around the old town? We can treat ourselves to fish and chips on the beach too!'

Queenborough High Street as depicted in an engraving by H. Adlard, from a drawing by T. M. Baynes, published in 1830. Apart from the now tarmac-coated roadway and minor changes fronting the church, little has changed.

Queenborough High Street and today little has changed except for that modern pest the automobile!

The skipper thought, 'That's if we don't get blown away or washed off the beach.' He chose, though, not to voice those thoughts!

'The boy would enjoy it too', the mate added to reinforce her view.

The skipper nodded sagely. It being dark the mate hadn't seen his response, so, after what seemed like an age since her last words, she asked, 'What are you thinking?'

The skipper looked across the darkened cockpit where he could just make out the mate's face, dimly lit, in the orange glow that oozed from the cabin, and said, 'Sounds good to me.' Then, silently in his mind, as he smiled at the mate, he said to himself, 'What's to be has to be.'

The next day the wind had eased somewhat, but was still deemed of a too great an intensity to do anything other than go ashore for a long day out. After landing, the youngest member of the crew was allowed to scamper off towards a chandler's that sold little ten pence bags of sweets. After hauling the dinghy to the top of the old concrete hard (for this was years before the floating causeway had been installed) the skipper and mate ambled along the high street. They took their time, for a change, to look more closely at this little waterside town.

The mate said, 'It's at times like this you can look up and around you: above the lower levels that bounded the pavements there is something more, much more.' So they surveyed and took in what was actually there. 'We', the mate said slowly after a while, 'and others walk up and down this street time and time again, when visiting, not noticing. Many of the buildings in Queenborough hail from a bygone age, some date back over three centuries, others are much older.'

The skipper said, 'Date plaques give this or that, but the heart of many are likely to be much older, having likely been rebuilt when the known age was given. Look at the Town Hall; it's a quaint building with an overhanging upper story. It has the look of

Blue Town High Street. Victorian housing overlooks the high brick wall that denotes the boundary of the old naval dockyard. Workers' entrances, lined with stone, have now been bricked in and the modern port beyond is shrouded from gaze.

a far more prosperous time too, as do many of the buildings we're passing. I bet the old church could tell a tale or two.'

Outside an old rambling building, with wide and deep-looking fissures in its walls, Fig Tree House, they waited while the little crewmember caught them up. He had had a little excursion of his own and wanted to tell the world about it, so there was nothing for it but to let him do just that, for a while, as it had all spilled out in a verbal torrent!

The skipper grinned to himself because the mate had, at one time, had a strange wish to own the building outside which they had stopped, considering that it would have made a nice home. In the garden a fig tree had, over the years, spread itself in a tangled interwoven branches, covered in a profusion of broad, flat leaves, which, in the late summer when they were there, partly hid a dark front door. It looked eerie and forbidding to the skipper – not at all the nature of his mate!

Turning out of the ancient high street they passed by the old school house, dating back, to the Education Act of the 1870 or thereabouts. The buildings were forlorn and not in use. It was a sad indictment of the area's town planners. The skipper made one of his usual comments about this! On a later visit to this town, during another year, they found that the old school had a new use as a community centre, giving the building more life.

On the same side of the road, just before the railway line to Sheerness, an area of rising ground ended in a low hump. This was the remains of Queen Philippa's Castle. Queen Philippa was given the borough as a wedding present by her husband, King Edward III, who had the castle built. For years it dominated the surrounding area, controlling the passage of trading craft – a lively source of income as this area was in the midst of the major industry of the time, wool.

The train journey from Queenborough hadn't taken long and before they had time to settle, the skipper having been barely able to glance through his newspaper, the

... fish and chips enjoyed on the seafront

train clattered over a set of points into Sheerness. They soon found Blue Town. Here, too, was a museum worthy of a visit. The mate said, 'I vote we all have a coffee, or what ever, to include the lad, and a cake at that bakery back a while, before going to the museum.' There was no resistance: all cheerfully and quickly acquiesced!

Blue Town was an old part of Sheerness, but it is likely to have altered by now, in the constant demand these days for change by town planners and others. Blue Town was a Victorian-era housing development that formed outside the ancient naval dockyard to house the influx of workers which had come to the place, as the navy increased in size to police the burgeoning British Empire. The houses were largely built of seasoned timber. The timber had been used by the dockyard authorities as payment to the workers when the Navy Board was short of funds.

In recent times the docks, now no longer with the navy, had expanded to astonishing proportions, burying in its growth a large area of mud-flats which fringed the south-eastern edge of the Medway shore under acres of concrete. A constant stream of imported cars maintained a permanent cover on the concrete; other goods arrived there from all over the globe too. Some of the exporting nations, now independent and flourishing, were once part of that massive empire which had been protected by ships built and serviced here.

After a visit to a seaside fun fair, a pleasant lunch of beautifully cooked fish and chips was enjoyed on the sea front. They had been wind blown, but remained warm and dry. No small vessels were seen to be moving and the mate and skipper firmly agreed that the day had been well spent indeed. It had been fun.

Later, on their way back to the Queenborough waterfront, the mate dropped into a butcher's shop and obtained some local sausages which they planned to have for their supper that night – these had been had obtained from here before. They had been especially enjoyable with mashed potatoes, beans and fried onions – washed down with a glass of red wine. Later, those sausages were polished off in that same way.

Taking a circuitous back route back to the waterfront and their dinghy, they sauntered round the old harbour. The harbour sat in the tidal creek that still wended its way round the back of the high street and was once the economic centre of the town. Here sat a somewhat motley collection of fishing vessels, many of dubious origin and seaworthiness, it seemed. It had a beleaguered, almost terminal, look. A visitor now, though, would see a different place: it now has a fresh vibrancy – a look of wellbeing from its industry of inshore fishing.

Queenborough Creek on a nice day is still a hive of activity for inshore fishing and pleasure, where nets can still be seen being repaired and hung out to dry.

The mate had noted, on a previous visit many years before, that a mass of old hulks sat in an inlet opposite the quays. She'd asked, 'Are those broken hulks all old spritsail barges over there?'

The skipper said, 'Well, I think so. A lighter or two could be amongst the morass. But, I can see the remains of several stems – those would have been sailormen. I don't suppose there is an accurate record.'

A visitor now, walking this same route, won't see any of this. The inlet has been dredged out and filled with pontoons and numerous boats ill-suited to the local environment, the skipper thought. They seemed to sit peacefully enough, well for what they were doing – perhaps the intention of their owners: they rarely moved it appeared. Along the quays, too, the fishing boats have a more purposeful look: the inshore fishing industry has improved. A wet fish outlet has opened up where locally caught produce can be purchased too. Reluctantly, they headed back for the hard, led by their tired young crewman.

Escape next day was on the skipper's mind as he clambered aboard in time for the local forecast. This was good news. A southeasterly of force three to four was promised, with fine and dry conditions. It sounded grand indeed. An early night was ordered as the evening set in. The conditions had, in comparison to the earlier conditions, become almost benign, with a near calm that hung above the creek ... it looked good indeed for them to make the final passage home. 'No sitting out under the stars tonight', said the mate, prompting the skipper out of his reverie!

The skipper only nodded as he acquiesced to what was in effect an order from the mate and he reluctantly followed her below, sliding the hatch over as he did so.

The alarm, to catch the early forecast from their local radio station, had sounded all too soon and the skipper turned out to put the kettle on for coffee. Looking outside he saw that the wind was still from the southeasterly quarter, but was now only light to moderate in strength. A sun shone between fluffy clouds that passed over a sky of deep blue; a sky clean after the period of easterlies that they'd had. Things looked good and a decent passage home beckoned. The forecast did not speak of anything untoward; thus a light cheerfulness spread through the skipper and his mate.

A breakfast of toast and cereal was soon consumed and cleared away. The skipper, though, had not eaten a lot. The mate thought that he was thinking of the passage – she had not eaten much either. The skipper went on deck and left the mate to tidy the boat for sea. The youngest member of the crew had decided to stay put in his bunk – well he'd dragged himself and his sleeping bag out from the fo'c's'le to set himself up between the centre plate box and cabin side on the after side of the dinette table. He looked comfortable the skipper had thought. His mother had detected a spot of something, however: the boy looked a bit off colour. However, at the time she had not given it a great deal of thought.

Out on deck the skipper was busy. He put a reef in the mainsail just in case the conditions outside were stronger than under the sea wall where they still sat. They were soon ready.

The tide still had an hour to run when they set off, sailing away from the mooring they had been attached to for the last few days, watched by and waved at by various crews from other yachts. The skipper smiled at the mate as she came back aft, coiling the mooring line. As she handed the line to the skipper he had seen that his mate had an apprehensive look. He understood it had been perhaps why she had not had a lot to eat at breakfast. She'd lost her usual colour.

Clearing the deep-water ship berths along the Sheerness shore inside Garrison Point, the skipper slid the boat across the channel to the Grain Spit side, as was his custom, slipping the boat between the old fort and buoy that surged in the tide along the edge of the deep water channel. It was then that the skipper saw that there was a bit of a sea running outside and along the ship channel. As a precaution he said to the mate, who he noted was then looking a bit green about the gills, 'I'm going to keep close to the shallows, but not too close: look at those rollers over there', pointing to emphasise.

The mate pointed further out in the channel: a small yacht, not much more than about seventeen foot, plunged into deep troughs and then reared up at a seemingly impossible angle, dipping its foredeck and stern into the seas, in a violent rocking motion.

Then they met them too. Their boat rose up and dropped back down in a rapid rocking-horse motion, which felt and was ugly. The skipper indicated to the mate to keep a firm grip. Looking astern at the tender trailing in their wake, the skipper had wanted to lengthen the painter: the little boat seemed as if it wanted to dive under the stern as the stern made another rapid trajectory upwards, burying the foredeck in a mass of confused water and froth which ran back aft, spilling overboard as it came. During his glance astern, the skipper saw the rudder as it boiled in completely broken water. He struggled to keep the required heading. The boat, though, stuttered, staggered, lost drive with the sails a-shake and then drove robustly forward again. Thank goodness we have the tide with us, the skipper thought.

The skipper looked at his mate suddenly: his attention, for what seemed an age, had been on the job in hand. He realised that she was trying to get his attention. She was asking gravely, looking positively ill too, for probably the third or fourth time, 'Shall we turn back?'

There followed a period of silence; the silence seemed an eternity to the mate. The skipper's mind was in a whirl of the possible consequences of that manoeuvre. The silence was not broken by the mate. It all lasted for less time than it does to write.

They shot out like a 'bat out of hell', the mate had said later to a friend; as for turning round, in those rollers … the skipper just said 'No!'

The mate slid below, unable to contain what was going on inside her!

Nearing the outer Grain Spit buoy, well out of the channel stream, it became much more bearable. Then, as if operated by some magic switch, things had suddenly quietened to little short sloppy seas that slapped and teased the boat, and they were off on a broad reach, leaving a boiling white wake. It was then that the skipper was aware that the mate was mouthing that she had had to go below.

Later, much later it had seemed, she reappeared, briefly, looking a little grim. She announced that last night's supper had gone straight through her. The boy too had also suffered. Thinking about this the skipper too had a feeling that all was not well with his innards!

In the calmer waters over the Grain Spit they gradually turned north. The skipper watched the echo sounder as he followed a three-metre contour – sufficient water for them. The wind was then on the starboard quarter and it pushed them along at what seemed a phenomenal speed. Out in the open, though, they found that the breeze was fresh, around force five, and with the reef in the sail was glorious – if one could have enjoyed it!

The boat rushed across the shipping channel; it slapped banged and scrunched its way through the short waves that had built up against the last of the ebb. A shower of water droplets was occasionally cast up and as these passed over the bow, they dampened the deck, which had nearly dried from its earlier soaking, darkening the foot of the jib too. The boat was thoroughly enjoying this sail. The crew were not. The mate had not reappeared on deck and, with the boy, was below, wondering which end would need attention next …

The skipper again tried to get the mate's attention: he himself had had a sickness build up inside which did not bode well – the feeling, a dire needed to be relieved … this was to no avail. The skipper sailed grimly on, heading for the buoy that marked the shallow, at low water, entrance to the channel that lead towards their home moorings.

Sensing a change in the boat's movements, the mate's head appeared in the hatchway, 'I feel better', she had said brightly, her eyes pricked by tiny tears. So, coming out into the cockpit, she was somewhat surprised when the skipper had quickly pointed to the

… a bucket full of spray … catching the mate full on!

On a different day a squall, in the distance, blots out the Medway while *Whimbrel* slips towards the welcome calm beyond Southend Pier to work her way westwards up the Ray. (Courtesy of Ian Kemp)

next buoy and, without another gesture or word, shot below. While there, he felt the boat rise up and crash into some rollers, but he had not cared ...

Returning to the deck, he said, 'It was those sausages.' Then looking more closely at the mate he had seen that water was dripping from her smiling face. Whilst below, a bucket full of spray had been cast up and it had flown across the boat, catching the mate full on! They had both laughed: it was funny how just along the edge of the shallows this invariably happened in such a chop.

With tears welling just beneath the surface, the mate said, 'Sorry, I didn't realise you were bad too.' She, too, was then much relieved at the skipper's protestations that he was now all right.

What a joy it had been, to them all, to reach the sheltered water of the Ray Channel and take stock of what had happened: they had all suffered from food poisoning. They had coped, but it could have been so very different, indeed ... the purveyor of those stores responsible for their ills, they found on a visit the following year, has closed down – shame!

13

What a Waste

She had sat alongside the company wharf, rapidly gaining a forlorn look. The decision not to maintain her the previous spring was telling, after another hard summer at the beck of her masters. For nearly a decade she had taken numerous charter parties here and there. In the summer months, too, she had followed, shorn of her famous racing rig, in amongst other spritsail barges that had continued to race on this river. Now, however, her sailing days were over.

Men had started to come aboard during the autumn. Her mast was lowered for the last time. A watcher would have seen her sails and rigging being carefully removed, followed by her topmast, sprit and mainmast. The masts were lifted off by the dockside crane, which was busy for a while yet, removing all her winches and such like.

One of the men, a man who had sailed on her, was almost brought to tears, mumbling to his work mate, 'She was a fine sailer, especially after being done out for the races.' Looking up at a younger man, he said that they had better get the masts and main rigging wires laid out as directed by the foreman. 'Expect this lot will get sold or something', he mumbled as they had worked away.

The younger man, intrigued, had started to ask some questions about life in the yard before he had arrived, a year back; his companion recounted a lot of what he knew. Finally finishing with this particular barge, 'She were sheaved with another layer of planking back in the fifties, you know – that's another layer of planking over the original outer layer. She were better then, faster too, to take on the crack racers from that other river, the London River. Good as them she were, and on her day she were the best too – any one would tell you that.'

'Her sails were a picture, white with a huge brown crescent in her topsail, her billowing headsails in them races were a sight, I tell you. She had a huge balloon jib, a bit like a yacht spinnaker, a russet brown it were, with a white crescent in it, that was the company logo, see.'

'I was … I was mate of a sailing barge and then a motor barge, latterly as skipper. I was … the foredeck hand on … on this one … for the races, that is' he had said with sharp intakes of breath. He'd turned away as he finished: he had to hide the choked-up feeling, the welling up and near rush of tears which would have been evident to the youngster. The day's work was finished so he had an excuse to continue walking away and had done so, thus preserving his feelings for himself.

The men continued to work away for a few more weeks, until they had completely stripped off all her sailing gear. They removed the engine and stripped out all the cabin joinery fitted after her racing days were finished. Learning that all was done, the office had arranged a tow with one of their tugs. This was organised for a week or two's time, to take the old girl to a place of rest while the men in the big office decided what to finally do with her.

During that waiting time many people came to the edge of the wharf and looked down on this faded jewel of the river, for many years the flagship of the fleet. Could not she have been sold to someone who would have expended time, effort and money to do what ever was needed? But then (but not now, alas) a fair number of younger barges were still trading as motor barges, though their days were numbered too. Was it one of these that the old barge's masters had in mind? Were they going to recycle the old barge's gear?

Just before the tow arrived, a messenger came running into the shed, where the yardmen were having a well-earned cup of tea, panting and trying to pass his message but not being able to break into the men's time-honoured ritual. The workmen looked up casually from their tea and tab nabs, which on that day was a huge hunk of rich dark fruitcake, made by the wife of the foreman. One of them said, through a shower of crumbs, 'Slow down, for gawd sake … slow down … what is it you say is wanted off that old barge? … the dead eyes yer say? Come with me, we'll go for a look.'

With that, the man set down his tea and wandered over to the quayside. Looking down at the barge hull, he said, 'Look, see there, they've bin removed, tell 'em up in the office, they're off, and in the stores.'

The messenger was a girl, young in years, intelligent-looking and showing a spark of curiosity. She was very new to the office. She asked, 'What was she like – I've never seen one of them. Is she in one of the pictures up in the big offices?'

'I dare say', the old man murmured.

Then the workman's eyes had glazed over for a moment. Choking back emotion borne of many years, he had then recounted in a brief few minutes the glory days – well just some of them – a taste, of barging, the racing and the joy of being chosen to crew this old girl.

'They were grand years, lass, but hard at times too. People tend to be glassy-eyed and romantic about them days now. And, as I say, they were hard days but this lot weren't too bad to sail for', looking up towards the office, 'and I'm still working 'ere aren't I,' as he finished he had to quickly wipe an eye before the girl could see the tear that was about to roll, un-checked, down a cheek.

The young lass had wanted to know what was going to happen to the old barge and the workman, with a long drawn out sigh, said, 'I don't know lass. She be going somewhere down river is all I've bin told.'

'I doubt if we'll see this famous racer sail again though.'

'She gave them Thames lot a run for their money too. I'll always remember that.'

With that the old boy and the lass returned to the work they had been doing previously.

The day of the tow was breezy with an overcast sky, almost leaden looking; low-level clouds scurried beneath and threatened squalls. It would be a boisterous final passage for this old girl. The flood tide was making rapidly as the tug had arrived off the busy little yard, creeping across the shallows it ranged alongside the old hull. Crewmen leapt aboard her and fastened mooring lines round her cleats, which had not been removed.

At the top of the spring tide cycle, the old girl was towed down the river and laid in the marshes along side a sea wall. It was near the entrance to a creek leading up to a dock; here she sat for some time. She quickly took on the look of a derelict; she was forlorn, her holds open to the weather, she took on water during the winter rains and her planking started to come away from her transom: her hull did not like the angle of the berth she had been pushed into. It was twisted. What was going to happen to her?

One day, late on in summer, on an evening tide, a group of lads turned up in a barge boat, powered by a spluttering outboard engine, coughing noise and fumes that

Above: The *Sirdar*, 'the Queen of the Medway', rigged and set up in her prime, racing into the entrance of the River Medway. Beyond her can be seen the gaunt stone and concrete fort on the edge of the Isle of Grain and one of her competitors, the *Dreadnought*, one of three barges from the other river, the Thames. It was three against one and still she did exceptionally well! (From an original print by Leslie G. Arnold, courtesy of Keith and Marian Patten)

Left: The lovely *Veronica* in her prime – it was her swansong too. (From an original print by Leslie G. Arnold, courtesy of Keith and Marian Patten)

... a group of lads turned up in an old barge boat ...

shattered the peace of that isolated spot. Their wake on the calm water was marked by an oily trail that drifted on the ongoing tide up the creek, after they had come alongside the old barge. The lads then started to do some work.

A watcher would have seen them attack the fastenings of a section of rail: it was in good condition. One of them needed the piece to finish a job on another barge – he's the skipper of our little yacht but was then many years younger. The job was for his dad. The dumps, blind bolts driven into the decks outer board, were cut through and a long piece of rail had soon splashed over the side.

In the calm of the approaching evening a tow line was fastened to the length of timber. At that point the expedition had gone un-noticed by the world. Dusk was approaching, but as they were about to move off a loud hollering erupted from a position too close for comfort. The outboard was away in a moment, for once, and the boat with its tow and exuberant pirates was soon out of earshot or chance of recognition. The headland to the east had soon hid them!

The trip was later toasted, over a pint or two in their village pub, while the barge lads recounted to their village friend and helper that day how they'd had all sorts of things from other old barges over the years. To this day, the skipper of the yacht and his old pal still have fond memories of that foray.

Eventually it was obvious that the old girl had been forgotten. She had been left to rot away, slowly and silently, in her own little world, in that lonely marshland place. She had rapidly become a hulk, lifting on a few of the tides, but often not. Soon she would break open, like the fate of many of her sisters, from the pressure of the tides and shed her side planking to leave only her timbers as a testament to her existence. Bird-life had started to use the nooks and crannies about her decks for nesting, for even in her first summer lying there grasses had started to grow in sheltered corners where seeds had found an opening or moisture to germinate.

However, the mooring lines that had been attached to some posts on the sea wall, by the tug men, weren't up to much: nobody expected her to float for long. They fell apart. This would not have mattered had she not remained semi-buoyant.

On an unusually high spring tide, at the dead of night with a mist hanging over the creek, she floated free of her expected grave. It was quiet and very still; no breeze could be felt, only the tide-borne draught that swirled a mist about its surface. The normal night sounds of curlews were missing too: they remained quietly in their roosting places. Silently the old girl drifted on the last of the flood a little way up the creek, a shadow to any watcher, coming and going as the mist whirled about her. At the top of the tide, she stopped as if suspended in a cloud, then slowly at first, and then with a little more speed, she gathered pace as if underway, as the ebb set in properly: a voyage all on her own.

A tug that crept cautiously, through the mist, in from the main river towards a mooring buoy out in the deeper water off the end of the creek, was suddenly confronted by a ghostly silhouette coming down on the tide. The skipper thought it looked at first as if it were a rigged barge, with no lights showing, sailing in the mist, but as the gap closed, only the hull took on any real shape, the assumed shadow of sails and spars had disappeared.

Circling the strange hull, it dawned on the tug skipper that it was the wreck that he had seen, so often, sitting up in the marshes against the sea wall further up the creek. He came alongside and his crew made a line secure, before continuing towards their destination. The men wanted to get home after a long day working on the river, but the old hulk had a fair amount of water in her, and seemed to be settling lower all the time.

'What's to do?' he had thought aloud, 'No one's going to be up to talk to now.'

He then called up the river authority, who asked what he thought, being on the scene.

'I'll have to moor her in the shallows in case she sinks', he tentatively suggested.

That was agreed and so that was what the crew did, running her up into the shallows and securing her with a kedge anchor from the tug, before getting back to their own mooring.

The outcome of this little excursion by the old barge was for her to be towed round to a dead end creek, away over the marshes, where she was pushed up a bank. There she was rammed by the tug, to break her hull open: they were to make sure that this was her final berth.

Her hull, then open to the heave of the tide borne waves, soon began to break up. It was not long before a barge that had once been the queen of the Medway – the lovely, graceful *Sirdar* as she was called – and famous too, as the old boy earlier in the tale had testified, had become almost indistinguishable from the cord grass covered shore upon which she now rested ...

It was late summer and the skipper of the little clinker yacht was sailing alone for a couple of days. He had come into this quiet backwater: he had meant, for some time, to seek out the remains of the barge that had gone on a voyage alone, and that of another he had known in his childhood too.

Years before, as a boy, on another barge which had also been his home, he had had the privilege to sail alongside two gaily painted ladies with clouds of sail during the early years of the 1960s. The two ladies had vied with each other, those many decades ago now, to be crowned champion of the rivers. The skipper was, as has been said, one of the lads that had gone on an expedition in a barge boat to remove, for reuse, a section of rail from one of them. He had done similar things on other hulks, too, dumped in the marshes in a backwater nearby.

Finally the skipper had made it. On a hot and balmy day, with a gentle breeze, he poked his yacht up into a little creek leading to a place known as Bedlam's Bottom. With the ebb having only a short period to run he let go the anchor as the boat's keel scraped the muddy bottom. In that position the two ladies were nearly in sight, but by now they were old and in an unknown state.

All around that anchorage was an almost flat tidal mud basin from which only a few humps of marsh rose up from the desert-like landscape. The area was extensively excavated for its blue clay by brick makers during a hundred years of brick making. The brick works were based at a little place up another creek nearby. The landscape seemed unnatural, as if hewn by an outside force. It had a hard bottom that

... the skipper went off ... to find his two old ladies ...

shimmered with the previous tide's pools and run-offs. Gutways wended their way across this panorama, running in torturous twists and turns, fed by numerous gullies which themselves were fed from the numberless pools.

Soon, the young flood had made enough and the skipper boarded his little lug-sail dinghy, and sailed off to find his two ladies – old ladies.

One of the barges, the *Sirdar*, had remained in sail for some while after the last of the trading owners had elected to end the racing that had been taking place since the Victorian era. The other was the *Veronica*. She'd been sold to become a houseboat, and a 'no racing' proviso had been made at her sale, it is said: they, the trading owners, would not allow it!

For a number of years the *Veronica*, the one that became a floating home, had the word '*Belle*' added to the end of her original name. She sat at a berth under the hills of the old town of Chatham, later being moved to a Barge Museum with the intention of a rebuild. This venture failed and she too was towed round to Bedlam's Bottom, to rest peacefully and decay quietly in this eerie environment.

As the tide crept over the flats the skipper slipped effortlessly over the shallows until he could not steer to sail. Then he gradually poled up to what still had the look of a sailing barge, sitting in amongst a morass of other hulks. The bow of the barge seemed to float, ghost-like, her stem erect and sturdy; her sheer line still gentle and sweet. On her starboard side, though, the skipper noticed that her bow was collapsing; her windlass bitts were resting at an angle on the remains of her side planking. It was an eerie and evocative sight. It was, dare it be said, a little troubling to the skipper, for he'd felt an awesome sadness at the old vessels lingering demise.

Looking forward to the stem, across the emptiness of her missing decks, the *Veronica* presented a sad sight. The steel structure that held her together and supported her outsized racing rig survives intact; it will do for many more seasons.

For a short while he had sat looking up at the remains and mused: he was back with his siblings aboard their sailing home where they always had had an excellent view of those gaily painted racers, because, more often than not, they'd have been bringing up the rear of the staysail fleet in their usual place. There they were able to watch the champion racers surging towards them with clouds of billowing creamy cotton canvas straining every seam, every stitched thread, bow waves curling as if trying to climb aboard them. It was a fantastic sight. Those last crack racers of the champion class, of which these two old ladies had been members, always started a short time after the rest of the fleet, catching up and sailing through the slower vessels in such a grand manner, as if to say, 'Stand aside, for we're the queens of the fleet.' The skipper had never forgotten.

The skipper climbed aboard, tying the dinghy painter to a rigging chock. His eyes rested on tiny patches of white, the paint her hull had been coated with, still attached to the steel band around the edge of the covering board. He looked around. In the hold, the mud was up to the level of the top of her steel keelson, which remained, to the end, straight with no hump amidships. Her broad transom and stern quarters had gone, but the bulk of her sides remained standing.

On departing from this old lady, the skipper, sailing away, looked back at the bow of the hulked barge and on down her intact port side. A lump welled in his throat, his mind full of memories past – how firm they had remained – how strange, he thought!

'I'll remember you, not as the *Veronica Belle*,' he'd said, 'you were the famous *Veronica*.' Then he added, with more than a tinge of sadness, 'I'll always remember you, in all your glory. You were a sister to my old home too: both of you were part of Parkers' fleet, sailing out of Bradwell.'

Glancing back after checking the dinghy's direction he gave a last solemn shake of his head. The sun-burnt face with its shock of bleached hair atop moved slowly back and forth as the hulk merged into the others that surrounded the poor old barge in her resting place.

She seemed to float – ghost-like – her stem erect and powerful – her gentle sheer intact – the yacht's skipper rowed away – remembering ... the *Veronica*.

In amongst the cord grass-covered shore the skipper found the *Sirdar*, the Queen of the Medway, her starboard side had gone, her hull open as if half a sardine tin. Her doubled hull is clearly seen and too to the discerning eye, remnants of her trademark rustic brown paintwork. In the distance, her racing competitor, the *Veronica*, keeps her company in the lonely vigil of their lingering death.

The skipper continued to head away across what had become a vast lake of flat water stretching round the far crescent-shaped shores and round to his own yacht, her hull now floating above the hump of clay which had earlier obscured her.

Pointing his little dinghy in the direction of a dark patch in a sea of cord grass on the distant shore to the south, he concentrated on sailing for a while. The light breeze of earlier had nearly faded away, but enough remained to keep the little lug-sailed dinghy moving over the languid surface of the water. Around him small fish plopped as they jumped in the shallows, chasing shrimp.

The other barge – although barge would something of an overstatment, for the remnants did not amount to much – rested in a bed of cord grass below the edge of a field used for grazing cattle. Hoofmarks abounded around her remaining port side: it was quite probable that she still had a use – as a place for the beasts, milk cows or beef cattle, to scratch their backs upon.

The skipper, after tethering his dinghy, walked slowly around what remained of the barge. Her starboard side had completely disappeared – the side that had been burst open by the tug, in all probability. The skipper had heard a report too that the barge had been burnt, but he saw no signs of that. Part of her port quarter lay buried in the mud, with remains of her deck carlines protruding amongst the long stalks of cord grass. Her stem had gone. There was little trace of her forward curves, and at the aft

The skipper's memory had this picture – a wonderful and memorable view of the *Veronica* grandly overtaking her gentler rigged sisters, chasing her rivals the *Sirdar* and *Sara*, in her dash for the outer mark. Garrison Point and its old fort, topped with a smaller building than it has now, are in the background. The barges are (left to right) *Veronica*, *Dreadnought*, probably the *Anglia*, *Henry* and, in the distance, the author's childhood home the *May Flower*. (From an original print by Leslie G. Arnold, courtesy of Keith and Marian Patten)

end little remained except a stump – a remnant of her sternpost. A section of her port side remained intact up to the deck line. Amazingly, little areas of her trade mark russet brown paint had remained. Her doubling or sheathing to the side, in places was still intact. Her floors visible in places were in a remarkable condition the skipper had noted – but that was a feature of these old craft. The skipper had dreamt of her rising, a phoenix from the creeping cord grass, to once more grace these waters. He had grinned widely at the thought!

The skipper looked around as if to tell someone something important, and speaking into the gentle, saline-enriched breeze, looking in the direction of the sad remains of the *Sirdar,* he said, 'I sailed on you towards the end of the 1960s, as a passenger during a barge match, but little now remains of your hull. I can look, remember and visualise – I know what you were.' The memory had remained clear in his mind.

Eventually the skipper sailed away in his dinghy. He looked back to those two grand old ladies, resting in their tranquillity, slowly decaying in their final berths, and thought it was ironic that both of them would still be younger than many of the spritsail barges still sailing. He muttered, 'One would have been a hundred and the other only a little older.'

As his words drifted away on that warm, heavily saline-scented summer breeze, he took one last sorrowful look backwards, towards the now darkened smudges, as those two old sailormen merged into the environment. The skipper had spoken and only the sea birds would have heard him: it had been quietly, very quietly, his voice quivering, a little, but it had had firmness too: 'What a waste … What a *waste*!'

14
Autumn Moods

The skipper and his mate had set off from their moorings during the late morning on a gorgeous early autumn day towards the end of September. It was warm and sunny with high, fluffy, white clouds that moved slowly across a deep blue sky. The wind was a moderate and from the northeasterly quarter, which gave a slant across the estuary. It had had a chill in it, they found out, compared to the comfortable land temperature. That chilliness had been picked up, of course, from the cooler estuary waters.

Winds for the weekend had been forecasted to be moderate on the Saturday, calm overnight with a light variable breeze on the Sunday. Those were just the right sort of conditions to ensure a balance between good sailing and a pleasant, pleasing stillness to the evening.

When departing from their short and shallow creek, the mate sat and watched a number of common terns. The terns had been perched on some old posts, which imperceptibly waved in the run of the tide, along one side of the creek where it too was fringed with cord grass. They, the terns that is, were taking off, swooping about the boat and then later alighting again. Close by a tern was seen hovering, wing and tail motions in unison some distance above the surface, it had dived into the water, running over the shallows, to come up with a minute silver fish clamped in its bill. The fish glistened and glinted in the sunlight, as the tern headed for a fresh perch to consume its hearty meal.

'They'll be on the move in a month, or so, and be gone until the spring', the skipper said.

Quickly leaving this all behind them, they enjoyed, at times, what was a boisterous sail across the London River. For a day or two the tides had been exceptionally high, even for springs, and the flood was surging up the deep-water channel. On the edges of this, a number of times, they had thrown up a curtain of spray as the boat scrunched down into the troughs of some of the deep rollers. The mate complained loudly when caught by the droplets, but relished the ever-changing colours of the water as its facets alternately collected and lost colour from the sky above.

After having to put in a short tack to ensure they cleared the outside of a buoyed firing range which that sat over the flats bordering the Kentish shore, they were able to free off the sheets, gradually, as they took a curved route round the end of the Isle of Grain. Soon they had reached the old gaunt grey fort, a relic of many defences of our realm. The fort had sat alone, a sentinel, seemingly in the midst of nowhere when the tide was up, on the edge of the shallows, for centuries. It was a useful landmark! After clearing the fort the sheets were freed right off for a riotous run into the river beyond. The boat, scrunching her clinker edges, was bucking and surfing over the rollers set up by the forces of wind and a fast current. The skipper and mate knew how these fairly benign conditions could change on the ebb, having experienced them on more than a few occasions in the past. For then they had revelled in it!

The tide at the entrance was, at the time, still in their favour and their speed over the ground, accordingly, was approaching hull speed. Watching the mate, from his perch opposite her, the skipper had thought what fun it was and envied her trick at the helm as she expertly worked the boat. The boat of course could have gone a little faster with her big genoa up, but all three seemed to be enjoying the romp!

Some two seasons earlier the skipper and his son had, on a passage between the Maldon River and Harwich, logged an average speed of over eight knots in this clinker sloop, between the two piers that entertain the shoreside holidaymaker, along the edge of the Tendering peninsula. The skipper reckoned it the fastest sustained passage that they had made, the tide being on the whole in their favour, with the wind abaft the beam. A pristine white plastic yacht seen coming out of the Colne after them had taken an age to catch them. Eventually it had. Shortly afterwards the boat had broached badly, it rounded up sharply, then righted itself. The crew were then seen to rapidly pull down her mainsail. Ah well, that was all history.

Back to the present, though, the mate, having helmed for a fair while, wanted a break and told the skipper that she would prepare something hot, as the breeze had got to her. It was decided to partake of a drop of soup, which the mate promptly got on with, quickly emptying a tin into a pan to simmer gently.

Looking up from stirring the soup, the mate had looked up towards the skipper and said, 'Do you remember that winter sail over here a while back, when in the late afternoon sun we had soup and cheese crusted rolls, it was much colder then, but we didn't feel it until later. It's the wind direction that makes the difference, isn't it?'

The skipper smiling at his mate had nodded with an affirmative.

Coming down the river towards them were a myriad of gaffers of every type: smacks, smack yachts, ancient cutters and newer varieties. The skipper had called down the hatch to catch the mate's attention and said, 'Look, you must come out and see this', so, reluctantly putting her book down (for she would read at any time or moment that presented itself), she popped her head outside.

Cockleshell Hard, Port Victoria, and once, for a short time, the Royal Corinthian Yacht Club were based here. A disused jetty bisects the hard, but the beach is still a little jewel; the Grain power station dominates the environment. Grain Fort is on the far right.

The skipper, pointing, indicated that the gaffers were spread out right down the two reaches in view, to a point of marsh away in the distance. 'It must be an Old Gaffers' regatta', he said, following up quickly with, 'I didn't know that lot sailed on this river – they do round on the Swale, sure we know, because we've seen them.'

'You're the expert on these matters', his mate said quite pointedly!

'Come on,' said the skipper, 'what do I know about gaffers?'

The mate, appreciating the sight, had lingered a few moments before turning back to the stove and the gently simmering soup.

Sailing along past a sandy shore, known as Cockleshell Hard, the skipper mused about this place being the site of the Royal Corinthian Yacht Club; well, it was close by anyway, before the move to the Burnham River. He recounted too that Erith had been the club's original base on the Thames. 'Both of those previous places were now a little below the Crouch', the skipper thought aloud. That river, the Crouch, it was now said by some, was the Mecca of east coast yachting. Looming large over this stretch of the river was the bulky monstrosity of a huge oil-guzzling power station, which when operational spewed fumes into the atmosphere which landed upon mainland Europe. Its ominous shadow was always felt over the river: created a wind vacuum in certain conditions too.

Returning to more immediate matters, the skipper looked at the water and noticed that the ebb had now set in. They had started to surge over rollers induced by a wind over ebb situation; it was soon beginning to affect their ground speed. After waiting for an approaching freighter to pass by, they crabbed across the tide to the shallower southern shore. Clear of the tide rip in the main channel they made better progress too.

Earlier, when the skipper had watched the huge bulky freighter leaving her berth, he had known that he would have to wait for her to pass before their move across the channel. He gazed at her and marvelled at her sheer size: a huge container ship crewed by a mere handful or so of human beings. 'Glad I'm not still doing that', he said to

Ships in the river ... they are huge and dwarf all around them.

himself as she had passed by, for he had been an engineer officer on ships. Ships now have become ugly leviathans: functional, but largely without grace. Even the *crème de la crème* of shipping, passenger ships, have become graceless palaces with little or no sheer, lacking in all sight-pleasing pleasures, being what they are – floating hotels.

'There are a few, but all too few, graceful ships now', said the skipper, his thoughts far off in the different, less complicated age that he had known.

Along the southern shore, sailing along the shallows to keep out of the worst of the tide, the mate pointed to the barge hulks up in the marsh, and turning to the skipper said, 'Do you remember? It was on our winter sail along this same shore, you promised to tell me about those barges, barges from your childhood. You still haven't fulfilled that promise.'

The skipper nodded, thinking, 'Hey, wait a minute. I did do so a while back, in the spring', but not speaking aloud, as his concentration was directed on a curving change of course to enter the stretch of water that a great number of other yachts were seen to be heading into as well. The water, Stangate Creek, was a broad channel running virtually north and south from the main river. The tide was pouring out round the nose of its eastern side, throwing up an area of disturbance. Their clinker hull scrunched its way through this, the rudder kicking at times with the forces from opposing swirls running along the keel.

The mate, for the time being putting aside her forgetfulness to find out about the barge hulks in the marshes, looked instead at an out-of-place piece of high ground sitting at the nose of the sea-walled landscape. She noticed, too, the tide sluicing through the upper-level marsh grasses at the foot of the stone-faced wall, realising that it had indeed been an exceptional tide. She thought of the latent forces and power bound up in a mere backward and forward flow of water, marvelling. On that ground beyond was the first of a line of power pylons stretching away southwards across the low marshland. Near its base sat a hut; the mate wondered what it was for.

The skipper, perhaps in tune with the mate's thoughts, said, 'You know, a tunnel was dug under the river here to run the power cables across when that great power station was built. It's big enough for people to use too – though it's not as far as I know a public right of way.'

What more does the mate need? She has her book and a succulent dish of samphire: the gentle smile says it all!

Moving properly into the creek entrance, the wind had come more on the beam. So, hauling their sheets, the little yacht tore over the swirling water, quickly leaving it to enter a calmer, more placid, but fast-running stream.

They were bound for a little off-shoot a little distance down Stangate, a creek that shot off to the west, with several twisting turns. The tide, as said, had been an exceptional spring, and the marshes at the entrance to the creek, known as Sharfleet, were completely inundated. The super-charged ebb swept over the marsh top, boiling as the flow tumbled from the edges, ripping off unseen chunks of clay and vegetation leaving them scattered over the flats where they would eventually, in time, turn to mud.

The stream was full of marsh-plant debris too. Grasses, pursalane and samphire (or more correctly, glasswort) stems were seen. The mate, seeing these, licked her lips, relishing the fresh flavour of the samphire that she had enjoyed just a couple of weeks earlier when they'd anchored for the night further up the main leg of Stangate Creek. She grinned broadly at the skipper too: he had rowed, in the dinghy, into the marshes to collect a bunch carefully cut from various shoots. He'd washed and rinsed the edible stalks, cooked them quickly, blanched, for a short while and presented them in a dish with vinegar, to his mate with love!

Terns were having a veritable feast: they dived into the disturbed water for the numerous shrimp and small fry that abounded, totally unseen by human eyes. They were feeding up, as were the birds that had been seen earlier, to be ready for their fast-approaching flight to their far off wintering grounds.

Taking care to ensure that their course maintained a decent distance from all this activity, the skipper instinctively felt his way in, having to come round onto a run, then a gybe over onto the opposite reach from that of earlier when coming into the main creek. 'Some poles driven into the marshes would be a good idea in this part of the world now', the skipper had said to the mate when sitting later over their tea.

Inside were a number of anchored yachts; some were in the process of settling their anchors and a couple were experiencing dragging problems. The mate said, 'It's deep in that part', remembering that they too had had a spot of bother here many years ago!

... terns having a veritable feast ...

The skipper, nodding, had explained that some parts had between eight to some twelve metres at low water; these were swirl holes, gouged away by the tide rushing through from the flats and river beyond the creek to the west. There was, too, a long spit of clay hummocks, hidden from about half tide, which needed to be avoided!

'Look,' he said, 'there's our friends' boat. They said they might end up in this backwater.' Giving a hearty wave, sailing close by, they quickly agreed for all to meet aboard the bigger yacht for aperitifs later.

'We'll sail on past into the bay. You take over while I drop and tie down the jib.' With that the skipper went forward to stow the jib; at the same time he prepared the mains'l halyard ready to drop that sail too. Next he pulled some twenty metres of cable from the locker, ranging it on the fore deck. Finally he freed the anchor from its lashings.

Going back aft the skipper and mate discussed the arrangements for anchoring. The skipper wanted to be in a minimum of two metres at low water, so, agreeing with the mate that eight was the present depth to aim for, they prepared to sail round in a loop. The mate would drop the mainsail while the skipper laid the anchor.

When the mate had judged her moment, she called out and brought the boat up into the wind. Going forward she dropped the mains'l, putting a couple of ties loosely round the sail for the skipper to sort out later. Meanwhile, the anchor splashed overboard, the skipper paying out the cable until it was on the bottom, releasing more chain as the boat made sternway, snubbing her and letting out more to bring the boat up sharply.

'I'll pay out a little more chain in a while after tidying up', he said to the mate, who was busy dealing with a scrum of sail sheets in the cockpit. 'It's good holding on this shore', he added while checking the depth and seeing that they would be in about two or maybe three metres at low water. 'The northeasterly will keep us clear of the tide line, but if it turns southerly and we rest in the soft mud at low water, it's no problem with our underwater profile.'

The mate then produced some afternoon tea and, to ward off the hunger pangs until supper, some ginger cake, which the skipper had spread with butter, it being, he said, 'The only way to eat it!' Refreshed, they both settled down in the cockpit to read their books.

The skipper, in a busy anchorage, was often found with a book; but many a time he didn't seem to progress through the narrative very quickly: the wonderful goings on in the world around generally attracted his attention. It was an afternoon of high drama, or could have been: a small yacht coming through from the main river beyond had attempted to cut across the spit of clay hummocks. The tide was then running fast over the tops of those, boiling and foaming beyond. The yacht had run onto one of the humps and was seen to be stuck fast. In just a few moments, the tide had dropped too far for any chance of getting off. The current held her. As the tide dropped she was left high and dry, eventually some three metres above the low tide mark. Fortunately for the crew, the little boat sat precariously on the top. All around was a rapidly sloping hard clay base littered with the remnants of huge chunks of Kentish ragstone, the size of buckets. The skipper thought of their early days of boating, saying to the mate, 'There but for the grace of God go I' – both had the same thoughts!

Casting his eyes across the mud-flats of what had been a huge bay of water, to the marshes beyond, the skipper looked at the remnants of an industrial past. An old jetty, its posts and some structure still intact, sat with washed-out infill forming a beach to one side. On the other side up a gulley sat the shattered remains of an old wooden lighter, slowly rotting away, and nearby a large steam boiler rusted slowly too: both now sunk deeply into the soft mud. The beach was partly composed of broken shell and a morass of pottery and glass fragments, but the most striking ingredient was clinkers, broken down into sand-sized grains, giving it a distinct black appearance. They had landed there some years ago to take a look. Some scrub trees and bushes hung on, clinging to the high ground above the highest tides, but obvious denuding of the banks by the highest spring tides indicated that soon it would all be tidal salt marsh.

As the tide dropped the skipper climbed into the sailing tender and prepared it for sailing. Calling to the mate that he was going, the skipper hoisted the lugsail aloft and cast off, spending an hour cruising around the anchorage looking at the various yacht types and having a few snatched passing conversations. The tide had by now stopped its mad rush through the backwater. The flats to the west being uncovered, the flow from the river had stopped and only the local marshes and guts were being drained. It made for easy and comfortable sailing in the little lugsail dinghy.

Later, returning to the boat the skipper found that his mate was fast asleep! Waking her he said, 'Come on, look lively. We've a date aboard the good ship astern of us.'

Some time later they returned to their own boat to prepare supper, leaving their friends to relax with theirs. They had all enjoyed a couple of aperitifs with some tasty nibbles, yarning about cruising and suchlike. With their own supper cooking slowly on top of the simpler cooker, the skipper had reflected on some of the points that had come up in conversation. He ruminated over boat sizes and the extent owners use bigger boats. 'The argument for additional comfort was hard to beat down; but at what point does size start to impinge on "sailability" with a limited crew of, say, one?'

'Some of those boats are so light, unless they've got the full compliment of crew aboard, they appear to need some ballast when sailing!' he said. Then, remembering the supper simmering down on the galley stove, quickly gave the pot a stir.

The skipper in his dinghy ... the breeze is light ... the sun has sunk low ... dusk has fallen.

The skipper hadn't finished, though, because he went on, almost without taking a breath. 'Remember that modern sloop we saw earlier today, yes she was fast – yes, but did you notice that three of her crew were sitting on the side decks hanging their legs over the side. That's no way for a family cruiser to be sailed!'

The mate looked up at her skipper and smiled, having heard all this before, and decided, wisely she knew, to say nothing.

After supper, the skipper lit the riding light and set it up the forestay for the coming night, while the mate cleared away the dishes. Then the skipper hopped into the tender for a gentle sail before the night closed in. The moon had risen; it wasn't quite calm, for a soft breeze still wafted down from the marsh tops high above the anchorage, bringing with it the heady scents of brine from freshly washed plant-life. It was intoxicating.

Calling out that he wouldn't go far, the skipper set off skimming across the now almost still water. The ebb had still a short time to run, but its strength had, by now, all but evaporated. Most of the boats in the anchorage were lit up with their cabin lights. Not all, the skipper noticed, had their riding lights up. Some of the crews were lounging in their cockpits, wrapped up against the early autumn evening chill, enjoying convivial chatter and perhaps a glass of something. Comments came floating across to the skipper. He himself hearing clearly every word said and chuckling, he whispered, 'They've forgotten that sound travels clearly over the water.'

The skipper, looking around suddenly, realised that the sky was taking on a darker hue. So, turning and sailing gently, he gazed up at the stars, now spread over the sky, as the gentle breeze wafted him along. A curlew loosed its plaintive cry over the marshes and another followed suit, both letting each other know of their respective presence. Other calls came too. The night was closing in. The skipper shivered, his life jacket no longer warding off the chilly air. 'Time for me to get back aboard the boat', he thought aloud.

Twinkling lights now shone from most boats; conversations were beginning to quieten, crews perhaps enjoying this evening, probably wondering if it were to be last before next season. The skipper revelled in the shadows created by the boat lights and the moon in the sky above. It was only about a half moon, but it sent the sun's reflected light into this little backwater, illuminating the surface in a bronzed glow.

Approaching his yacht the skipper was aware of a buzz of excitement from a group of smallish yachts rafted up close into the mud edge. A sudden flash of light dazzled the surface of the water and lit the tan sail of the dinghy into a deep translucent red. 'Did you get it?' A shout drifted across the water to the skipper as he had ranged the dinghy against the clinker sides of his own sloop, onto fenders, of course.

The mate, reaching down, took the painter and held the mast steady while the skipper stowed the sail and lashed it to its spars, before removing the plate and rudder. Boarding their boat, the mate said to the skipper, 'I bet you've had a good sail!'

'I did', he'd said, 'I did', grinning from ear to ear!

Over a coffee, laced with something nice to ward off the chill, they snuggled close, enjoying the end of the day. It was an early start in the morning, the skipper wanting to be away some two hours before low water, so with a general reluctance, they headed for their bunk.

Leaving the anchorage at first light, the mate said quietly in hushed tones, 'I think we're being watched!'

Sailing gently on a quiet southwesterly air, they serenely passed through the sleeping yachts. A window curtain or two had twitched, but no one else was out and about yet. Hauling the anchor always creates a noise and what with regular dipping of the bucket for water to wash off copious quantities of sticky, black, mud, it was not unusual to disturb someone.

'Look', said the skipper, pointing towards the three humps of clay, all that remained of the ancient point, 'the boat obviously got clear last night – she's not in the anchorage. Must have gone on elsewhere during the depths of the darkness.'

It was a gentle sail back to their club moorings, allowing plenty of time to ruminate and watch the world pass by. The tide gate at the entrance to the River Medway had been nicely timed, but before then and for a time after, when crossing the Thames going northwards towards Southend, they'd been passed by a myriad of sailors with chugging engine exhausts catching up time. The mate sat on the cabin top endeavouring to finish a book, knowing that the coming week ahead, back at school, would not allow for such moments, whilst the skipper enjoyed the sail – he had been in a sublime ecstasy – drinking his cup of nectar.

Later, waiting for the tide to make before being able to motor into their creek to moor, and while clearing up below, the mate looked fondly at her skipper and murmured, 'You know, that has been one of the finest autumn overnight sails we've had for a long time.'

'The best parts were seeing the tide flowing right over the marshes and the boiling water along the edges, the heady mixture of scents afterwards, your moonlit sail and sitting out together under the stars.'

'It'll do for now, it was so full of different moods. For you know, I love this time of the year – autumn – it's so nice.'

They both smiled.

15

Into the Sunset with One Little Hiccup

Sometimes the unexpected happens. The skipper of the little clinker yacht was called up by a sailing pal, who at the time was working away from home. It was just a few hours before he was to depart to join his next ship, in some exotic foreign part.

The voice on other end of the line had said, 'Dad's taking his boat up the creek, to be lifted out of the water. It's up at the usual place; any chance of you going with him?' The request was made in the serious tone the skipper had grown accustomed to. The voice continued almost in the same breath, 'I've told Dad that Wednesday is your day off.'

What could the skipper do but to say, 'Yes, of course I can'? it was the only option! Not that there was any question of his not doing so.

The friend went on to warn about making sure that the anchor was ready before getting close to the boatyard. The previous year his dad had almost ended up against a flood barrier: the little outboard engine had failed and the anchor rope was all tangled up. The crew, for that passage, had not investigated the forward end of the boat during the passage up the creek.

Disaster had only just been averted.

The date was dutifully written into the skipper's diary. The little clinker yacht's skipper was to be relegated to the rank of crewman. The friend had said that it was likely that another old buffer would be there too, to help.

The dad, skipper of the boat being laid up, was getting on in years. He had gravitated to sailing a nineteen-foot weekender after years of sailing and racing various classes of dinghy, much to the annoyance of close family and guffaws from friends at his local sailing club.

With a crew of one other, a person nearly of the same age, they'd pursued various club and foreshore combined club cups with a certain amount of success, sometimes sailing against the skipper of the clinker yacht. The guffaws were then on the owner and crew's faces! At the time the combined age of these two, hoary, old, salty sea dogs, was around 150 years. One could only applaud their efforts. The time had come, however, for the old owner to give up his own little yacht, but not to hang up his sailing shoes completely: his son, who had a large comfortable boat of his own, had promised his dad some sailing to offset his loss.

A few days before the expected passage, the phone had rung and the old boy ran through the plan, asking his pre-arranged crew to be at the foreshore-located yacht club by a certain time. It was some three hours or so before high water, so it would give plenty of time to get ready, and to make the passage.

'No problem', his crew had replied cheerfully, concurring with the timings.

The old boy went onto say that he would provide lunch and that another pal of his would be coming along for the trip too. 'He knows you', he had said!

The Essex Yacht Club headquarters ship, the *Wilton*, an ex-Royal Navy plastic (GRP) minesweeper, and their dinghy slip with storage racks alongside, where the last voyage began. An old timer, the pretty *Nancy Grey* slips past on a pleasant autumn afternoon's tide.

So, on a pleasant early autumn morning the newly assigned crewman, who as it turned out was very much the youngster, had arrived at the landing stage of the old boy's yacht club and stood daydreaming as he looked out over the tranquil water. A light, northerly it seemed, breeze wafted the scents off the land – a good direction. Over-ripe blackberries from tumbling brambles that fringed a fence along a railway line and the tangy saline aroma of seaweed mingled in a not unpleasant cocktail. A hail brought him up with a jolt and his contemplations snapped back to attention. A wizened old character, of a somewhat robust disposition, had appeared from behind a rack of stacked dinghies. He was waving. The hail, a wave and a call, came again, confirming the source.

'Are you the young chap who is going to pilot our vessel up the creek?'

'Our skipper has just gone out with the stores and some gear. He won't be long.' He then stopped and did a double take, saying, 'I say, you're ... err ... one of the barge lads aren't you?'

'Yes,' said the youngster, 'I was ... a long time ago.' He paused and was waiting for some irksome tale about his childhood life, before adding, 'The barge is history. Mum still lives in Kent and Dad has long hung up his boots.' He'd wanted to add, 'I don't always like to be reminded ...'

The old boy then recounted an occasion that he and another chap had looked after the barge's gaggle of kids while their parents were up in the town shopping. The barge, their home, was moored for a time, during a summer, out on the mud-flats off the old fishing village of Leigh-on-Sea.

As the owner of the boat ranged his dinghy alongside the pontoon, the youngster said, 'Look, here's our skipper.' He had a momentary feeling or perhaps just a little trepidation and mouthed to himself quietly, 'What have I let myself in for?' Later he

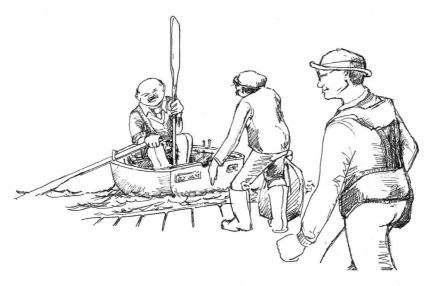

... with just a little trepidation ...

realised that a greater responsibility, than being a mere crewman, lay on his shoulders – but that was later!

Sitting on the centre thwart of his dinghy looking up towards the two dissimilar characters standing on the pontoon, the oarsman said, 'Ah, good, I'm glad you two have got to know each other. As we're all here we'll get off out to the boat. Come on, you young'n, up in the bow, oldie into the stern!'

The youngster handed his ditty bag down to the skipper then donned his life jacket before getting into the dinghy. He was followed by the other crewman. It was noticeable that the two old men were not going to wear life jackets – it was a surprise to the younger man – but it is often seen. Later he related this to his own boat's mate (his wife), who had then reminded her husband of the recent fatality on a nearby river: traversing between the beach and the boat was the most hazardous part of their recreational activity.

The old skipper rowed, with slow, well-practised strokes out to his boat, which swung on her mooring not too distant from the shore. Neatly slipping the dinghy alongside, the youngster was ordered out, and taking the painter with him he was followed by the other crewman. The skipper then clambered aboard too. It became apparent to the youngster at once that this was a small craft, as it had rocked to and fro with each and every movement made by the people aboard her. It was in reality no more than a large dinghy, or day boat, with a lid.

Going forward the youngest crewman looked casually into the anchor locker. As had been expected, and warned about, it was a tangle of rope and chain with the anchor buried beneath it all. Before starting to sort it all out, he thought that a tactful comment was needed. Looking back aft, with a grin, he casually said, 'Umm … while I'm up here skipper, I'll get this lot all ready – if err … that's alright.' Receiving an affirmative nod and a casual wave of a hand from the skipper the youngster had soon sorted out the anchor and cable. He coiled the line down into the locker, then the chain, and finally laid the anchor carefully on the top of the coils. That done he went back aft.

While doing all of that the young crewman had, in readiness for any quick action that might be needed, made a mental note of where things were about the decks, what ropes, halyards, went to what cleat. He made note, too, of the care that was called for underfoot, for he'd found the sloping decks greatly different from his own sturdy clinker sloop. For, although only a metre or so shorter than the youngster's own yacht, it was a much smaller vessel in volume and mass; hence why the crew movements had caused such motion.

The skipper of the little yacht, who from time to time had glanced up from getting the outboard engine ready for use, had issued instructions to his crew too, laying out the general plan for the trip up the creek. It was simple enough. The conditions were idyllic. All, it seemed, were looking forward to a pleasant autumn afternoon's sail.

The plan was for them to leave the mooring under sail, sail across the Leigh flats, out into the deep-water channel at the eastern end of Canvey Island, then run up with the tide. The light breeze was from the northeast and, if it held, would take them all the way up. Before getting under way, the skipper tied off the dinghy to the mooring buoy.

When all was ready, the skipper sent the youngster forward to deal with the mooring as he himself hauled out the jib, letting it flap briefly as the mooring was dropped into the water. Sheeting in the jib, they were off, gently reaching across the shallow water-covered flats beyond the foreshore. The little boat picked up to a leisurely pace, leaving a line of small ripples running out from the bow on each side. The sun cast a perfect shadow which moved with barely a curtsey alongside them.

Back aft, the skipper explained that in the cabin he had a bag full of ham and tomato sandwiches and a few little bottles of low-alcohol beer, enough of each to keep the wolf away and quench a thirst. It being quite warm, the skipper suggested broaching the luncheon stores at once while they had time to sit back, relax and enjoy it. Handing the helm to the youngster, the skipper immediately disappeared below to pass the luncheon and bottles of beer to the other crewman. He had every intention of enjoying this trip it appeared. The youngster, it should be said, declined a beer.

As the two old boys sat back in the cockpit, beer and ham sandwiches in hand, they watched the world go by. Brent geese could be heard noisily squabbling with each other on the fringes of some salt marsh at the eastern end of an island to the north of them. Mixed in with these could be seen a number of shelduck. Wildlife abounded here at this time of the year and it was always more than a pleasant sight. Local sailors often saw the best of it, when out on the water.

The island, strangely known as Two Tree Island, sat to one side of a navigable channel that ran up to Benfleet. The channel along that stretch is known as Hadleigh Ray. The island had been reclaimed over a great number of years using tons of waste generated by the many thousands of people who lived in the area. Being deemed full up, it had, some years ago, been transformed into a wildlife park. Its mid-section is fringed by a sea wall which fell away onto saltings and mud-flats to the east. The mud-flats were an important feeding ground, of international importance, for brent geese and other waders during the winter months. A road ran across the island to a hard, originally used by fisherman, but now mainly by sailors and ski boat owners. A few fishermen still based their boats near the end of the hard; one of them had given a cheery wave as the little yacht sailed serenely by. Over on the other side of the creek, salt marshes stretched away across to a sea wall that protected the low hinterland of Canvey Island from the sea.

Soon the moorings had been left behind and marshes again fringed the channel on both sides. The creek narrowed gradually too, to become a typical creek, with mud banks leading up to a marsh fringe where sea pursalane abounded and hung over the edges. Before that point was reached, they passed a semi-tidal pond within the sprawling marshland at the western end of the Two Tree Island. It had been created from old sea wall boundaries which had latterly enclosed low land, and it had not been filled with the detritus of man. Here, amongst other species, many pairs of avocet

Above: The green and pleasant land that overlooks the skipper's local sailing grounds. In the foreground are the remains of the Salvation Army barge wharf, General Booth's Wharf. Beyond the high seawall protecting the low pastureland brickworks once abounded. To the left and out of view upon the hills are the ruins of Hadleigh Castle, with the buildings of the Salvation Army farm and training centre running across the crests. This was once an industrial landscape, with chimneys and light railways.

... cormorants, oystercatchers, some ducks ... and little egrets ...

had successfully bred in recent years, and a number were seen feeding on a mud bank on the opposite side of the creek. The youngster had said to the old boys, 'Look at those avocets wafting their bills back and forth, sieving the shallows for shrimp and other creatures.' He grinned because he'd regularly come this way on his own boat.

The two oldies were seen to look wistfully across the water; it was as if with unseeing eyes, it seemed to the youngster. He looked away – leaving them with their thoughts.

What were their thoughts, as they gazed at the scene before them? The youngster wondered. Perhaps it was past memories, of times stretching back to their youth when sailing was a less complicated pastime. Those birds, avocets, were then rarely if at all seen: then pollution was the dominant feature on the tideway, but man had made progress since. The waterways were far cleaner and, largely, clear of rubbish. The environment was rejuvenated and the delightful sight of those birds had been made a reality again. The youngster, though, would never know what these thoughts were.

Passing the remains of an old jetty, the little yacht's crew reminisced about the industrial past of the area. All signs of it had all but disappeared. A huge brickworks had operated on the bottom of the hills behind the high sea wall. All that remained now were the gnarled and rotting wharf timbers fringing the creek below the sea wall. On the other side of the wall, just inland, the red brick uprights of a bridge that had carried a small-gauge railway from the works to the wharf over the main line railway, sat like an ancient monument with tufts of grass and elder growing over them. Around the hills beyond, the youngster knew, were scattered remnants of broken glass, pottery and bricks that protruded from the thin grass covering the ground along the numerous footpaths that abounded around the hills. It was a reminder, to those that recognised what they saw, of the past.

Cormorants and oystercatchers sat preening themselves on top of some of the posts. Some ducks were bobbing in amongst banks of glasswort, which was tinged with a brown, or redness, that showed up clearly from the light of the autumn sun beaming upon it: the sun too was beginning to show some late-afternoon colour by then. Soon those plants would die back, to be washed out into the marshes, providing, with other dead material, nutrients for new growth in the spring and beyond.

'Look,' said one of the old boys, which one didn't matter, 'there's one of those little egrets; they certainly weren't around when we were the young'n's age.'

'No,' the other said, quite strongly, looking up while stowing the lunch debris into a bag, then still thinking of the remark about the past he said, 'You remember,' looking at the other old boy, 'we'd have thought nothing of throwing this lot overboard, in them days – we shouldn't have done it – we abused the sea!'

The other, still thinking about the egrets, then said, 'I heard recently down at our club some chap muttering about global warming – what ever that is. There was a discussion about those white birds as well: they were connected with it – well that's what the chap said!'

The youngster chipped in, looking at the two old boys, 'You know, your club friend was quite right. Those birds are south European in origin and used to only visit the south coast of our country until about a decade ago.'

Looking around them the crew noticed that the sun, which had long passed its zenith and was well on its downward path, was much lower in the sky than they had realised. The afternoon tinge of earlier had turned to a golden glow. The light was cast across the near-placid surface of the creek, and along the marsh edges, where it reflected the fauna that covered banks onto the creek's surface. The autumnal colours were a splendid sight. Seablite, that quintessential marsh plant of the autumn, grew along the lower marsh line shouting out its purple-red colours; it joined with the various browns of other spent life that had all been tinged with a rustic glow.

On a day not unlike the old boy's last passage, a golden glow fringed the creek as a yacht sailed away down stream. (Photograph, R.A. Scurrey)

With a casual glance over the top of the sea wall lying close by to the tree-covered hills of the downs below Hadleigh, the crew could see that they were dressed in their autumnal colours that reverberated in drifts across the slopes. The trees were mingled with a scrub of hawthorn, blackthorn and sloe bushes. Colours ranged from the deep darkness of the sloes to patches of green, on some trees, with yellows, browns and russets. The sun, too, accentuated those hues to grand advantage for the crew of the yacht as it slid casually by.

The youngster had been offered another beer, but again refused – even though the proffered fluids were those little bottles of low-alcohol 'Euro fizz': it was lager. The two older boys had decided that the warmth of the sun was excuse enough for one more. Were they celebrating something? The wizened old boy had then laughed, looking at his old pal the skipper, and piped up, 'Hey, it's a good job the young'n came along; and by the way, had you told him that he was going to be in charge?'

Looking back at his old friend, the skipper of the boat had grinned, and continuing to grin said, 'No, but he's looked competent enough – don't you think?' Together they both laughed!

The youngster had taken it all in, smiled inwardly and said nothing. All aboard the little boat continued to look around them, enjoying the quiet passage, talking about this and that, something that is easy to do when sailing slowly and effortlessly on the tide. The passage continued in that reflective reverie.

All along the marsh edge the boat's ripples gently gurgled and sucked in and out of crab holes along the sheer clay wall, beneath the overhanging silvery-green sea pursalane: they were that close into the bank. It had felt idyllic to the youngest of crew, who loved that type of sailing. Wild oceans and tempestuous seas were for the other types: and they could keep it, the skipper had often articulated to people around him.

Then, as if to break the spell, the old skipper, the little boat's owner, looking at no one in particular, reluctantly acknowledged to his crew that the voyage was nearly done, so draining the last of his beer he said, 'Okay, let's get the engine started and then we'll roll up the jib.'

The owner had by then taken back the helm, and pottered up with the tide, the engine quietly ticking over. They were then passing through the moorings of a yacht club, the Benfleet. The crew quickly got ready to come alongside where ever there was a clear spot at the boatyard, which was by then rapidly approaching. All thoughts of the surroundings, the numerous boats and goings on, were dismissed as the youngster went forward, leaving the two old boys back aft. All of the crew were by then concentrating, competently in silence, during those last moments of the voyage. Off the boatyard the old skipper brought his boat round in an arc, slowing down the outboard engine, and shaped up for the slipway.

It was at this moment that the outboard engine spluttered, coughed, and died!

The youngster, up on the foredeck, was ready. He watched the way come off, before letting the anchor run over the side. Thankfully it had bit into the bottom immediately, and it brought the little boat up with a definite snub, as she swung rapidly with the tide. Letting a little more out, he then felt comfortable. That done, he took a quick look round, astern, and saw that they were sufficiently clear of the tidal barrier, but it seemed to loom ominously close: the tide, he saw, was sluicing round its supports. 'That was a close call,' he said to himself, silently blessing his seafaring pal's words of wisdom on the telephone all those weeks ago!

Had the anchor not held the youngster saw only too well the predicament that could have ensued! He waited and watched, ready to spring into action: back aft, the boat's skipper, cursing loudly, tried unsuccessfully to get the engine started. After fiddling with it for a short while he had had another attempt; it failed again. After some more muttered comments and threatening noises, he tried again. With an exultant shout from the skipper, the engine burst into life at the next pull. It stayed running. Up forward, the anchor was rapidly brought up to the bow.

Without further ado, the owner engaged the drive and gunned the throttle, and they shot over towards the sides of a sleek motor yacht where several pairs of hands reached out, either to hold on or fend them off. It could have been either: that yacht's sides looked very new! Whatever their intentions, they were greatly appreciated while the little yacht's crew got mooring lines fastened.

The skipper, looking at no one in particular, said with a broad grin, 'Well, that wasn't so bad – only one little hiccup!' With that he had gone ashore to announce his arrival to the boatyard.

It was not long before the growling boat lift, belching dark poisonous fumes from its tractor unit, had appeared, and the little yacht was soon plucked effortlessly from its proper place. While this was going on the youngster noticed that the sun was well down in the sky: it had begun to cast long shadows as the little yacht was hauled out, her bottom displaying a few barnacles and some weed trails.

As soon as the little yacht was firmly sat on a few baulks of timber and while the old skipper had a few words with the yardman, the rest of the crew, as instructed, cleared their belongings from the boat. Then the old boy climbed a ladder and then clambered into the little cockpit. Very thoughtfully he locked the cabin doors. Turning, he looked around the decks, then down at his two crewmen and, with a glimmer of a grin, he clambered back down to terra firma.

As the crew carried the bags to a car the youngster cast his eyes back and saw the skipper gently pat the aft quarters of his old girl. He was seen to say a fond farewell. His voice, the youngster felt, had a wistful affection: some parts had carried the short distance. Then he turned, looked about him, as if to get his bearings and walked, deliberately and slowly towards them: for this old sailor, the sun had set ...

16

Festive Cheer

Christmas, more than any other season of the year, is thought of as a time for the family. It is an occasion when family life becomes more greatly entwined, bringing together people who have to rub along. Some will spend their time trading off against one another; either to be of help to the host or jut to try to please. On the whole the skipper and mate had suffered little from these maladies, but some friction is inevitable.

The skipper and mate often reflected on this, especially as they got older, and had an unannounced common thought: 'We're lucky really. Many couples we know often say, "We've all been there", just so!' Therefore they continued to feel rather well-endowed with their lot.

However, there's always a first. For the skipper and his mate it was a number of years ago now that they sailed into their sticky situation. Both mothers had come to stay for Christmas. It must be said, though, that the experience couldn't in any way have been likened to more than a light breeze that had ruffled the surface of a placid creek. Both spent the first two days sparring, it seemed: both had wanted to be the first either to please the other or be of help in some domestic need. A little tedious, perhaps, or even amusing, depending upon your viewpoint.

The skipper, initially buoyed with the general bonhomie within the household and too with thoughts of getting some pleasant winter sailing under his belt, started to grumble. However, the mate was feeling the strain the most. Her mother seemed to find plenty of opportunity to buttonhole her and complain about this and that – she had reached the point of no return! Christmas Day had been negotiated, as if it were a torturous channel marked by ill-sited withies, with the odd semi-floating weed-infested plastic can, all designed to cause the unwary to run up onto the bosom of a waiting mud bank. Their passage, though, had been accomplished with serenity and tact. It had been smooth and untroubled. All had enjoyed it!

Boxing Day dawned bright and cold with a clear sky; it wasn't freezing and the sun although low in the sky had definite warmth. A good day beckoned. At the breakfast table, however, things were obviously frosty and seemed about to take a dive. A storm was brewing. The mate's mother was unhappy about something or nothing in particular and the waters were becoming distinctly muddy. The skipper had only one thought – let's escape to the boat.

Their boat was always kept in commission and she sat in a comfortable mud berth. She was built of wood so the skipper considered it the best place for her. The skipper and mate had enjoyed a sail together a day or so before Christmas, taking the opportunity to savour a period of calmness before the arrival of both of their guests. It had been a dull overcast day, but the breeze, although generally light, was sufficient for an enjoyable sail with a period of tacking: this had helped to keep the cold at bay.

During the sail the mate, thinking about coping with two mothers (one sitting in the warm at home and the other due to arrive on the morrow), had turned to the skipper and said, 'If it's nice on Boxing Day,' pausing as she'd flicked through the tide tables, 'We should be able go out. Look, the tide will be early afternoon.'

The skipper, being aware of that already, added, 'Yes, I'd already taken that on board. I'd listened to the week's forecast on Sunday; the weatherman indicated that it was due to remain fine throughout the coming week.'

'I'm sure we're in for a tetchy time this Christmas and it'll be nice to get out: we'll probably need it!'

The mate, almost speaking without thinking, had thought of responding with, 'It won't be my mum's fault.' But knowing that it probably would be, she had quickly changed her mind and said, 'That's a deal. Even if it's freezing cold we'll go – yes you're right, we'll probably need it.'

But that was a few days before. The skipper, his thoughts now back to the frosty atmosphere emanating from the kitchen, marshalled the clearing away of their late breakfast things, before he headed upstairs to find his mate and get ready for their intended sail. Entering their room he found her in a flood of tears and in no mood for anything, let alone a sail. It was apparent that his presence was not needed either: he'd been told to leave her alone, so, reluctantly, collecting his extra layers of clothing he had crept away from the house.

Their son had already slunk away to the yacht club. 'It's safer there', he confided later. The boy had helped to lift a boat up, for a member who needed to do some underside work with his boat up in the club's travel hoist, and stayed to put the boat back down again. Feeling distinctly cowardly, the skipper, too, had made his way creek-wards where the boat sat at her moorings up the short tidal creek located at the eastern end of the island upon which they then lived.

The boat's mooring was against a finger berth, which jutted out from the sloping bank of the creek. Running down the bank from the boat's stern was a channel which was kept clear with regular use. To reach the berth the skipper had to walk round the staging, which snaked across mud-flats, with a wide expanse of marsh fringing it on one side and moorings on the other. Half way to the boat, the skipper, with a momentary pause in his stride, stopped briefly, believing that he had heard a call from behind. The belief was more a hope: upon turning there was nobody in sight. Continuing onwards round the walkway, he noticed that the tide was making well and was already round the boat.

The tide, not quite a neap but in the lower half of its cycle, was forging slowly up the creek, creeping up over the flats beyond the moorings. The skipper thought aloud, and speaking to no one in particular said, 'I'd better get a move on, the boat's nearly afloat.' With that he stepped up his pace and shortly hopped aboard.

On the way round he had time to notice that some brent geese were already well up the creek. Foraging in the shallows, they waiting for the tide to rise into the gullies and gutways that riddled the marshes here about, to feast on any remaining weeds and succulents. Redshank were chasing each other over the mud, backwards and forwards, along the edge of the rising tide, wasting feeding time in their instinctive need to warn off an interloper upon their own little spot. This always made the skipper chuckle: while they squabbled the feeding ground had been submerged!

The skipper quickly removed the cockpit cover which kept the elements off his pristinely varnished cockpit woodwork. Unlocking the cabin, the washboards and cover were dispatched into their designated stowage. Moving inside, a sail bag containing the jib was shoved out of the fore hatch. Then, grabbing the boat hook, the tiller, the ensign staff and club burgee, the skipper went back on deck. Shipping the tiller and in the same movement unrolling the ensign, he fitted the staff into its socket.

The cover was soon removed from the mainsail and then he fixed the burgee staff to its halyard with the customary clove hitches and hauled it aloft, where it flapped lazily in the soft south-easterly air.

Pausing a moment to switch on the gas alarm, he put the kettle on, knowing that by the time he had hanked the jib onto the forestay and run the sheets aft, it would be on the boil. With a cup of coffee to hand the skipper made up the logbook with the weather and tidal information, before removing most of the mooring lines. Finding that he had a moment or two to spare, the skipper's thoughts had inevitably wandered back to the events of the morning – wishing that his mate had come with him, and feeling that, if left to their own devices, the two older ladies would sort themselves out.

Opening the engine water and fuel supplies, the skipper started the engine, which with its customary efficiency burst into life. Its regular use meant that it did not need to be winterised as was the case on a boat laid up. With the weather that is experienced in his part of the country, it was often a mystery, to the skipper, why so many boat owners laid up their craft. Countless fine days are experienced during late autumn, through the winter and on into early spring, so that it always seemed a shame: when he himself had enjoyed those opportunities, he had often looked pityingly at those boats sat ashore, forlorn and bereft, and those too left sitting on their moorings unused and, perhaps, unloved.

Slipping on his life jacket, with the engine running sweetly and the last of the moorings hung off on the jetty, the skipper was ready to clear the berth. He had started to move out sternwards when his attention was diverted by a plaintive cry, several bursts of a distant sound, like that of a curlew's call. He looked up from the throttle, an ear cocked, as he closed it down to neutral; the engine noise, with it, settled down to a murmur. The cry came again. Then he recognised the almost sorrowful strains of his own name.

.... a plaintive cry ... 'Wait, I'm coming too!'

The shout had emanated from across the mud beyond the berth; strangely, from about the position he had paused at earlier. Marching along as fast as her legs would take her and looking his way was the mate, waving excitedly. She'd called again and the skipper thought he'd heard, 'Wait: I'm coming too.' That was obvious!

The boat, barely afloat, sat captive in her berth and, with the skipper, contentedly awaited the mate. The skipper, who was deeply of the view that a boat has not only a soul but feelings too, knew it would be as happy as he was ... They had had this little clinker yacht for a considerable number of years, the mate having watched her being built, from the keel upwards, in the shipwright's shed. She had a particular affinity with the vessel and, like a child, the boat was part of the family.

Quickly arriving at the mooring, the mate, with an uncharacteristic leap, landed on the deck. Wiping her eyes, which were still showing signs of recent tears, she smiled and said, 'Let's go then.' Then with a grin, she plucked two Father Christmas woolly hats from her pocket. The skipper's hat had been swiftly removed as she had pulled the festive hat over his head. Giving him a hug she whispered, 'I've left them to it and said that we would be home later.'

Leaving the berth, the skipper set the mainsail immediately: the wind being from the southeast had given them an acceptable slant. Setting the jib, then coiling the lines and hanging them off, the skipper went back aft. The mate, at the tiller, hauled the sheets in and shut down the engine. Then they made slowly over the sluggish flood, on a close reach. The skipper lowered the centre plate a few turns to give the boat a better bite on the water.

The breeze was of sufficient power for them to work out of the creek, over the placid flow of the incoming neap tide, so they settled down to enjoy the occasion. No other craft left the creek with them. The sky was clear of cloud. High above them it was a deep blue and a weakened sun shone down and spread a little warmth. The ensign flapped lazily on its staff, under a conifer sprig. All was blissful. They felt festive.

The skipper on the day written about. Looking at the sky it could have been summer, except that it certainly didn't feel like it!

In front of them a gaggle of brent geese sat in their way. The birds, turning this way and that, looked towards the approaching boat and its crew, probably not sure what they were looking at. They swam, slowly at first, away, and then peeled off in outward directions, with increasing vigour, to clear a path. Some rose from the surface, with much noise and fuss, to alight a little distance off, looking back to make sure that they had not been followed!

The mate, who was looking away in the distance at the mass of bird-life along the shoreline, had begun to loose her concentration, and the boat's course started to deviate. The skipper speaking quietly said, 'I think perhaps that we should keep more over to the other side if we want to stay off the putty.'

The skipper, recognising that the mate's mind was obviously engaged elsewhere, and for now distinctly disinterested in the navigational needs of the boat, then suggested in a casual manner, 'Look, you go forward and sit on the cabin top and enjoy the sights. Go on, I'll take her for now.' With that the mate abandoned the skipper and went forward.

As they cleared the creek, the mate relaxed and, looking absently at the wonders of the natural world around her, fell into a period of quiet solace and reflection. After what seemed an interminable age, but in fact had been only a moment in time, her thoughts returned to the pleasures of being out on the water, saying quietly to herself, 'The mothers are old enough to look after themselves – I'm going to enjoy this.' Then as an afterthought, 'I'm sure they'll be busy nattering away, again, by now.'

The mate then concentrated properly and looking around she began to glow with a pleasurable awe: she loved winter sailing. Looking across at the marshes, at the extreme eastern end of the island, she saw grouped together on patches of sand, shell and shingle a huge number of knot with smaller groups of oystercatchers, all shuffling about on a diminishing area of land. Then, as she watched, a flock of knot rose up and swirled about, diving down towards the water, swerving up over the top of the boat's mast, circling round again with sharp changes of direction. It was fun to watch. Finally the birds had settled down again, until that is, a small number tried to join the massed throng, signalling a waltz to another tune.

Ringed plovers darted about too, alighting and rising from vacant mooring buoys. One, cheekily, had rested briefly on the cabin top and after giving it a peck or two, looked about, and seemed to gaze at the skipper, turning its head one way then the other, before it lifted off again, flying away into the distance, the skipper chuckling at its inquisitiveness.

A number of other craft of various descriptions were seen to be out, their crews enjoying the fine Boxing Day weather. Coming down the main creek running to the west between the island and the mainland, was the glorious sight of the barge yacht *Tiny Mite* motoring against the flood and southeasterly breeze. The *Tiny Mite* had been built round at Frank Shuttlewood's yacht and barge yard on the River Roach between the two world wars. She was flying a huge red ensign, nearly as big as the space for her topsail. She was set in fine detail against the clear azure blue sky, looking resplendent and a picture of sheer delightfulness. Her skipper, smoking a pipe, gave a nonchalant wave as they passed by each other. The reflections of her dark green topsides danced in the gently rippling surface. Later, together, the mate and skipper watched as her sails were set and with the tide still making, she started her run back up the creek westwards, the sun illuminating the tan colours, giving them a rustic russet glow, so reminiscent of the ubiquitous spritsail barge, her unique parentage.

Leaving their creek, the skipper set a course to reach across the shallows which ran northwards from their moorings towards the distant shore. There, an old fishing village still thrives at the water's edge, supporting a number of inshore fishing craft. Boats with giant 'hoovers' designed to suck up cockles, and others used for shrimping,

The *Tiny Mite*, a miniature spritsail barge in every respect, sat for a number of years at a mooring immediately below the Benfleet flood barrier. Close your eyes, just for a moment ... unfurl those sails ... picture her sailing ... the sunset glowing on the russet cloth.

nestle against a bank, piled high with countless spent shells. The skipper had often wondered how long the famed cockle could be sucked up in such huge quantities in the locality, but still it went on. Behind, up a steep hill, housing straggles up to the top. The skyline used to be dominated by an ancient church, but now, unfortunately, blocks of flats all but hide the church tower: in its day, down the centuries, it had been used as a navigation mark, by mariners approaching from the east.

Reaching the shoreline off the ancient village, the skipper put the boat round and started to head back the way they had come. Glancing back the skipper ran his eyes along the shore to the old boatyard, near the town's station. It sat on the site of some of the last oyster pits in these parts, now a maze of laid up craft. Eastwards, past the cockle sheds, was another boat builder. Well, it had by then closed, but it had in the past constructed a class of clinker craft, not unlike the skipper's own little yacht. It has since been reopened for boat repairs and one-off builds. Looking back at the mate and sighing for he was feeling whimsical, thinking about other things; he saw that she had awoken from her reverie too. The poor girl was feeling a little stiff and numb from sitting, so she had come aft, massaging her thighs, and asked the skipper if he would like a hot drink.

'Never thought you'd ask', he said, with more than a twinkle in his eye.

The tide, by now, was close to the turn. The sun too was showing signs that it had not long to go, for it seemed to be rushing towards the distant skyline to the southwest. Overhead, the sky was also changing colour. It was like a wide-spread rainbow, running from a near white, in the east, then from light blue through to dark blue overhead, to an almost indigo purple, before becoming tinted with the fiery orange of the sun's glow as it approached the horizon.

The sun reached for the horizon, the mainsail had been stowed and the yacht ghosted into the creek, in the path of sailors long gone. It had been a magical Boxing Day.

The mate, handing up mugs of piping hot coffee, smelling of something delicious – it was a good dollop of whisky – came back on deck clutching a number of mince pies. They stood together admiring and soaking up the beauty of the scene around them, munching the pies and enjoying the warming coffee, with its additional ingredient giving them an internal glow. Far away in the distance, the sails of the *Tiny Mite* could still be seen; they were as if black now, standing starkly against the skyline with its festoon of yacht masts. The masts were now lit up by the reflected rays of the setting sun, their lonely halyards clinking and clanking through the winter at the marshland yacht club which sits on the edge of the creek, some three miles distant upstream.

Letting out a huge sigh of appreciation and joy, the mate with her arm through her skipper's, whispered lovingly, 'This is so wonderful', and, continuing in the same vein, said, 'I'm glad that I rushed after you – it was a close call too. You'd very nearly gone!'

Looking around and disengaging himself (they were approaching the fishing craft moorings outside their creek) the skipper said, 'Look, you take over for a bit and I'll haul the mains'l down, then we'll potter up under the jib.'

The job was soon quietly accomplished: they did things on their boat as if 'one', it seemed to bystanders. It had come from many years of mutual understanding when on the water, and land too!

'We're making sweetly over the tide', the skipper chirped.

The sun was by now low in the sky; its warmth was no longer felt and the cold had begun to be more intense, but not quite numbing. On the slow sail towards their creek over the gently ebbing tide, more mince pies, warmed under the grill, and coffee were consumed. As they looked, they had marvelled at the world around them. A deep orange glow had been cast up from the sun, as it had set behind the hinterland of low-lying houses sitting behind the protective sea wall; it cast long shadows down the

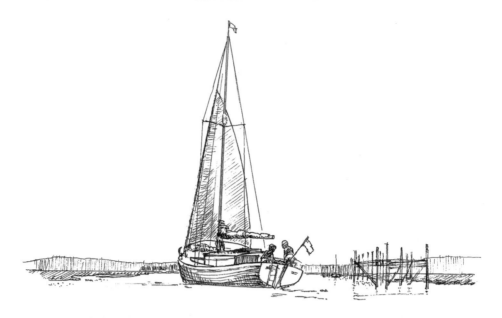

... under the jib ... we're making sweetly over the tide ...

creek. The almost smooth water was beautifully coloured as the gentle southeasterly breeze wafted them along. The boat's stem, as it cut through the water, sent gentle ripples outwards, contorting the reflected pictures. They watched too as the mirrored sky rippled in response. The creek's channel marker buoys hardly bobbed, but the skipper fancied that he had seen a delicate curtsey! It was enchanting.

The evening was setting in. Both of them had continued to stand quietly in the cockpit, listening to the chatter of the wild fowl, not saying anything and for a while they continued to soak up the magic: it was a magical moment indeed.

Savouring that magic, the mate had turned to the skipper and whispering quietly, said, 'The birds appear to be settling down', and had added with a little more emphasis, 'I hope those two at home have too.'

At home, unbeknown to the two out on the boat, all was aglow: their son, now back from his exertions at the yacht club, had dispensed sherry and settled everybody down. They were all jointly enjoying a television programme.

The mate after her momentary thoughts of those at home said, 'It's been an enchanting sail – here you take the tiller.' Giving the skipper a hug, 'I'm ready to get back to the warmth now, aren't you?' she had not expected an answer!

The skipper had the same feelings but had remained silent.

The light continued to fade quickly as they slowly made their way up the creek, past those numerous boats sitting, forlornly, at their moorings. The enchantment held as they closed their own mooring too. The skipper let the jib flap as the mate let it run down onto the deck. A few moments later, with sufficient way on, they had glided gracefully into their berth – in silence. On the way in, the skipper caught hold of the stern line, to gently pull the boat up, while the mate had made sure that they stayed put.

Looking towards the clubhouse, as they had left their dependable friend safely tucked up, a myriad of people could be seen silhouetted against the bright festive lights – enjoying themselves? The skipper, looking at his mate had quietly remarked, 'Shall we? But no ... let's not spoil the magic ...'

Bibliography

Ardley, Nick, *The May Flower A Barging Childhood* (Tempus, 2007)

Blake, John, *Sea Charts of the British Isles: A Voyage of Discovery Around Britain & Ireland's Coastline* (Conway – An imprint of Anova Books Company Ltd)

Coote, J., *East Coast Rivers* (*Yachting Monthly*, London, third edition [revised] 1961)

Harber, J., *East Coast Rivers* (Nautical Data Ltd, Westbourne, Hampshire, 2001)

Parkhill, Gordon and Cook, Graham, *Salvation Army Farm, A Vision Reborn* (Shield Books, 2008)

Simper, R., *River Medway and The Swale* (Creekside Publishing, Lavenham, Suffolk, 1998)

Stalley, A.R., *Whitstable History Series No.4. Last One Down the Slip* (Friends of Whitstable Museum and Gallery, Whitstable, Kent, 2005)

Taylor, Frank, *A History of Faversham & Oare Creeks and the Faversham Navigation* (Chaffcutter Books, Ware, Hertfordshire, [second printing] 2002)

Tripp, H. Alker, *Shoalwater & Fairway* (Conway Maritime Press, new impression 1972, originally published 1924)

Magazines: *Coast & Country incorporating East Coast Digest* (Parrett & Neaves Ltd)

Further Reading

There is a wealth of further reading that can be enjoyed, dating back to Frank Cowper's *Sailing Tours Part 1,* first published in 1892 by L. Upcott Gill, 170 Strand, WC, London, and then in 1985 by Ashford Press. The reader will find that this book is still relevant, in many respects, to knowing the east coast, of which the River Medway, the Swale and north Kent coast is an accepted part, but strangely, was not included in Cowper's *East Coast* book. Dick Durham in his book *On and Offshore* (Ashford Press Publishing, 1989), mimicked Part 1 of the *Tours* with the addition of a visit to the Swale and Medway.

The well-known sailing yarns written by Maurice Griffiths briefly touch upon the area written about in this book, but like many others, little is said that is nice: he was not a fan.

There is another old book available, if one searches for it: *Swin, Swale and Swatchway,* by H. Lewis Jones MA, published by Waterlow & Sons, 1892, which tells of cruising in these waters during the Corinthian age.

There are, as far as I am aware, only few other sailing books that wander into the lower edge of the extensive cruising grounds of the East (Anglian) Coast of England. Two of these are *Shoalwater & Fairway* by H. Alker Tripp (new impression by Conway Maritime Press, 1972; originally published in 1924) and *Sailing Just For Fun,* by A.C. Stock (published by Minerva Press, 1998). They do not stay long, being mere fleeting visits only.

It is hoped that the eyes of many a reader, sailor or landsmen, old hand or new, may well be opened to fresh and exciting discoveries and to look anew at the fascinating expanse that is the northern Kent marshlands and the southern edge of Essex along the Thames estuary: an area permanently entwined by its geography of silt-laden waters, shifting sands and mud banks. Therefore, I hope dear reader that you relished the voyage and crave for more, as I always do.

Nick Ardley
June 2009